No Ordinary Hotel

BOOKS BY ADRIAN WALLER

Theatre on a Shoestring

Adrian Waller's Guide to Music

Data for a Candlelit Dinner

The Gamblers

Soulikias: Portrait of an Artist

*Writing! An informal, anecdotal guide to the
secrets of crafting and selling non-fiction*

*The Canadian Writer's Market,
Eighth Revised Edition*

*No Ordinary Hotel:
The Ritz-Carlton's first seventy-five years*

No Ordinary Hotel

THE RITZ-CARLTON'S
FIRST SEVENTY-FIVE YEARS

BY ADRIAN WALLER

Véhicule Press

MONTRÉAL

Book design by J.W. Stewart
Cover photograph by Leon Thomas
Special editorial assistance by Nancy Marrelli
Typeset in Goudy Old Style by Zibra Inc.
Printed by Les Éditions Marquis Ltée
Bound by L.G. Chabot

Canadian Cataloguing in Publication Data

Waller, Adrian, 1936-
No ordinary hotel: the Ritz-Carlton's first seventy-five years

Includes index.
ISBN 0-919890-86-5

1. Ritz-Carlton Hotel (Montréal, Québec) — History.
I. Title.

TX941.R52W34   1988 647'.9471428101   C88-090376-7

Canadian distribution
University of Toronto Press
5201 Dufferin Street
Downsview, Ontario M3H 5T8

U.S. distribution
University of Toronto Press
340 Nagel Drive
Buffalo, New York 14225-4731

Véhicule Press
P.O.B. 125, Place du Parc Station
Montreal, Quebec H2W 2M9

Printed in Canada

For the Ritz-Carlton's staff,
which is rare indeed —
cheerful, alert, hardworking,
meticulous, and civil,
even when pressures mount
and the day seems never-ending

ACKNOWLEDGEMENTS

I am indebted to several members of the Ritz-Carlton Hotel's senior staff, particularly the following, who gave me invaluable help and encouragement: Diane Roch, the director of marketing, René Gounel. the general manager, and Fernand Roberge, the executive vice-president and a member of the board of directors. Nor can I overlook the hard work of my editors, Joan Naimark and Nancy Marrelli, who made this a better book.

My gratitude also goes out to those kind people who lent or traced photographs, or who unearthed valuable information and contributed personal impressions of the Ritz-Carlton Hotel: Marie Baboyant, research librarian of the Montreal Municipal Library, who worked tirelessly on my behalf; The Rt. Hon. Edward Heath, MBE, MP, a former British prime minister, of London, England; Senator Royce Frith of Ottawa; Magda Sabella, the Ritz-Carlton's public relations officer; Helen Dearlove of the Bell Canada Telephone Historical Collection, Montreal; Catherine Lowe, manager of historical research, Bell Canada, Montreal; Yolaine Toussaint, assistant archivist of the Bank of Montreal, Montreal; J.A. Shields, the corporate historian and archivist at Canadian Pacific, Montreal, and Nancy Williatte-Battet, the archives assistant; G. Drummond Birks, president, chairman, and chief executive officer of Henry Birks & Sons Ltd., Montreal; Alfred Hirmke, food and beverage manager of the Ritz-Carlton Hotel; André P. Laurendeau, coordinator of the Audio Visual Service at Dominion Textile Inc., Montreal; William A. Murphy of the National Library, Ottawa; Madame Yvonne Contat, wife of a former Ritz-Carlton general manager, of Brigham, Quebec; Anne Monette of Montreal, daughter of the hotel's second manager, Frank Quick; Dean Shaldon, editor of *Canadian Interiors*, Toronto; Dale Huston of the Côte Saint-Luc Public Library, Quebec; Pierre Demers, a former Ritz-Carlton executive chef, Côte Saint-Luc, Quebec; J.A. L'Ecuyer, a former Ritz-Carlton financial controller of Ste-Julienne, Quebec; Nicholas Stahl of Stahl, Nicolaidis, Fukushima, Orton, Architects, Montreal; Robert Lemire, chief historian at the Canadian Centre for Architecture, Montreal; Claudette Daniel, secretary of the Canadian Centre for Architecture, Montreal; Peter Kilburn a consultant for Richardson Greenshields of Canada Ltd., Montreal, and the chairman of the Ritz-Carlton's board of directors; Fernando Monserrat

ACKNOWLEDGEMENTS

of the Fraser-Hickson Library, Montreal; Maureen Sullivan of CN
Hotels, Montreal; Jodi Post, director of sales and service, Hotel
Newfoundland, St. John's, Newfoundland; J. Raymond Denault,
president of Canadian Microfilming Ltd., Montreal; Jacques Des
Baillets, a nephew of a former Ritz-Carlton manager, Montreal; Frank
W. Graham, Newfoundland Sports Archives, St. John's, Newfoundland;
Daniel Doheny, Q.C., vice-chairman and secretary of Ritz-Carlton Inc.;
Monique Bélanger of Ogilvie Mills Ltd., Montreal; Robert Smith,
Lachine, Quebec; Pierre Joly, the Ritz-Carlton's director of personnel
and his secretary, Josée Gobeille; Ingrid Tcheki, assistant administrator
of the Hotel Association of Greater Montreal; Jack Goodson, president
of Hotel Printing Ltd., of Montreal, who collects old menus; Denis
Catroun, editor of the Ritz-Carlton's in-house newsletter, *Ritzogram*;
Denyse Papineau, Toronto; Sarah McCutcheon of Sarah McCutcheon
Art Contemporain Inc., Montreal; Mark London, architect and planner,
Montreal.

Numerous other Montrealers provided invaluable glimpses into the
Ritz-Carlton's life, its staff, and its patrons, and I am sincerely grateful
to them, too: Pauline Rathbone, Douglas Fales, Patricia Madeline Ford,
Roberta Coyle, Suzanne Viau, Marjorie Martel, David Shaughnessy,
Pearl Webber, Vivianne M. Silver, John Bertram, Raymond Caron,
François Smet, Jacky Ross, Madeleine Boyer, Pierre Ranger, Roselly
Miller Kershaw, and Susan Spier.

Contents

CHAPTER ONE

Grande Dame
of Sherbrooke Street

*"Chances are you have never stayed
at the Ritz-Carlton in Montreal. Most people don't.
Most people can't afford it. But then that's what is so nice
about the old Ritz. It isn't for most people, is it?"*

WEEKEND MAGAZINE

Darkness has long since fallen, and on the gentle southern slopes of Mount Royal, the grand hotel is hushed, its bars and restaurants closed, its brocade curtains drawn against a full moon and the neon-lit city sprawling below.

Down in the black and burnt-amber lobby the crystal lights are twinkling, and there are signs of life. International flights into Mirabel Airport have been delayed by a blizzard and now, at half-past three in the morning, there are three late arrivals: a sociology professor from Cape Town, a General Motors executive from Amsterdam, and a billionaire from Bahrain.

The night bellman has been waiting to greet them. When he has settled them into their rooms and cleaned and delivered the last of twenty-three pairs of guests' shoes, he will be free to go home, like the floor waiters who have scrubbed and closed their kitchenettes, and the night maids who have stored their surplus hot water bottles and blankets and left 323 guests — one of them actor Christopher Plummer — sleeping. Then, the only movement in the lobby will be a man with a mop and a bucket of water, and a trolley full of cloths. He must clean the white-marble floor and the trim, and polish the brass bannister of the gold-carpeted staircase that reaches up to the mezzanine and two large antique floor chandeliers flanking the entrance to the little oval foyer.

Nothing much stirs in the hotel's main kitchen, except the ladle in the night cook's hollandaise sauce. Even though eggs benedict is not on the "Night Owl" menu, he is preparing it anyway, for a couple who enjoys eating late, very late. He is also broiling a steak for the Amsterdam auto executive, a regular guest who never fails to check in famished.

His white coat and tall hat gleaming, the cook has one eye on the eggs, the sauce, and the steak, and the other on twenty-dozen croissants, twelve dozen muffins, ten dozen sweet rolls, and nine dozen Danish pastries that must all be ready for breakfast. By the time this is served, at 6.30 a.m., the hotel will have started to spring fully to life again, with the day staff, and renewed vigour. The restaurants will be adorned once more with smart suits and leather briefcases, and will rustle with morning newspapers.

Later in the morning, the front desk's day shift staff will have deposited an account of the previous day's work for senior managers to see. The hotel, this will show, was busy enough yesterday but, with additional reservations and fewer departures, it promises to be more so today. Besides, to the banquet manager's delight, all the salons have been booked — for twelve private luncheons, nine private dinners, and the late night wedding reception of a patron's daughter.

This is Montreal's venerably ornate Ritz-Carlton Hotel in the act of what it enjoys being most — itself. A chunky, grey-yellow limestone building with fluttering flags, a satisfyingly luxurious marquee, and cordial, unhurried service, it has been called "prestige" by *Vogue*, "a synonym for elegance and comfort" by the *Reader's Digest*, and the best hotel in North America by the *Denver Post*.

To those who savour it most, though, such as the group of discriminating bankers polled by a company called Institutional Investors, it is one of the finest hotels in the world, and decidedly unique. Through long, impoverished years, the Ritz-Carlton has survived to take its place among the oldest inns of its kind anywhere in Canada — a privately-owned and impeccably preserved example of gracious hostelry in the Old World tradition that harkens back to the long-gone era of grand hotels known only in Europe.

Its 240 lofty, high-ceilinged rooms rich with chandeliers, fireplaces, and soft, bulky sofas, have earned it accolades as a bastion of refinement and elegance and a haven of care, kindness, and unflagging hospitality of the very highest order. "Canada abounds in sanitary places to eat and sleep," said *Quest Magazine*, "but in all its length and breadth there is only one truly great hotel, the Ritz in Montreal."

The sentiment has been echoed afar, and seventy-five years after its birth to a handful of St. James Street tycoons who confessed to an insatiable appetite for stylish comfort, the Ritz has also become inseparable from the city it has enhanced, and an integral part of Canadian history. It has coddled the rich, flattered the famous, and catered to the sophisticated needs of anyone else who could afford to be among its guests.

More Ritz-Carlton patrons than anyone has ever dared to count, have been celebrities — a veritable kaleidoscope of them, whose names read like pages from *Burke's Peerage* or the *International Who's Who*. The hotel's immaculate doormen have doffed peaked caps in summer, or fur hats in winter, to haughty heads of state, jet-setting aristocrats, and world-renowned policy makers by the score: the Duke and Duchess of Windsor, for instance, the Duke and Duchess de Bourbon, the King of Siam, Lord Baldwin, Sir Anthony Eden, Sir Winston Churchill, American President William Howard Taft, French President Charles de Gaulle, Israel's Prime Minister Golda Meir and her defence minister Moshe Dayan, Italian prime ministers Giulio Andriotti and Bettino Craxi, and nearly every Canadian prime minister since Sir Robert Laird Borden.

Marshall Joseph Joffre of the French Army and United States Chief Justice Charles Evans Hughes have basked in the Ritz's splendour. So has Lord de l'Isle, Prince Karim Aga Khan IV, Congo President John Hatzebetros, and the Shah of Iran.

"The Shah's stay," remembers Dean Shaldon, editor of *Canadian Interiors*, "gave me the pleasure of interviewing his wife, the most beautiful woman I have ever set eyes upon. Appropriately, whenever I think of her, I immediately see myself reclining at the Ritz because the princess and the hotel somehow seem inseparable. They both know and respect luxury, yes, but they are both so strikingly refined, discreet, inherently uncomplicated, and so redolent of an era gone by."

Many personalities have likened the Ritz to some of the stateliest homes of Europe, and have been quick to admit that this originally drew them there. Not long before he died, the popular performer Liberace called the Ritz-Carlton "simply a gorgeous place to be!" And the legendary concert pianist Artur Rubinstein, himself the epitome of gentility and warmth, always said, "When I am in Montreal I can't ever imagine myself staying anywhere else."

Opera tenor Beniamino Gigli, Douglas Fairbanks, Rita Hayworth, Charles Boyer, and Linda Darnell were among the first personalities of stage, screen, and concert hall to stay there regularly. Since then, as the hotel's reputation for plush rooms and exquisite cuisine has reached across oceans, its showbusiness clientele has amounted to an endless register of fortune, fame, and glitter.

Glenn Ford slept there, as have Carlo Ponti, Catherine Deneuve, Gene Kelly, Jessica Jackson, Petula Clark, Paul Newman, Robert Redford, Lee Majors, David Niven, Robert Mitchum, Burt Lancaster, Ella Fitzgerald, George C. Scott, Charles Aznavour, Margot Kidder, John Wayne, and British actor Basil Rathbone, whose chocolate voice reverberated through the ballroom when he recited poetry there for the League of American Women in the early 1950s. Elizabeth Taylor, reputed to be a hard-to-please connoisseur of fine hotels, agreed to the Ritz's Royal Suite in 1964 as the site of her hurried marriage to Richard Burton.

Phyllis Diller, Gina Lollobrigida, and Neil Diamond have indulged themselves in the Ritz-Carlton, too, as well as David Bowie, Bill Cosby, and Bob Hope. Peter Ustinov once showed waiters in the hotel's Intercontinental Restaurant his talent for dialects; Harry Belafonte revealed to room service a passion for watercress sandwiches; in the hotel's main restaurant, the Café de Paris, the gargantuan Soviet weightlifter Vassiliu Alexeïev predictably rejected the Ritz's paper thin "Steak Charles" in favour of three massive sirloin steaks, one after the other, at the same sitting.

"The big, hungry Russian wanted the whole steer," a waiter observed, "so we gave it to him. Why not? We work at the Ritz, remember."

Over the years, explorer Sir Edmund Hillary, fashion designer Pierre Cardin, and one-time world heavyweight boxing champion Gene Tunney have enjoyed extravagant Ritz hospitality, too, as have Jacqueline Picasso and television commentator Mike Wallace. Actor Donald Sutherland often stays there when in Montreal to watch Expos' baseball games, and nearly every major international musician has found it a distinctive home-away-from-home while appearing with the Montreal Symphony Orchestra, including violinist Yehudi Menuhin, concert pianist Vladimir Ashkenazy, and maestros Leopold Stokowski, Josef Kripps, Sir Thomas Beecham, Zubin Mehta, and Arthur Fiedler.

"When it comes right down to it," a retired head porter once declared. "It's not so much a question of *who* has stayed at the Ritz. Much more to the point is who *hasn't*."

On the steamy night of July 31, 1976, Prince Philip, alone in Montreal after the Queen had returned to England following the

Olympic Games, dropped into the Ritz for dinner. Only a few days before, he had attended a state banquet there. Now alone, and lusting after another delectable meal, he had returned. "I like this place," he told the manager who escorted him into the main dining room. "I get the impression you are running a really splendid hotel — one of the very few really good ones left, I should say."

Many wholeheartedly agree. "In an age when mechanization seems to be replacing the human touch, when elegance is derided, and the egalitarian world seems imminent," the editor of *Weekend Magazine* once noted, "there is still the Ritz. But egalitarian it ain't."

It isn't, of course. It was never intended to be. Beneath the hotel's quiet dignity and formal front, however, there lies a generous and idiosyncratic nature that has endeared it to millions, even those who could never hope to stay there. As Robert Halliday, a busy attorney of Potsdam, New York, puts it, "The old place has a heart and a soul that makes it a helluva lot of fun for ordinary folk like me."

In truth, he and his wife, Gloria, could easily afford a suite in many hotels just as luxurious, anywhere. But the Ritz-Carlton — the "Grande Dame of Sherbrooke Street," as it has come to be known across time — is less expensive than many of its competitors and not nearly as ostentatious or pretentious. It appeals so much to the Hallidays that they have been known to tackle the first leg of the 140-mile journey from their home by jeep, and the second by train. Whenever they have, says Halliday, it has celebrated a determined effort to escape the telephone, savour Ritz service, and appreciate the people — both staff and guests — who have given the hotel the peerless personality that has thrust it into a class all its own.

One such person the Hallidays liked to meet was a jovial French-Canadian named Pierre Demers who, in nearly four decades as the Ritz's executive chef, garnered eight Culinary Olympic gold medals. He once invited Bob and Gloria Halliday to take the battered service elevator down to the hotel's kitchen, with its deep sinks and big, box-like ovens, to actually watch him prepare their favourite Ritz dinner, *chicken grand'mère*.

For all his acclaim, which stretched around the globe, Demers remained refreshingly hospitable and humble and, in so doing, came to epitomize the Ritz-Carlton's social and community spirit. He got to know Ritz "regulars" so well that he would welcome them to his home for an eight-course gourmet dinner cooked from recipes he had collected while working with some of the world's greatest chefs in Paris and New York, and which he had refined and adapted to meet his customers' tastes.

More than once, he received a telephone call from a Baltimore businessman who asked, "Hey, chef! What's the salmon like today?"

"Good, Sir, as usual," Demers would reply confidently. It inevitably sufficed to spur the man to board the next flight to Montreal to sample both the meal and the inimitable decorum of the waiters who served it.

Decorum had become a Ritz-Carlton way of life. One wintry night, a desk manager heard a Salvation Army band carolling a few blocks away and, without putting on his coat, dashed into the street to invite it into the hotel to play for the guests. With its gleaming brass, decorated fir tree, and the cluster of musicians blowing lifeblood into silver trumpets, the lobby suddenly took on the appearance of an expensive Christmas card.

For a Montreal psychologist, however, the Ritz proved itself a friendly refuge when he needed friendship most. That was on the night he and his wife separated and he arrived at the hotel fatigued and worried, and fully intending to check into a room where he could gain the composure and the strength he needed to search for an apartment the following day. For a while, the man sat on a lobby chair collecting his thoughts, and fell sound asleep. When he awoke in the morning, he discovered he was still there and that rather than disturb him, or ask what he was doing in the hotel, one of the lobby staff had covered him with a blanket.

Under its outward formality, the atmosphere at the Ritz-Carlton has always been so relaxed and natural that staff and regular guests have come to know each other well, and been inspired to help each other out. On one of several visits to the hotel, British newspaper baron Lord Northcliffe discovered a front desk clerk unusually glum. "What's up, old fellah?" he asked him. "You weren't like this the last time I was here."

True to the hotel's policy of expecting staff members to refrain from sharing their personal lives with guests, and certainly not lumbering them with their problems, the clerk would not reveal why his spirits were down — until he could no longer withstand the weight of His Lordship's prodding. Only then would he admit that he was worried about his wife, who had been taken to hospital that morning to give birth. He had been so busy, he confided, that he had not even found the time to phone to ask how she was, or if he were yet a father.

"But we can do better than telephone her," Northcliffe said with a wink. "You shoot off to the hospital and see her, and I'll hold the fort for you."

During the thirty-five minutes the clerk was away, His Lordship answered the telephone and admitted a party of wealthy Americans to their rooms. Later, consulting their lists, the management ascertained with relieved delight that the group had been assigned to the correct accommodation.

For many years, a retired banker walked into the steamy Ritz kitchen each week with bags of the tomatoes he had grown in his garden. He wanted the staff to peel and serve them not just to himself, but to anyone else who happened to be lunching that day and who enjoyed tomatoes as much as he did. The executive housekeeper, meanwhile, shopped regularly for a retired Canadian army captain named Gordon H. Murray. She bought his socks and pyjamas and instructed her department to clean the Boer War sword he had hung proudly above his dresser, and to polish his World War I medals.

Murray, by the way, an Englishman, first entered the hotel for a meal one night in 1949. Too tired to catch a return flight to London that day, he checked into room 614 instead, where he stayed. Over nearly three decades he displayed a dignified military posture in deftly tailored English suits, seated on a blue-velvet *directoire* chair in the Oval Room, formerly the main dining room, where he read his newspapers and letters. As he succumbed to age and was less inclined to read, he became as much a part of the lobby as those big standing chandeliers that took the night cleaner more than an hour to polish. He sat as straight as a ramrod in his own special chair, his hands on his walking cane, and nodded approvingly to all who entered or departed the Ritz, whether he knew them or not.

"Dear Captain Murray didn't just *live* here," the housekeeper used to say. "He belonged here. He *was* the Ritz."

Murray, in turn, a lanky, bald man with a white military moustache, insisted, "This place isn't so much a hotel as a state of mind. Anyone who doesn't know where they are and how they must behave here, shouldn't ever bother coming in."

When he died in his suite in 1975 at the age of ninety-two, three members of the kitchen staff placed a wreath on his lobby chair, where it stayed for three days.

Times at the Ritz have changed now, but not appreciably. The Captain Murrays and the Lord Northcliffes, and all they connoted, have been replaced by a newer set, which is just as accommodating, and just as appreciative of all that the hotel offers. A Grand Prix Bar waiter once lent a customer $50, and got it back; a barman in the Maritime Bar will never forget the time he presented a man with his bill only to watch him sink his hand deeply into his pocket and slap a bullet on the counter.

"If I had a gun," the customer said, "I'd give it to you right here and now so you could load it and kill me. I've left my cash in my other trousers, and my wallet, credit cards and all, is on my dressing table at home. As sure as eggs are eggs, I'm in the Ritz — but penniless!"

"There's no need for me to kill you, Sir," said the barman, who had never seen the customer before. "Pay us next time you're around." The man did, three weeks later when he arrived to retrieve his bullet which the barman had kept safely aside for him in a brandy snifter.

Not long ago a globe-trotting stockbroker, one of many regular guests who habitually phone ahead to pre-arrange their menus, asked for *cassoulet* to be accompanied by a bottle of Brouilly 1977. The wine, which the man wanted placed in his suite exactly three hours before his arrival so that he could enjoy it at proper room temperature, was already in stock in the hotel's cellar. The meal, however, which was not on the menu, was a different matter.

"If that's what the customer wants," the chef said, "that's what the customer gets." To gather the ingredients — white beans, sausages, and salami — two members of his kitchen staff walked several blocks in the snow to buy them from local grocery stores. The dish was served, and the client asked that it be ready for him whenever he arrived on numerous subsequent visits spread over many years.

While the hotel's culinary prowess is legendary, so is its near-holy consecration to goodwill. The managers label it "service;" guests call it "pampering of the very highest quality." Ask the two doctors who arrived from California one Saturday night. Their luggage, they found to their horror, had been damaged in transit, and the shirts they had planned to wear at a conference the following day were badly stained. Their quandary was certainly not helped by the knowledge that all dry cleaners were closed until Monday.

"Don't worry about it," said a maid, calmly. "I'll take care of it for you."

"How?" asked the doctors.

"You'll see."

The maid took the shirts home and returned them a few hours later freshly-washed and ironed — "with compliments of the hotel, and hoping to see you both here again some time."

Ritz-Carlton house detectives have babysat and porters have continued the long, faithful custom of walking patrons' pets. On one occasion they were entrusted with a tan chihuahua that belonged to opera soprano Lily Pons, who was widely known in the world's most prestigious opera houses for her fiery temperament.

It was understandable, then, that when Miss Pons telephoned room service late one night for a filet mignon, the staff began to quake. The floor waiter hurriedly passed the order to the sous-chef, who cooked the meal instantly, and set it out neatly with spinach, new potatoes, and freshly-picked fiddleheads. It was delivered to the diva's room post-haste, steaming hot, in a copper casserole.

At breakfast the following day, the chef received a $2 tip from Miss Pons, and a note from her secretary:

> Thank you very much for the fine filet which you so kindly provided last night, so terribly late though it was. You will be very pleased to know that Madame Pons' little dog, who is enjoying his stay here at the Ritz-Carlton Hotel as much as we are, was enormously pleased with it and will doubtless be asking for more helpings before the time comes for us to leave. Thank you again.

Ritzmen have met important guests at railway stations and airports, taken them to their rooms, complied with their whims, and seen them off. One long-serving doorman known as Victor remembers escorting a woman to her New York-bound train when it suddenly started off while he was still placing her luggage on the overhead rack. Undaunted, he disembarked at Westmount, the next station, and forty-five minutes after setting out, returned to the hotel by taxi.

"Where have you been?" the head porter asked, worried that something might have befallen him.

"Doing my job," Victor replied casually. Nothing more was ever said about his absence.

Another doorman, who patrons knew for more than thirty years as Jamieson, was also a typically faithful observer of the Ritz way of doing things. He developed, out of dire necessity, an uncannily tactful knack for solving awkward situations, which was the envy of colleagues. For instance, he once saw a long-time patron's daughter, who was given to all manner of antics when she had been drinking, trying to "steal" the coat rack being used by a small gathering in a mezzanine salon called the Blue Room.

"Dear me, that is *such* a clumsy thing, Madame," Jamieson declared sympathetically, springing to the woman's side from his post beside the main entrance as she manoeuvred her burden — heavy with mink coats — from the elevator and halfway through the lobby toward the street. "Please allow me, Madame, to assist you."

His plan was perfect. He ushered the woman gently into the revolving door and followed her. She was discharged outside while he, having surreptitiously left the coat rack behind him, was in a single motion returned to the hotel. With the typical British reserve always so admired at the Ritz, he asked a porter to return the rack to the Blue Room, and no one else in the hotel that night needed to be any the wiser about what had happened.

Such amiability, chivalry, and concerns for the public's well-being at the Ritz-Carlton have prompted Manhattan stockbroker Harry Minden and his wife, Beryl, to make concerted efforts to spend at least two long weekends there each year, to bask in what they call "the mulled splendour of our favourite hotel." Like the Hallidays, they could also afford to stay in most hotels, anywhere. But ever since they first sampled the reliquary Ritz-Carlton while attending a friend's wedding there in 1963, they have come to consider it a "bastion of elegance, refinement and sensibility," and have always hurried back.

Minden remembers once paying the cashier by cheque, and another time not at all. Not, at least, for several days. That followed the hot summer afternoon he lost the briefcase containing his wallet, cheque book, and files. It was eventually discovered wedged between a sofa and a wall in a Ritz-Carlton bar, but not until several hours after Minden had departed for home. The hotel mailed the briefcase with a covering letter wishing him and his wife well, and Minden sent a cheque for his room, a thank you card, and a few dollars to defray postage costs.

"When you talk about the Ritz," he says, "you're really talking about an institution that has distinguished itself by being honourable, trustworthy, and good. Yet it still finds time to serve world-class food and offer world-class rooms. It's the kind of place that we must cherish and preserve."

Indeed, it is this curious blend of Old World tradition and the bright efficiency of the present that gives the hotel its unmatched appeal. Its talent is to offer white-tie service among eighteenth-century decor, for example, yet encourage business meetings and welcome numerous outside groups to hold their quiet dinners or annual celebrations there.

Not long ago, a bowling club banquet was beginning to get slightly out of hand in the Oval Room and a group of celebrants was attempting some daring acrobatics from a nearby balustrade. One of the men suddenly toppled like a nine-pin and, anticipating the problem, a waiter on his way from the hors d'oeuvre table darted forward to break his fall.

Fortunately, neither man was seriously hurt. The bowler was a little bruised, the waiter shaken and bemused. He scrambled instantly to his feet, nonetheless, and, before picking up his tray and scooping up the mess of unwanted food, straightened his clothes and managed a slow bow from the waist.

"Excuse me, Sir," he said. "But will you be expecting anyone to join you?"

To the guests, the panache of the Ritzmen makes the hotel rare, indeed. It is a hostel of character, charm, and dignity, and is most certainly synonymous with luxury and class. It is authentic. It is welcoming.

Today's patrons like the Mindens and the Hallidays express this differently. To them, the Ritz-Carlton Hotel has come closer to livery than to service, closer to charm than to convenience, closer to home than to hostelry, and closer to the past than to the future. Other inns, schooled in time-motion thinking, they will tell you, offer a new kind of service, antiseptic, instantaneous, and impersonal. At the Ritz, though, the philosophy, barely altered since its opening, has been fondly passed down and, like all loyal patrons, they feel it.

"When Gloria and I have checked in, shaken hands with the staff, had a cocktail, a fine dinner, and gone to bed," says Bob Halliday, "we tell ourselves over and over again that we are entrusted to one of the last great hotels."

Harry Minden has never met Halliday and would like to one day, if only to swap a few yarns about the hotel, perhaps, or share his experiences there with someone who will value them almost as much as he does. "Quite frankly," he says, "it's hard to imagine a better place to stay, or walls that tell more stories. The tales the Ritz can tell — sometimes inspiring, sometimes picaresque — are doubtless a reflection of twentieth-century life refracted through a golden lens. You can't help but wonder how a magnificent old place like this first came about. I'd sure like to have witnessed its beginnings."

CHAPTER TWO

Four Tycoons,
and the Ritz Idea

*" The most satisfactory accomplishment of all
is to enjoy life and help others to enjoy it, too,
even if it does mean spending money. "*

CHARLES HOSMER, RITZ-CARLTON FOUNDER

The Ritz-Carlton was a dream. It was the dream of a group of Montreal investors who regretted that their city lacked a hotel to cater not only to their own tastes for caviar Astrakhan and Grande Fine Champagne de Napoleon 1800 served by white-gloved Continental waiters, but to those of visiting Europeans.

True, they could take their visitors to the Windsor Hotel, and did. But these men were St. James Street tycoons, mostly, and prominent among the 25,000 residents of what was then called Montreal's Golden Square Mile. This, an area bounded by Guy and Côte des Neiges streets to the west, University Street to the east, Cedar and Pine avenues to the north, and Dorchester Boulevard to the south, was said to have contained more than seventy percent of the entire wealth of Canada.

Most of those who lived there wore the opulent look of long-standing success, and those St. James Street tycoons were by no means an exception. Accordingly, they visualized a hotel they could call their own and, financially, it would not be beyond their reach. They had always known what they wanted, after all, and through determination and effort, had got it.

These men were drawn from many parts of the great business spectrum. Invariably, they had started out as accountants, solicitors, or small manufacturers, perhaps, but had ended their careers as financiers, bankers, or industrialists. They then pioneered work about which they initially knew absolutely nothing, amassing considerable fame and formidable fortunes on the way.

Sir Herbert Holt disliked liquor, barbers, pomp, publicity, the press —
and high society. But the idea of a new hotel for the city's elite intrigued him.

There was Dublin-born Herbert Samuel Holt, the dream-driven power magnate, a brilliant engineer by profession who, while still in his early twenties, had built several American and Canadian railways, including stretches of the CPR. He formed the Montreal Light, Heat & Power Company, and served on the boards of numerous corporations, eventually controlling nearly 300 of them. When the Ritz-Carlton was born, he was president of the Royal Bank of Canada, a position he retained for twenty-six years.

Dour and introspective, Herbert Holt never gave up thinking. The writer J. Herbert Hodgins once said of him that when he contemplated a project, he "looked forlorn, like a boulder resting alone on a hilltop." Holt, who stood a massive six-foot-five and sported a handlebar moustache, disliked liquor, barbers, and high society. More than anything, though, he hated pomp and publicity, and he shunned the press. He once turned down an interview by saying, "I am certain anything favourable you might write about me would only give the Communistic yellow press another opportunity to vilify and lie about me."

Not surprisingly, Holt rarely made friends. One of his colleagues, R.O. Sweezey, called him "a ruthless, lonesome old cuss," but conceded that he was "fundamentally sound and honest." Holt was, and he possessed a genius for leadership.

His greatest assets were vision and ambition, and these manifested themselves in countless successes that won him accolades by the score, including his knighthood. To colleagues Holt was "the builder of the Dominion" and "the quietly analytical genius who worked like a silkworm in his own cocoon." To the public, however, he was Canada's unpretentious millionaire, and a man they never knew or liked.

Sir Herbert Holt contrasted sharply with another Ritz founder, the friendly, outgoing Montreal-born financier and industrialist Charles Blair Gordon with whom he was often seen. Gordon had learned to manufacture cotton so well, first at the Standard Shirt Company and later at the Canadian Converter Company, that, in 1909, he was able to organize Dominion Textile Ltd., become its first president — and earn the sobriquet of Canada's Textile King. That year, he was knighted for his work, and became a director of Molson's Bank.

As illustrious as Holt and Gordon were two additional Ritz founders, the industrialists Hugh Montagu Allan and Charles Rudolph Hosmer.

Although one of thirteen children, Montagu Allan, as he was known for most of his life, was never left wanting. He was born in Montreal, son of the owner of the Allan Line of steamships, which he later inher-

Sir Charles Gordon organized Dominion Textile Ltd., and earned
the sobriquet of Canada's Textile King. The Ritz-Carlton, however,
utilized his expertise and influence as a banker.

PHOTO COURTESY OF THE BANK OF MONTREAL ARCHIVES

ited. His prominence had begun to grow when he was in his teens (shortly after changing his name from Hugh Andrew to Montagu to avoid being mistaken for a cousin) and already a successful merchant.

He was president of the Allan Line at only twenty-one and went on to become an official of more than a dozen large firms, each of them different: the Montreal Rolling Mills Company, the Canadian Paper Company, the Acadia Coal Company, and the North-West Cattle Company. He earned his knighthood mainly for outstanding philanthropy, most notably the donation to amateur hockey of its Allan Cup. His leisure time was spent helping the Society for the Prevention of Cruelty to Animals and serving as Master of the Montreal Hunt.

Charles Hosmer, on the other hand, was almost entirely self-made. He was born and educated in tiny Coteau-Landing, Quebec, thirty-five miles west of Montreal. At twelve, he swept a junction station-house of the Grand Trunk Railway and cleaned kerosene lamps, while keeping his eyes on the job ahead. Each day, he listened to the intermittent clicking of the telegraph key that announced each train, and studied by night so he could decipher what he heard.

Learning Morse code, however, was only the beginning for Hosmer. By fourteen, he had learned to communicate through telegraphy. He eventually became so proficient at it that by the age of twenty-one, he was appointed superintendent of the Dominion Telegraph Company. By the age of thirty, he was the dynamic young president of the Canadian Mutual Telegraph Company, and five years later manager of the infant Canadian Pacific Telegrams, which he built to international importance.

If that were not enough, he had already begun to serve simultaneously with more than ten other organizations, including the growing Montreal Gas Company. He was also launching sizable business ventures of his own, everything from mining and paper making to hydro and flour-milling, that soon spanned the country. One more — something as small as a hotel — may well have imposed upon his time, but certainly appealed to his nature.

In this respect, Hosmer was the antithesis of Herbert Holt, with whom he did business, and considerably more akin to Charles Blair Gordon. He was portly and jocund, and he radiated gentility.

These men spearheaded the impassioned drive for the hotel on behalf of friends and colleagues, and were bolted faithfully to the belief that it would be an asset, and certainly not a hindrance, to a growing Montreal. With the exception of the unsociable Holt, the founders spent many of

Sir Montagu Allan was president of his father's Allan shipping line at only
twenty-one and went on to become an official of more than a dozen large firms,
each of them different: the Montreal Rolling Mills Company, the Canadian
Paper Company, the Acadia Coal Company, the North-West Cattle
Company — and the Ritz-Carlton Hotel.

PHOTO COURTESY OF CITY OF MONTREAL ARCHIVES

their off work hours in the St. James Club, the Montreal Club, the new and ultra exclusive Mount Royal Club, or the Canada Club, in which they held simultaneous memberships. They joined clubs that suited their travels — the Manitoba Club in Winnipeg and the Rideau Club in Ottawa. When they were in London, England, as they often were, they sipped sherry with aristocrats in the Empire Club or the Marlborough Club.

Wherever they went, however, they found either that the food was wanting, or that the tables were too close together. This, they complained, prevented them from conducting their "deals" over a fine dinner, and in absolute privacy. So, in an orgy of divine inspiration, they began to envision a club of their own — a dignified sanctum in which they could wine and dine their wives, and meet colleagues and clients in style. There, they could smoke, drink, and eat in peace, without having to meet their employees. To Herbert Holt's delight, they would be able to shut themselves away from reporters and hide from the prying eyes of competitors in any number of available rooms.

It would be, too, a luxurious home-away-from-home for friends, wives, even mistresses. It would be exclusive, quiet, and unique. It would be a new hotel.

None of the founders, however, had any knowledge whatsoever of hoteliery — just finance and good business. This, it transpires, proved to be sufficient. Their awesome, combined talent for administration and investing was a force to be reckoned with, and it had been derived largely from what they all did have: a talent for seeking advice and accepting it, and an innate ability to surround themselves with the most competent people available. On the strength of this they surged ahead.

During frequent visits to London they had all become enamoured with London's Carlton Hotel, a friendly, club-like institution that functioned affluently at the corner of Pall Mall and Haymarket, which runs between Trafalgar Square and Piccadilly Circus. Consequently, the founders at first proposed to model their "club" after the Carlton, and enticed two of its directors to sit on their board.

One new associate was Lionel Guest, the gentle but grave son of Lord Wimborne, whose family homestead, Wimborne House, stood next door to the Ritz Hotel in London. The other was the irascible Harry Higgins, who had recently ended his career as a Royal Guardsman to become the London Ritz's solicitor. After seeking to augment his income at the racetrack, and at last confessing his failure there, he was ripe for another business venture, even one that entailed investing overseas.

Charles Hosmer was born and educated in tiny Coteau-Landing, Quebec, thirty-five miles west of Montreal, where at the age of twelve, he swept a junction station-house of the Grand Trunk Railway and cleaned kerosene lamps. He and Sir Montagu Allan spearheaded the drive for the new hotel.

PHOTO COURTESY OF CP RAIL CORPORATE ARCHIVES

On Christmas Eve, 1909, the six founders formed The Carlton Hotel Company of Montreal Limited and vowed, even though they were busy, to continue to refine their concept. It evolved from a small club to a large club, to a small hotel, to a grand hotel. It would be administered by businessmen for businessmen. But, strangely, it would never be required to make huge profits. "The mere accumulation of wealth cannot bring enjoyment to any properly constituted mind," Charles Hosmer said. "But there is satisfaction in using wealth for the promotion of things that add permanently to the world's progress."

The company's final mandate was to "erect and operate a first-class residential hotel," and the directors pledged to finance it jointly. Overnight, its assets totalled $2 million which was divided into 20,000 shares worth $100 each. For these, there were many eager buyers; the company now had the money for a suitable building, in a suitable corner of the Golden Square Mile.

Early in 1910, before even convening their first meeting, the directors bought a mansion on the north-east corner of Sherbrooke and McTavish, and the land surrounding it. The property had once been owned by the prominent Montreal businessman Jesse Joseph, who was credited with importing the city's first cargo of tulip bulbs from Belgium. The sale, by his family shortly after his death, caused much controversy. It was public knowledge that the philanthropic tobacco magnate Sir William Macdonald had contemplated buying it to donate to the McGill University campus. The land had originally been part of the estate of Simon McTavish, the legendary fur trader, and abutted the lands of James McGill, which embraced a farm and two apple orchards. The public felt that the site was unsuitable for a hotel development, and said so.

The Carlton Hotel Company drew all manner of critical onslaught from the city's academic world and the public at large. Letters to Montreal's newspapers accused the directors of putting money before the future of youth and their community. One called the idea of building a hotel on university land "the proposed desecration of scholastic sanctity."

After much negotiation, the hotel's founders proved that their word was their bond. Despite their somewhat stolid, hard-bitten appearances as they went about their daily business in their black coats and white, wing-collared shirts, when it came to community affairs they were unflinchingly understanding. With the polish and reserve that has never ceased to be a Ritz-Carlton trait, they agreed to sell the property to Sir William Macdonald for exactly what they had paid for it "so that campus life could continue unscarred by development," and so he would be free to present it to the university, which he did. The Carlton Hotel Company then began to search for a likely spot elsewhere.

By that summer, it had found one: a piece of land that had once been owned by Henry Mulholland, a wholesale hardware merchant, just along the road at the corner of Drummond and Sherbrooke streets, where today the hotel still presides over the most fashionable area of the city. The seller, by the way, was the Montreal stockbrokerage of C. Meredith Company, in which Sir Charles Gordon also held a directorship. He served there with another of the Ritz-Carlton's first major shareholders, the eminent Montreal banker Hartland Brydges MacDougall. A Canadian army major in the front line during World War II, MacDougall had become one of Meredith's senior partners and was there to serve both the company and the new hotel.

Conflict of interest? Maybe — particularly when you consider that shrewdly anticipating its value to the hotel's founders, the C. Meredith Company had bought the land only a year before selling it to them. But the men involved in the deal were all part of a closely-knit business world anyway and, at times, it was impossible to separate them from virtually every business move they made. Not only did they attend the same clubs, but they sat together in some of the most prestigious board rooms in the country — Ogilvie Flour Mills Ltd., for instance. The formation of the Ritz-Carlton Hotel, then, was private enterprise at its very best, even if it was blatantly incestuous.

According to the deed of sale, the price for the lot was "One dollar...but with other good and valuable consideration." Meredith, it transpires, also received $787,500 in preferred shares in The Carlton Hotel Company of Montreal for which it paid $318,404 in cash. It expected the balance of $469,096 to be covered by "goodwill, benefits, and advantages," which were never fully explained. From then on, though, as a major shareholder, the firm would have some say in the Ritz-Carlton's future.

Whether or not the hotel was to make Sherbrooke Street what it has since become, or whether "Montreal's Fifth Avenue" would enhance the Ritz-Carlton, is still cause for contention. But it remains that the transformation of this part of the thoroughfare into one of note had already begun. The comfortable, impenetrable Château Apartments were about to rise up just across the road. So was the Building of the Art Association of Montreal, now known as the Montreal Museum of Fine Arts. Indeed, the hotel's founders envisioned that in this part of their Golden Square Mile lay the future of Montreal. A lot more would happen there, they predicted; Sherbrooke Street would one day sport exclusive shops and emerge as the social centre for Montreal's English-speaking elite. For a hotel which would one day bask in acclaim, this was an ideal location.

The site was magnificent, too. Once finally in place, the building would command a panoramic view in every direction. Tree-laden Mount Royal rose to the north, the St. Lawrence River and the Victoria Bridge to the south. On a clear day, the Lachine Rapids could be seen, with the Adirondack Mountains sprawling faintly in the distance beyond. To the east of the site was open space, an uncluttered vista of outlying, fast sprawling districts reaching down to the St. Lawrence as it curled past Pointe-aux-Trembles.

In the immediate vicinity was a forest of trees shading stretches of imposing homes. This leafy corner of the Golden Square Mile was calm and untroubled, and spared the seemingly endless noise of traffic in the commercial district just beginning to form on St. Catherine Street, only a hundred yards downhill. In this tranquility, the great hotel would one day dominate one expansive region like a cathedral staring out across a valley. But when exactly? "Soon," said Charles Hosmer.

To superstitiously avoid opening their hotel in 1913, the founders set themselves a deadline. They wanted to open the Ritz-Carlton with a huge gala ball on December 31, 1912. There was a lot left to be done, then, and time was running out.

No sooner had Mulholland's house and several stables on the site been demolished than the foundations of the dream were laid. In only weeks, the huge limestone shell was beginning to rise under the watchful gaze of two firms of architects.

The building had been designed by the distinguished New York City firm of Warren & Wetmore, which comprised two able partners. The older of these was Whitney Warren, a largely French-trained architect; the younger was Charles D. Wetmore, a graduate of the Harvard Law School. During the first three decades of this century, they had made Manhattan virtually their own, designing a slew of hotels, including the Biltmore, various commercial buildings, particularly the Stewart & Company Store, and several railway terminals, most notably New York's Grand Central Station.

While working on the Ritz-Carlton, Warren & Wetmore had, by law, to have a local representative to supervise the project. One was not too difficult to find. The firm simply assigned a junior architect, Montreal-born Frederick Garfield Robb, who had joined the firm in 1910. On his return to Montreal, Robb's first office was at the corner of Stanley and St. Catherine streets, his second in Phillips Place, off Phillips Square. Here, he established his own firm and oversaw the intricate job of constructing a building that conformed exactly to Warren and Wetmore's plans and specifications.

By mid-1911, work was well underway. Robb had assigned sheet placing, shoring, and excavation to the George A. Fuller Company, at a cost of $57,630. The lowest and successful bid to install the steel beams had been submitted by the Dominion Bridge Company, which wanted $147,000, a price Robb felt was too high. He accepted the tender, but convinced the company to do the work for less — $137,360.

The moment the shell of the building was complete in August 1911, contractors began the painstaking job of finishing it inside. More than seventy men employed by the Montreal firm of R. De Vigan & Company cemented and plastered walls and applied stone slabs. Workers from the William Rutherford & Sons Co., also of Montreal — "wholesalers and retailers in all branches of mill work" — installed railings and balustrades.

Three firms sent specialists from Ontario: the Lautz Company of Toronto, dealers in foreign and domestic marble, and J. & J. Taylor Ltd., manufacturers of cast iron safes. When the building was more than half completed, the Otis-Fensom Company of Hamilton installed the public and service elevators. Montreal's richest men would soon see their dream a reality.

There was one more detail to consider, however, and it was important enough for the directors to convene the first meeting at which they would all be present. Astonishingly, particularly in view of their combined success in business and commerce, the investors' discussions about the hotel had been somewhat piecemeal. The complex job of drawing up partnership agreements between them and devising shares had rested entirely with their lawyers.

Virtually all their conversations about the business itself, and how to refine it, had taken place by telephone or over a drink or two at the Mount Royal Club, which gives credence, perhaps, to the oft-held theory that huge financial deals are not, by any stretch of the imagination, made solely in the board room, but on golf courses, in locker rooms, or in saloons. This one had been no exception.

Now, though, during the early evening of January 12, 1912, the men decided it was time to meet in one place at one time to consolidate their philosophy, and share their enthusiasm. Besides, they knew that Charles Hosmer, who at the age of sixty was considered the "grandfather" of the group, had something important to suggest to them.

That meeting, in the Mount Royal Club, was chaired by the board's new president, Lionel Guest. Sir Montagu Allan later headed the company, resigning in only a matter of days when business pressures mounted as his Allan Line was being absorbed into Canadian Pacific. So from 1912 on, Hosmer took over. Meanwhile, he had solicited new support. Hence there were two new faces among directors at that meeting — Thomas Joseph Drummond, the fiery, Irish-born iron magnate, and Montreal-born William Massey Birks, about to become chairman of his father's Canada-wide company, Henry Birks & Sons Limited.

Lionel Guest called the gathering to order and invited Charles Hosmer to speak. Had Hosmer not wanted to make his announcement, it seems, the men might have found no good reason to meet that night at all, and the first collective meeting of the hotel's major investors may never have taken place.

Charles Hosmer had an idea which he needed to share. Even at this late stage, after the company had been formed and construction started, he wanted to pursue a slightly different tack. His cohorts listened intently.

During visits to Europe around the turn of the century, Hosmer said, he had met and befriended an energetic young Swiss hotelier whom the pleasure-loving King Edward VII had dubbed, "The hotelkeeper to kings and the king of hotel keepers." His name was César Ritz, he had opened his first hotel in Paris in 1898, and it was already the talk of Europe's cafè society as a haven for the rich, and an elegant place in which to be seen.

"If, gentlemen, we can persuade Mr. Ritz to some way lend his name to our venture or endorse it," Hosmer told his associates, "then we will be guaranteed instant good fortune. Mark my words."

"All very good, Charlie," said Sir Charles Gordon, who had also met Ritz in his travels. "But we will have a lot to live up to, if you don't mind my saying so. We might not be able to do it."

"We will," Hosmer replied quickly. "We will indeed. With what all of us around this table know, think, and can find out, we can do it."

The suggestion did not go unnoticed by Lionel Guest and Harry Higgins. They knew Cèsar Ritz better than anyone.

Thomas Joseph Drummond, the fiery, Irish-born iron magnate became a
director of The Ritz-Carlton Hotel Company Limited shortly after
construction of the building had started in 1911.

PHOTO COURTESY OF CITY OF MONTREAL ARCHIVES

"Monsieur Ritz is open to any suggestions," Higgins said. "And he is a man of great wisdom and encouragement. I can assure you of that."

After the meeting, the investors visited the construction site, then Hosmer went home to write César Ritz a letter explaining, in detail, what he and his colleagues had undertaken. Within weeks, on his next visit to London where Ritz had an office, Hosmer called in to see him and was both relieved and delighted to find him receptive.

César Ritz had already begun to advocate his technique — and sell his name through his newly-formed Ritz Hotel Development Company. Besides the hotel in Paris, it had already fostered eighteen others across the world, including those in London, Madrid, Lucerne, Naples, Rome, Evian-Les-Bains in France, New York, Philadelphia, Rio de Janeiro, Saõ Paulo and Guaruja, Brazil, and Buenos Aires, Argentina. The company was also sponsoring restaurants on three luxury ships of the Hamburg-American Line: the SS *Amerika*, the SS *Kaiserin Auguste Victoria*, and the SS *Imperator*.

Ritz told Hosmer that for a fee of $25,000 he would be happy to help any group of financiers who were prepared to underwrite the cost of a suitable building. But there was one major proviso. He needed absolute assurance that he would always be their mentor and guide, and that the standards established by his Ritz Plan would be closely adhered to.

"I see no reason," he added, "why we can't all work together to make the Montreal venture a prosperous one, and be exceedingly happy doing it."

Elated, Hosmer caught the next steamship back to Canada to advise his colleagues to pay the money, and rename the organization The Ritz-Carlton Hotel Company of Montreal Limited. They needed little persuasion and did so instantly. The corporate name was legally altered by Canada's Secretary of State, William James Roche, on March 5, 1912.

But César Ritz's permission to allow the Montreal hotel to enter his "family," Hosmer explained, had not been given easily. When it came to associating himself with other people's projects, the old man was decidedly uncharitable, and not without reason. He and a staff of salesmen had built a fine reputation and a huge corporate empire, and they were not about to destroy either through haphazard risks or poor decisions.

No one knew hotels like César Ritz, and he had learned about them the hard way. He was born in 1850, the thirteenth child of a poor Swiss shepherd and his wife. They never believed their son would one day perpetuate the family name, let alone revolutionize the hotel industry

William Massey Birks was recruited onto the Ritz-Carlton board as his father's Canada-wide company, Henry Birks & Sons Limited, beckoned him to take over the chairmanship.

and give the world new standards for luxury, but that is exactly what the boy did. He rose from that humble parentage — in the huddle of weather-beaten cottages in the village of Niederwald, overlooking the Rhone River — and the job, at age thirteen, of helping his father tend sheep on the mountain slopes, to become a social arbiter in the fashionable *haut monde* of the gay 1880s and the even gayer 1890s.

It was just reward. He was blessed with the virtues of ambition, courage, and taste, and strove for excellence in everything he did. He did not, however, consider that his life had really begun until 1867 when he left Switzerland for Paris, where be became a waiter at Voisin, which was then considered the city's most fashionable restaurant.

One story goes that while he was there, he dropped a bottle of wine and a disgruntled diner snarled, "You'll never make it in this business." César Ritz, still in his teens, went his own way quietly and later teamed up with the celebrated French chef, Auguste Escoffier, with whom he had had a magnificent apprenticeship, working with him in several famous European establishments, including the Carlton Hotel, where he had first met Charles Hosmer and Charles Gordon.

While in London, Ritz decided to return to Paris to find a suitable site for a hotel of his own, and eventually persuaded Marnier La Postolle, an old friend and the originator of Grand Marnier liqueur, to lend him the money to do it. The rest quickly became history.

César Ritz agreed to allow the Montreal venture to use his name and his Ritz Plan in exchange for guarantees that Hosmer and his men would accede to a barrage of conditions. They did. Charles Hosmer, Sir Herbert Holt, Sir Montagu Allan, and Sir Charles Gordon agreed with the demands and collectively drafted a letter to Ritz thanking him for his help.

From his experience in Paris, César Ritz discovered that integral to the success of any fine hotel was location. It had to be a "convenient" place, yes, but removed from noise and congestion. Preferably, the hotel needed to be an "oasis unto itself," ideally overlooking a public park or square.

The rooms of all hotels to which Ritz would lend his name were to be comfortable to live in rather than merely attractive to look at. Food and beverage services had to be second to none, not only in the quality of its preparation, but in its presentation as well. The offerings of the wine cellar, he said, should appeal to the "finest connoisseurs."

César Ritz considered service to be the most crucial aspect of what he called the "perfect" hotel. Providing the absolute last word in service, to the minutest detail, and maintaining its quality, he said, meant ensuring that the number of employees always exceeded the number of guests!

It was, quite obviously, a sign of its times, and a demand that could not always be honoured. Others that Ritz put forward, though, could and definitely had to be. Any hotel that bore even part of his name, he insisted, had to conform closely to what the Ritz Plan considered absolutely imperative: washrooms, and possibly a bath and a telephone, in every room.

On each floor, Ritz wanted a kitchenette fitted with an electrically powered dumbwaiter that dropped down to a main kitchen directed by the finest available chef. By having these, he fervently maintained, the Montreal hotel would ensure that all room service meals, "unspoiled by strong sauces," would be of the finest quality and could be served course by course and, like most people wanted them, hot.

César Ritz stipulated, too, the appointment of an around-the-clock valet service to clean shoes, maids to wash clothes and press them, and a head porter who would sit behind a separate desk inside the main door to trace lost luggage, order theatre tickets and cabs, give directions, answer guests' questions, and be available at all times to walk their pets. If necessary, Ritz said, the head porter was also to make reservations in other hotels, even in those establishments, like the Windsor and the Queen's, that were considered Ritz-Carlton competitors.

Finally, the hotel's public areas should be well appointed with tasteful furnishings, an abundance of plants, fine paintings, and plenty of comfortable seating. And the lobby itself? In general, it needed to be small enough to create warmth and intimacy and make loiterers obvious to the staff day and night, yet sufficiently large to avoid overcrowding should an influx of guests arrive all at one time.

Above all, Ritz said, the lobby had to have a front desk that was tucked into a corner so it would not be a focal point, and a wide, curving staircase from the mezzanine so that on special occasions women could make the most dramatic entrances possible and show the full effects of their gowns.

Such an occasion, of course, would be the auspicious opening, and it certainly would not be an ordinary New Year's Eve party. Before it took place, however, there loomed another crisis.

In November, 1912, the City of Montreal wilted under public pressure and refused to grant the hotel a liquor licence. A war of words ensued. The city, represented by J.A. Roberts of Dominion Alliance, contended that by allowing the Ritz-Carlton to serve alcohol, too many young students would be encouraged to drink. "This establishment," Roberts said, "is far too close to McGill University for the comfort of the people."

The Ritz-Carlton assigned Lord Shaughnessy, the pinch-lipped president of the CPR, to state its case. He argued that the students were already drinking freely anyway, in a nearby restaurant called Broker's whose liquor licence the hotel would be happy to buy. In fact, he added, the restaurant had already told the hotel's directors that it would be prepared to sell them the licence, because it was considering closing. "Perhaps it would be a good idea if the city permitted this arrangement to go forward," Shaughnessy said. "That way, it will not be issuing another licence, but merely transferring one already in existence. It would be allowing an honourable, worthy establishment the chance it sought to satisfy its clientele."

In the following days, the city reviewed the hotel's application more favourably. Lord Shaughnessy further maintained that allowing the YMCA on Drummond Street to serve drinks and not the Ritz-Carlton, created unfair competition. The city finally agreed with him, and the licence was granted on December 10, 1912, with only days to spare before the opening event. Two days later, *Le Devoir* carried a public notice announcing the city's plans to extend Drummond Street northwards from Sherbrooke Street to make way for new homes.

So important was the Ritz-Carlton Hotel to Montreal, that the inauguration celebrations would become one of the decade's biggest social gatherings. The city's best-known socialites, civic leaders, and businessmen would meet at a gala banquet and ball. "THOUSANDS MAKE MERRY TONIGHT," announced the *Gazette*. "New Hotel Will Accommodate 350 Guests On Its Debut. Special Features Promised By Managers."

One of those features would be an exquisite gourmet feast; the other the appearance of the little orchestra Signor Eugene Lignante had taken to Pittsburgh and New York, and which had now been hired to lead the celebrations.

This would be another extravagant night for socialites, and they could drink and make merry to their heart's content.

CHAPTER THREE

And a Good Time
Was Had by All

" The Ritz-Carlton Hotel at Montreal is more one link
in the marvelous growth of a creation started
through the ingenuity of a Swiss farmer."

CONSTRUCTION MAGAZINE, 1913

They came by car, cab, and buggy, mostly from the Golden Square
Mile, and some arrived on foot. It was the most elaborate parade of
wealth and good fortune that many Montrealers had ever seen,
particularly those among the thousands who had no choice but to watch
from outside. Not even a spiteful wind that cut down Sherbrooke Street
and blew little drifts of snow against the Ritz-Carlton's steps deterred
them. The spectacle resembled a modern-day Hollywood Oscar night,
with ordinary people celebrating New Year's Eve by craning their heads
to see who was there.

They glimpsed Lord and Lady Shaughnessy, for instance, and Sir
Herbert Holt and his wife Jessie Paton, who were making a rare public
appearance, and imagined for the moment that they were one of their
associates, privileged and powerful.

Montrealers had heard a lot about their newest hotel and who would
be at the opening. For nearly two years, news of its progress had spilled
into city newspapers at least once a week. Now, at last, they could see
it for themselves — the twenty-first in the mighty Ritz system. Directors
of The Ritz-Carlton Hotel Company of Montreal, meanwhile, stood back
to view the results of their endeavours, and their illustrious monument
to the city they loved. As the building neared completion, a *Montreal
Daily Herald* editorial proclaimed:

> The citizens of Montreal may, and in fact, do feel that in their new
> hotel they will have the finest and most artistic building of its character
> in the Dominion of Canada. They realize that the standard already

Many of the earliest patrons, nearly all of them residents of the Golden Square Mile, arrived at the hotel on foot. Some of them, however, as this picture shows, came by horse-drawn buggy.

PHOTO COURTESY OF THE RITZ-CARLTON COLLECTION

established (by M. Ritz) has been raised a trifle higher in this resultant of genius, through a broad experience with all phases of the work and a studied handling of the aesthetic capabilities.

On that New Year's night, the crowd admired a building that cost a little more than $2 million — completely within the investors' budget — to both erect and equip. According to William Henry Atherton's *History of Montreal*, however, published in 1914, it had an actual real estate value of only $663,330. Nonetheless, the Ritz-Carlton Hotel was assessed by city planners as Montreal's fifth most valuable structure, twice as expensive as the YMCA, six times that of the Imperial Tobacco Company's headquarters in Little Burgundy, and infinitely more attractive than either.

The hotel had been built in the fashionable Adam style, so called because it had been fathered in England at the turn of the century by two architect brothers, Robert and James Adam. Most new buildings throughout the Commonwealth in the early 1900s were Victorian or Georgian and, for the most part, bulky and fussy. The Adam brothers, though, had brought to the fore a refreshing new concept of design. It harkened back to the Classical period of architecture which had been preoccupied with shape, proportion, and delicacy and, unlike the extremely decorative Baroque period which preceded it, was characterized by a sparing but highly effective use of ornamental plaster and stone work architects call terra cotta.

The Ritz was, indeed, a magnificent example of Adam architecture. Externally, reported the trade magazine *Construction*, its general appearance was "a masterpiece of refinement and dignity. The terra cotta trimmings at the window openings, and elsewhere, are in perfect harmony with the limestone, which gives the structure a feeling of solidity and strength."

The building rose majestically for ten storeys with its interior reflected in its exterior. The lower of two horizontal courses marked the base of the building, which consisted of the ground and mezzanine floors. A narrow frieze above it denoted the first, or servants' dormitory floor. The cornice above this indicated the guests' quarters, or, as the management called them, "sleeping apartments."

The three top storeys above the second cornice was rich in ornamentation, and demonstrated both its artistic and its practical use. "It is well to notice," *Construction* said, "the natural blending of this with the yellow-grey limestone and how much the former material expresses the latter."

The balustrade at the top of the building rested upon an extremely high base, allowing it to be viewed and enjoyed without craning too much from the street directly below. Balconies protruding over Sherbrooke Street from some of the top floors provided a break in the two central divisions and lent an additional aesthetic value to the overall architecture.

A huge, black-metal, glass-covered marquis, or parapet, stretched westward from the Drummond Street corner for nearly 100 feet and provided shelter for guests the moment they climbed from their cars and headed toward the main entrance. The entrance, which housed a public telephone booth, comprised a little vestibule between two sets of doors.

Those lucky enough to attend the opening night gala marvelled at the interior — the work of Montreal's socialite decorator, William T. Castle — particularly the lobby, where Lionel Guest and Harry Higgins welcomed the first patrons. César Ritz would have been as proud as Castle was happy. The lobby's solid, white marble floor was covered in places with sumptuous Oriental rugs. The walls were made of imitation Caen stone positioned above a Hauteville marble wainscot. The same marble adorned the counter of the front desk.

According to Ritz's wishes, this had been tucked — with the cashier's office beside it — into the left-hand corner of the lobby against the northern street wall, so as to spare all who entered the hotel from having to gaze into an obtrusive workspace and the bustle that would certainly accompany it. "All mercenary suggestions," wrote a *Herald* reporter, "are removed by placing the office where it is readily accessible to the main entrance, elevators, etc, and at the same time in an inconspicuous location."

Opposite the office, and on the lobby's southern wall, were the elevators, screened from the rest of the lobby by mirrored partitions. From their vantage point behind their counter, front office clerks could see who went up to the rooms, and who came down, while guests sipping tea in the lobby need be none the wiser!

When they passed through the revolving door, which was flanked by two other entrances with polished brass handles, all who entered the hotel were, in fact, confronted with the fine set of glass partitions that separated the main lobby from the Palm Court. "This inspires one with a feeling of restfulness and deep content," said the *Gazette*, "making the entry into the restaurant beyond a matter of ease and grace, a feature often objectionable on account of opening directly from the lobby."

What the reporter really meant to say was that the Palm Court, an enclosed reception area, provided a buffer zone which prevented a direct view of diners from the lobby and spared them undue noise.

When invited guests poured in on opening night, Sir Charles Gordon, Sir Herbert Holt, and Charles Hosmer, were sipping shooting sherry and sucking on their pipes in the Palm Court, which was attractive, indeed. It had been made particularly inviting by a number of small Antoinette tables and wicker chairs which had been arranged neatly on the soft, thick-piled, green Wilton, a carpet of the very highest quality.

Subdued lighting was provided by sixteen wall lamps and a magnificent centre candelabrum containing 150 bulbs made to resemble candles. Extra, decorative, lighting shone from behind the cornices and provided a soft glow that accentuated the cream walls above the marble wainscot.

At the southern end of the Palm Court, a short, broad staircase led to a large landing, which had a brass balustrade that matched the banisters of the lobby stairs. Beyond this was the sedate Oval Room. It was seventy-eight feet long and fifty-six feet wide, with three huge windows, one looking east onto Drummond Street, one looking south into an alleyway, and the third facing the Dutch Garden, which was to be used in summer for small parties and luncheons. The Oval Room also had a curving, thrust stage large enough for a twenty piece orchestra.

Most of the Oval Room's lighting came from a slightly-domed Adam ceiling with its abundance of elaborate moulding — a myriad of bulbs hidden behind a circular cornice. The room's walls were cream, matching the tablecloths; the carpeting was two shades of old rose. The lighter of these matched the silk tapestry of the chairs, the darker shade the heavy curtains that hung from beneath impressive valances imprinted with the hotel's crest.

The Oval Room was designed to accommodate 250, but at eleven o'clock that night it was stretched beyond capacity, for it was there that the hotel's very first diners sat down to a full-course dinner in the authentic Ritz style:

Caviar Astrakhan
Consommé Viveur
Truite au bleu, Zolkhaus
Selle de Chevreuil Grande-Duc
Gelée de Groseilles
Désirs du Prince de Galles
Salade Argenteuil
Pêches Melba à la Ritz
Corbeille de Fruits

One of the first photographs of the Ritz-Carlton ever taken reveals a snow-bound Sherbrooke Street stretching eastward and what appears to be yet another mode of patrons' transport — a sleigh.

PHOTO COURTESY OF THE RITZ-CARLTON COLLECTION

The feast was accompanied by a choice of fine, imported wines, and followed by liqueurs.

Looking to their right when they entered the main door, patrons saw — across the length of the lobby and beyond the cloakroom, the Ladies' Dressing Parlour, and the Gents' washroom — a foyer. Also partitioned off with glass, this provided another buffer zone, this one between the lobby and the Grand Ball Room.

The foyer had a separate entrance off Sherbrooke Street, which allowed direct access to the manager's office. This was on a grey, marble floored landing halfway up the big, curving staircase, with its black iron and brass rail, that led from the foyer to the mezzanine.

Here could be found the Smoking Room, the Grand Ball Room balcony, and the Oak Room, so called because of its oak wainscot and paneling. It had silver wall lights, too, and oak tables, and enough chairs upholstered in green to match the carpet, to seat 160 people.

One of the most attractive mezzanine salons was the Blue Room, designed for private gatherings. It was put to immediate use, for on the hotel's debut several families preferred to celebrate alone rather than to join the crowd. Said a *Gazette* social note:

> Lord and Lady Shaughnessy will entertain at a large supper party at the Ritz-Carlton Hotel tonight. Covers will be laid for twelve, the others expected to be present being Sir Thomas and Lady Tait, Mr. and Mrs. Kidd, Mr. and Mrs. W.F. Shaughnessy, the Misses Shaughnessy, Edith and Marguerite, Mr. Redmond and Mr. Meredith Smith.

A little way along the corridor, in the Grand Salon, Sir Herbert and Lady Holt presided over their own dinner to celebrate the Ritz-Carlton's birth and the coming of the New Year, and invited ten guests, which included their sons and their sons' fiancées.

The first floor above the mezzanine would belong almost entirely to the servants, most of whom were already living in the hotel. It had bedrooms, dressing rooms, dining rooms, and a lounge, as well as sewing and supply rooms for bedding and crockery. At the end of a long passageway near the elevators, were special facilities for visitors: the men's shoeshine stand and barbershop, and the women's hairdressing parlour, which was furnished with porcelain washbowls and mahogany chairs upholstered in grey.

All the other floors had been designed exclusively for guests. The cor-

The Ritz — particularly its Oval Room, shown here — was immediately hailed
as a magnificent example of Adam architecture. This style was fathered
in England at the turn of the century by two architect brothers, Robert
and James Adam. Externally, reported the trade magazine *Construction*,
the hotel's general appearance was "a masterpiece of refinement and dignity."
So was the Oval Room.

PHOTO COURTESY OF THE RITZ-CARLTON COLLECTION

ridors had tan Wilton carpeting that bore dark brown edging, and which had been laid on cement floors finished with marble that ran part way up the walls to a copper dado.

The accommodation itself comprised 164 double rooms, seventy single rooms, and twenty-seven suites, all with cream, washable-plaster walls and grey silk curtains. Bedrooms were lavishly equipped with brass beds, commodious built-in wardrobes — or cupboards — and mahogany dressers, tables, armchairs, lamp standards, and trunk stands. The sitting rooms, and most salons throughout the lower part of the hotel, each had a sofa, a dining set, a writing desk and matching chair, and a commode.

On the second floor was the Vice-Regal Suite, which stretched westward from the north-east corner of the building, above Sherbrooke Street, for the length of four ordinary sleeping apartments. At the eastern end of the suite was the dining room, with windows in two outer walls. It had a long mahogany table with matching chairs, and a beautiful Adam arch which separated it from the living room, or reception area. This was predominantly old rose and was informally, but lavishly, appointed with two love seats, three chesterfields, several floor lamps, and three crystal chandeliers.

Off the living room was a small antechamber that contained a gaily-painted chest and a dainty, tapestry-covered chair. This, in turn, opened onto a large, elaborately furnished bedroom with a four poster bed of highly polished walnut, a matching dressing table, chifferobe, and writing desk, and a floor-to-ceiling clothes cupboard with long mirrors set into each of its three doors. One large window was curtained with old gold netting and the draperies themselves were of rose and gold brocade.

West of the main bedroom was an intimate private sitting room complete with four deep-cushioned chairs and a settee upholstered in rose damask, a writing desk, and a marble-topped carved table. Beyond, was a second bedroom, which also had a four poster bed, as well as an adjoining sitting room complete with fireplace. Tucked inconspicuously away at the western extremity of the Vice-Regal Suite were the valet's quarters, with a single divan bed, a dresser with a table lamp, and a small closet.

The bowels of the great hotel consisted of three basement floors crammed with the kind of amenities and equipment that visitors are never supposed to see. On the lowest level was the elevator pit, a row of coal bunkers, all manner of container tanks, a central vacuum cleaner system, and the three 750-horsepower boilers used to feed the radiators in winter.

An artist's impression of the new building, drawn around 1913, used on the cover of a banquet menu during the hotel's early days.
PHOTO COURTESY OF THE RITZ-CARLTON COLLECTION

All hot water piped up to toilets, bathrooms, and kitchens, however, was steam-heated by two thermostatically-controlled boilers which could supply 3,000 gallons per hour. One of these supplied needs above the ground floor, the other those below. Because the lower basement floor was sunk more deeply than the city's new sewer, seven 250-gallon cast iron compressed air ejectors were required to collect and thrust the refuse upwards for more than twenty feet.

The sub-basement — "the cellar floor," as staff would come to call it — above the lower basement, was largely taken over by the hotel's air conditioning system: four giant, multi-vane fans, each servicing one particular area of the hotel by blowing fresh air through ten-inch galvanized steel ducts. One fan, for instance, cooled the lobby, Oak Room, and Oval Room, another the wine cellar, Grill Room, Oyster Bar, and main kitchen on the floor above.

The air conditioning system was completed by fresh-air intakes fitted with filters made of galvanized wire netting and cheesecloth, and several large fans which sucked stale air away from bathrooms, restaurants, and other public areas, and released it at the rate of 90,000 cubic feet per minute — with exhaust fumes from the boilers and water heaters — into the rear alleyway.

Besides the Grill Room and Oyster Bar, the upper basement floor — directly beneath the lobby and the main restaurant — housed the "trunk" rooms where guests could deposit unneeded luggage. The elevator motor room could also be found there, as could twenty-seven lockers or storerooms, three tailor shops, the blower room, and the main kitchen. With its four electric ovens, and a chain of deep sinks occupying one complete wall, it was considered the most advanced kitchen of its kind in North America. Said *Construction*:

> Adhering strictly to the attractive and cleanly policy maintained throughout all departments, the kitchen walls are built of white glazed tile and floors of nine-inch square tile. Connecting the kitchen with all floors are electrical dumb waiters equipped with special heating apparatus underneath, for the purpose of keeping meals served to the various floors warm. Corresponding lifts without the heaters administer to the cold storage needs. All liquors, etc., are served from a special bar attached to this department.

The Ritz-Carlton's refrigeration plant consisted of twenty-two five-ton ice machines and fifty cold-storage boxes that were cooled with brine. One high-pressure system serviced the cold-storage boxes placed in kitchenettes on each floor. Next door was the filter plant. Believe it or not, all cold water used throughout the hotel was purified with alum and pumped through four 200-gallon filters containing an eight-inch layer of screened gravel, several wire strainers, and three feet of sand!

The upper basement floor also contained a long, narrow barber shop for members of the staff and patrons' servants, and a little hallway at the bottom of a flight of steps leading to the upper foyer.

Conveniently, the foyer from Sherbrooke Street also provided separate access to the hotel's biggest room — the Grand Ball Room. This, ninety feet long and forty feet wide, was large enough for 400 people to attend banquets, receptions, balls, or concerts. From the piers of the balcony, which was really a chain of adjoining galleries of varying breadths encircling the entire room, hung lights that were encased in etched-alabaster glass globes finished in dull gilt. The walls, of smooth duresco plaster, were decorated with white wood trim, gilded metal, and heavy, grey silk curtains that matched the upholstery of the balcony rail.

Here, under the Ball Room's gargantuan chandelier, that dangled from another impressive Adam ceiling, nearly all the guests on that opening night would crowd excitedly. But not yet. Lionel Guest and Harry Higgins led their invitees into the Oval Room for dinner at 10.45 p.m. Gaiety there was silenced at midnight, but only temporarily, when a busboy was ordered to dim the lights. This he did by descending the foyer steps to the control panel in the switchboard room next to the kitchen and pulling down a huge lever as if he were drawing water from a pump.

Simultaneously, the drummer in Signore Lignante's little twelve-piece orchestra on the Oval Room stage, commanded the diners' attention with the rumble of a roll announcing "God Save the King." At this, the guests stood at their tables in silence. Then came "O Canada." As midnight struck on the grandfather clock, which rose as tall as Sir Herbert Holt near the Palm Court, the orchestra played "Auld Lang Syne" — and the cream of Montreal "society" rose to their feet again and joined hands. "In this melody," said the *Gazette*, "the guests joined in heartily."

When dinner was over, they trooped back through the Palm Court and into the lobby, and made their way into the Grand Ball Room to find it festooned with balloons and streamers. There, on a sprung floor of quartered oak, they swirled away the night until 2 a.m., when they began to trickle home to bed. The Ritz-Carlton Hotel had been built and admired, and was now officially open. That glittering New Year's Eve banquet and ball, though, had taken on an extra, special meaning.

CHAPTER FOUR

Premier Patrons,
Premier Hotel

"As I grew older, I continued coming to the Ritz.
There were many parties. But for me the highlight
was the dinner my father gave me for my
thirteenth birthday. It was a glorious, warm
June evening, the dinner was in the Garden,
and my joy knew no bounds."

DR. MARY MUNN, A BLIND PIANIST

In the shafts of cold light that pierced down through the drab of the following morning — January 1, 1913 — the hotel opened for business. Many of the people who stopped by on that first day did so purely out of curiosity, clutching newspaper reports of the previous night. "Ritz-Carlton Opened Its Doors for First Time and Made an Auspicious Debut," headlines in the *Gazette* announced. The report said:

> Picture to yourself a huge oval room, perfectly proportioned and charmingly decorated in the Adam style, filled with a well-dressed throng with the handsome dresses of the ladies blending well with the rose of the curtains and of the lights, the whole charmed by the music of a first-class orchestra, and you have an idea of the scene.
>
> The spectacle was certainly a new one to Montreal, and the brilliance of it was reminiscent of Paris, and was a living evidence of the fact that Montreal has become one of the world's important centres.
>
> Anyone who saw the inside of the hotel as it was a week ago, must have found it difficult to believe that he was under the same roof last night, when he saw the restaurant, so lately a wilderness of paint and plaster filled with tables, shining with silver and decorated with pink and red carnations and ornaments, and with the entrance adorned with palms and azaleas.

The large kitchen staff, assembled for the hotel's 1913 opening, gathered in the Grand Ball Room for this picture. Note the ballroom's attractive arches and the fashionable potted palms that were to be seen in abundance throughout the Ritz-Carlton's public rooms.

PHOTO BY GORDON

The hotel lobby was still flower-strewn when the first paying guests arrived to see that the tariff had now been placed in a little black frame behind the cashier's desk.

Single Room and Bath, from: $3.00
Double Room and Bath, from: $5.00
Bachelor Suite with Bath, from: $7.00
Suite of Rooms with Bath, from: $8.00

It was expensive, indeed. But not for those who would become Ritz-Carlton "regulars." They included all the hotel's directors; Senator Robert MacKay, the tenacious merchant and capitalist; Lord Shaughnessy and Edward Beatty, his general manager, who propped up a squat bulldog's body with tiny feet; all the directors and major shareholders of Ogilvie Flour Mills; and J.K.L. Ross, who would spend the next fifteen years squandering the $16 million fortune left to him by his father. He rented entire trains, not just private rail cars, in which to travel Canada, bought eight Rolls-Royces and seven yachts, and hired thirty-seven servants in his forty-room Peel Street home. He spent a lot of his money at the Ritz.

Everyone, it seemed, went there on that first day. "The attendance was a notable one," said the *Herald*. "The fact that the hotel was so well supported is ample proof of the wisdom of the directors of the Ritz Hotels in choosing this city for the site of a new establishment."

These patrons, most of them men, began a tradition. They eventually lunched daily in the Oak Room for $1.50, dined at least three times weekly in the Oval Room for $2.50, and sipped "le five o'clock tea," as Cèsar Ritz had called it, with English muffins or scones in the Palm Court, for 30 cents. And when they were absent, their wives and young daughters were supporting the hotel for them, often alone.

The Ritz was safe and fashionable, and it would grow to become not only a sanctuary for the founders' children, but their colleagues and clients, too — and, in turn, *their* wives and children. In time, it would become the province of relatives and friends — anyone, that is, so long as they fitted the Ritz mould. If a customer was unknown to a "regular" or looked in the slightest unsavory, a founding patron or shareholder simply passed the waiter a note which read, "Don't serve this fellow again. He doesn't fit in." The command was instantly obeyed.

The ideal Ritz-Carlton patron was rich, trustworthy, refined, and known to at least some of the others. If he did not immediately appreciate what he found in public rooms — the European decor, the comfortable

1918 Christmas Dinner menu cover.
COURTESY OF THE JACK GOODSON COLLECTION,
HOTEL PRINTING LTD., MONTREAL

chairs, the paintings, the smell of fine cigars — he belonged elsewhere. And money or not, he was dissuaded from ever returning.

All who entered the Ritz-Carlton could not help but admire it. A brochure extolling the virtues of Montreal hotels enthused that the Ritz-Carlton was "situated in the most aristocratic" part of Sherbrooke Street. It added:

> To pass through its stately portals is to enter into an atmosphere that charms and soothes. There is no rush, no noise, no bustle — not the slightest suggestion of the commercial spirit which is everywhere evident in the great city of Montreal. Deep, colourful rugs on the marble floors muffle the footstep. High-backed, carved oak chairs, grouped conveniently about small tables, extend an hospitable welcome. Desks placed against the wall provide an opportunity for and assure privacy for writing of that odd note which must be posted immediately.
>
> If it is tea or dinner hour, the subdued strains of the stringed orchestra may be heard from the Palm Court or the Restaurant beyond. In a word, the guest has entered into the most perfect substitute for his home that the art of hotel management could devise.

Nor could visitors ignore the elevator boys' smart khaki uniforms, the cloakroom attendants' blue satin knee-breeches, or the doormen's deep-brown bearskin hats. Above all else, though, they revelled in the punctilio of its first manager, a Prussian named Rudolf Bischoff, who had spent many months hiring a fleet of more than fifty waiters from Europe. "The hotel has been made ready in time for the occasion by this man's almost superhuman efforts," said the *Herald*, "and a willing staff that he has so ably selected and trained."

The directors thought so highly of Bischoff that they once noted with characteristic benevolence — and even recorded it in the minutes of their monthly board meetings — that he was unwell. "This poor gentleman," they said, " has a very nasty cough and should be allowed whatever time he needs away from his post to recuperate."

Bischoff chose to continue working, though. There was so much to do. Running the hotel was one thing; trying to please the patrons was another. Suddenly, there was an influx of them, especially after the hotel was listed in the November, 1913, telephone directory. The number itself had a smooth, musical ring, and it lingered on the tongue like fine cognac: Uptown 7180. "This is a Private-Branch Exchange," the directory said, "connecting all Departments and every Room."

About two-thirds of the Ritz-Carlton's rooms in those early years were

MURRAY HILL TAXIS LTD.– PACKARD FLEET– MONTREAL

LOUIS SAMUELS
President

Many Montreal companies, it seemed, wanted to be associated with the Ritz for promotional purposes, and the Murray Hill Taxi Company was no exception.

PHOTO COURTESY OF THE RITZ-CARLTON COLLECTION

occupied by guests who lived there permanently, for about $29 a month, and had their own telephone lines installed. They included men like Hugh MacKay, a director of Montreal Light, Heat & Power and of Canadian Breweries, and William Bog, superintendent of the Bank of Montreal. For several months after his return from England, where he had managed the London office, the Bank of Montreal's flamboyant new vice-president, Sir Frederick Williams-Taylor, lived at the Ritz-Carlton, too, while builders erected his greystone townhouse around the corner on Mountain Street.

Unlike many of his cronies, Sir Frederick was never to merely strut into the hotel's lobby. A big, bearded man wearing a flowing black cape and roll-brimmed hat to match, he *swept* in — looking more like the man portrayed on a bottle of Sandeman's sherry than an internationally known banker. Although unique in appearance, Sir Frederick was to become the absolute Ritz-Carlton patron. "Servants are much easier to find and keep in Montreal than they are in Mayfair," he said. However, he and his wife, Jane Fayrer Henshaw (Lady Williams-Taylor) entertained their house guests in the Oval Room, held private dinners and parties in Ritz-Carlton salons, and organized large, expensive dances in the Grand Ball Room so that their daughters could "come out" in style as debutantes.

Each year, numerous moneyed Montrealers took Ritz-Carlton suites for several months at a time while their townhouses were being redecorated, or to escape a marital row. Most permanent guests moved in with their own paintings, furniture, even drapes, however, treating the hotel as a residence-cum-private club where they could luxuriate in Continental hospitality for as long as they could afford it.

"When it comes to hotels," said a North American travel guide published in 1913, "the Windsor and the Ritz-Carlton appear most often in the social columns of Montreal newspapers. Of the two, the Windsor, steeped in tradition, appeals to men of affairs, while the Ritz is by far the most elite and comfortable."

Among those first permanent residents was also a woman who had sailed for a quiet holiday from Liverpool, England.

"How long will you be staying, Madame?" the desk clerk asked her.

"I'll let you know," she replied.

She was still in the same suite fifteen years later when the hotel's maintenance department was finally able to persuade her to allow workmen to paint it. Until then, she had steadfastly refused to admit them, fearing that any work done might detract from what she had

Patrons called him "Humpty Dumpty," which was an apt nickname indeed.
But his real name was Frank Quick, the hotel's second manager, who
welcomed guests with Cockney hospitality — "Hello, my dearies! How nice to
see you at the Ritz again! Make yerselves at home, and if there's anything I
can do, don't hesitate to ask."

PHOTO COURTESY OF ANNE MONETTE

originally "fallen in love" with.

"You leave my rooms exactly the way they are," she had said, consistently. "I absolutely love them, and I don't want you spoiling them for me!"

That same woman died in bed at the Ritz, having been there for two decades.

At the outbreak of World War I, the hotel braced itself for precarious times, and Rudolf Bischoff announced his resignation. "I am an alien," he said in a letter to the directors, "and for this reason, I can no longer perform my duty here." The directors understood. They noted in the company minutes that the war "had affected poor Mr. Bischoff badly." Like all too many of the hotel's first patrons, they were sorry to see him go. But should he one day want to return, "at the close of this horrible war," they said, a job would await him.

Only days later, however, Rudolf Bischoff returned to Europe, taking nearly two dozen of the hotel's most experienced, German-born waiters and cooks with him.

Bischoff's successor was a man very much his opposite in both looks and style — a cheerful Englishman named Frank Quick, who had emigrated to Canada in 1904 and spent ten years with the Canadian Pacific Railway's fledgling hotel division. He had managed the Banff Springs Hotel first, then the Royal Alexander Hotel in Winnipeg, and later Le Château Frontenac in Quebec City, where he had learned to speak French.

Actually, the Ritz-Carlton entered into a unusual agreement with the CPR to "borrow" Frank Quick for two years to help put the hotel back on its feet during a period in which experienced administrators were harder to find than waiters. "It is with the utmost pleasure that we loan this fine gentleman to you, to help wrest your establishment from these difficult times," said a letter from the CPR to the Ritz board. "We are sure you will be well satisfied with him." When his temporary assignment was up, though, Quick decided that the challenges involved in managing the new Ritz-Carlton Hotel were sufficient to induce him to stay permanently.

Patrons, meanwhile, had come to call him "Humpty Dumpty," which was an apt nickname, indeed. Frank Quick was short and exceedingly rotund, a physical characteristic which he did little to alleviate. He was said to have chain-smoked large cigars, and enjoyed three, sometimes four, hearty meals a day, following each with two stiff cognacs. "My father never really liked it when people said he was Humpty Dumpty," says Anne Quick, now widow Mrs. Anne Monette, "but he accepted it graciously. If that was what the guests wanted to call him, it was fine with him. They were the most important thing in his life and, I can tell you, he slaved day and night to make them happy."

Every morning, almost unfailingly, Quick, who originally hailed from the London suburb of Paddington, parked his bulk at the cashier's desk from where he bade departing guests farewell, and greeted those who were just arriving. This he did with the kind of hearty Cockney hospitality that some of the more established patrons found foreign to their ears — "Hello, my dearies! How nice to see you at the Ritz again! Make yerselves at home, and if there's anything I can do, don't hesitate to ask, dearies."

One of that era's few surviving Ritz-Carlton residents remembers that shortly after she and her family had moved into the hotel to spend a winter, her husband told one of their sons not to make too much noise. "If you persist," he said, "you'll get us all thrown out."

For a moment, the boy thought. "No, no," he said after a while, "that won't happen at all. When we first moved in here I heard Mr. Quick tell us the hotel was all ours!"

In effect, that is probably what Quick *did* say — "Make yerselves at home, dearies. The place is all yours! You see if it isn't!" And he would accompany each such salutation with a laugh so hearty that it bellowed in all directions — through the lobby into the foyer, through the Palm Court and into the sobriety of the Oval Room, and beyond the big doors into the street. Numerous patrons later claimed that Frank Quick could have stepped out of a Charles Dickens' novel. He was Mr. Micawber perhaps. Or he was Mr. Bumble. More likely, he was Mr. Pickwick — generous, accommodating, and always so meticulously attired in white, wing-collared shirts and cutaway tailed coats that did little to hide his corpulence.

Frank Quick's outwardly hospitable air was deceptive. Beneath the handshakes, the laughter, and the brisk half-run walk that transported him through the hotel, he bore problems which he valiantly sought to conceal. Under his stewardship, Ritz-Carlton standards had begun to slip and it was not entirely his fault. Good workers able to maintain the rigidly high quality of service, Quick complained, had become increasingly hard to find because "too many suitable young waiters, bellboys, and cooks had joined the colours" to serve Canada overseas. He was the victim of circumstance, and this was not always so readily acknowledged.

"D'you realize, Mr. Quick," snapped Lord Shaughnessy, as he swept from the Oval Room down through the Palm Court to pick up the lobby telephone one evening, "that one of *your* bellboys has just paged me in the restaurant — *out loud!* What in God's name is this place coming to?"

"I'm very, very sorry, My Lord," said Quick.

"Just don't let it happen again!"

Poor Frank Quick looked terribly ashamed and promised it would not. And for the most part it did not. He tried his utmost, meanwhile, to maintain business by training local people to rise to the Ritz occasion, and by inspiring his chefs to prepare quality food, even in the face of wartime shortages. He also embarked on the hotel's first advertising campaign, preparing all the copy himself on his office typewriter, and mailing it to newspapers throughout Europe and the United States.

THE RITZ-CARLTON HOTEL

The latest in the famous Group of
RITZ HOTELS
and the Headquarters in Eastern Canada
of the Touring Club of America
A Ritz-Carlton large green touring Automobile meets all the
RIVER BOATS
Passengers arriving from Europe are met at
Steamers, and every assistance given with Baggage, etc., etc.

One thing Frank Quick never omitted to do was tell prospective customers that the Ritz-Carlton was part of a Ritz empire that functioned well on both land and sea, and which was growing all the time. Much more important was that he extolled the virtues of his own hotel. "Every one of the sleeping apartments of the building," he wrote, "commands an uninterrupted view over the most beautiful tree-embowered residential section of the city. Thus the visitor is always assured of quietude and comfort."

Quick's campaign had a good effect. With him at the helm, the hotel's international reputation slowly began to extend well beyond the clients of the men who had built it, though it would be a long time before it would make sufficient profits to sustain itself. For the most part, it remained a social hothouse which catered prolifically to the special and eclectic needs of the St. James Street millionaires, their business contacts, and their women.

In the board room, meanwhile, the founders could not hide their disappointment. Although their hotel had been built during a construction boom, they ruefully conceded, wartime shortages and an acute lack of

One of the Ritz-Carlton's green touring cars, photographed in 1913, that transported American guests, and their many pieces of luggage, to and from river boats anchored in Lachine.

PHOTO COURTESY OF THE RITZ-CARLTON COLLECTION

visitors had stunted its growth. Most of the major shareholders, and nearly all of the directors, would need to subsidize it for many years to come. It was left to Sir Charles Gordon, Sir Montagu Allan, and Charles Hosmer, in fact, to finance the Ritz-Carlton from their private incomes for the rest of their lives.

As best he could, Frank Quick tried to ensure that the losses were minimized. To make money, he allowed some outside organizations to use the hotel, as long as they did not spoil its ambience. Off-duty officers of the Royal Canadian Militia were often to be seen there, and one was Colonel Jean-Jacques Vautelet, commander of H.Q. 4, Military District. He rode up on a black horse, dismounted in a clicking of heels, threw his reigns to the doorman, then strode up the steps for tea in the Palm Court where, according to one young observer, Murray Ballantyne, son of Charles Colquhoun Ballantyne, Minister of Marine and Fisheries in Sir Robert Laird Borden's Conservative government, he helped create "a mood of tense, buzzing cheerfulness." The colonel's horse, meanwhile, spent the afternoon dozing in a stable at the rear of the property on Drummond Street, where bellboys tended guests' pets: a dozen dogs and cats, two hamsters, and a parakeet who had been annoying other residents.

The buzzing cheerfulness, however, was muted and the hotel's flags lowered to half-past when, on May 7, 1915, two of Sir Montagu Allan's four children, Gwendolyn and Anna, drowned as the Cunard steamship *Lusitania* was torpedoed and sunk off the Old Head of Kinsale, Ireland. Not long afterwards, Sir Montagu's only son, Hugh, a fighter pilot, died in action while flying over German lines. Thankfully, there were other, more pleasing occurrences at the Ritz-Carlton during World War I.

Among several small functions Frank Quick permitted at the hotel was an annual music competition which, to this day, remains firmly implanted in the memory of one of its participants, Mary Munn. Music was Mary's life, and that competition at the Ritz so inspired her that she eventually earned a doctorate in musical arts from Boston University. Her parents, Mr. and Mrs. D.J. Munn of Dorchester Street, as it was then called, were patrons there, and remained so for many years. Each time they mentioned the hotel, their daughter's imagination was fired with "a sense of elegance and excitement."

There were times when the child yearned to see the action —the swirling dances, the glittering parties, the elegance of the permanent guests — for herself. But she knew she never would. She had been born blind.

Lord Shaughnessy, president of the CPR — and a loyal Ritz-Carlton patron. "D'you realize," he once complained to Frank Quick, "that one of your bellboys has just paged me in the restaurant — *out loud!* What in God's name is this place coming to?"

PHOTO COURTESY OF CP RAIL CORPORATE ARCHIVES

Despite her handicap she developed a keen sense of the hotel, and has always appreciated the chance it gave her. By allowing the competition into its Grand Ball Room, the Ritz enabled her to make her musical debut. Dr. Mary Munn writes:

> When I was five years old, my piano teacher, Catherine Hammond-Smith, informed me that I would be playing at her pupils' recital in the Ritz-Carlton's Grand Ball Room. I was so frightened that I assured her, "Mummy would never let me." However, Mummy was honoured that I was considered good enough to be included in the program.
>
> The day arrived, and my performance — all thirty-eight seconds of it — went without a hitch. Mrs. Hammond-Smith and my parents were pleased, and I liked the experience so much that then and there I decided in my heart that when I was grown up, I would give a long, full concert like those which my parents attended — and, of course, it would be in the Ball Room of the Ritz-Carlton Hotel.

Some months later, little Mary Munn performed again in another students' recital in the Grand Ball Room, despite a severe ear infection which had followed an attack of measles. Her courage did not go unnoticed. She remembers:

> Our duet was the hit of the evening, and as I was waiting for Daddy to get a cab, I felt a tap on my shoulder, and a lady said, "Miss Mary, here is a present from the manager of the Hotel." The present was a five-pound box of Page & Shaw chocolates, and a card reading, "With compliments from the manager to a brave little girl who played so well and would not let her teacher down."

That manager, by the way, was Frank Quick, always generous, always kind, and always the first to encourage youth. So much so that when he welcomed guests, daughter Anne, a child of three or four, was often there with him, standing silently in a massive pall of cigar smoke, trying to fathom the significance of each "important" guest.

"Now curtsey for the lady and the gentleman, Annie," Quick would say. And Anne Quick would respond in a flood of girlish pride, providing a splash of family warmth that helped give extra charm to the Ritz-Carlton during its early struggling years when it needed it most. Almost without exception, guests appreciated it. That is why most of them kept coming back, which was essential to business, and a credit to Quick's managerial abilities.

To further attract clients, Quick drastically slashed room rates, a move which was bold enough to warrant national attention — coverage in *Hotel and Travel*'s edition of June, 1915:

> It will be recalled that last summer this well-known member of the famous international Ritz-Carlton group of hostelries made a material reduction in its rates and began catering more extensively to the requirements of the better class of commercial trade. The Ritz-Carlton at its inception was planned to appeal to the same class of people who patronized the other houses of the same name or managed by the same interests in leading cities in many parts of the world, but the idea didn't work out.
>
> Not that Montrealers and visitors here didn't have the price to pay but this being an intensely commercial city, it is quite naturally to be expected of the metropolis of one of the most rapidly growing countries in the world, a very large percentage of the transient trade was furnished by businessmen, and they, in many instances gathered the impression that staying at the Ritz-Carlton meant living in an atmosphere of depressing formality whereas such is far from being true.
>
> The service at the Ritz is different, it is true. But it is intended just as much for the tired businessman as its is for the wealthy leisure class whose time is largely taken up by social engagements. There is none of that garishness which is to be found in many of the ultra-modern hotels, but for home-like comfort, attentiveness and courtesy it is impossible to find a more desirable place to stay than at the Montreal representative of the great Ritz system.
>
> Realizing that an effort would have to be made to dispel this erroneous impression, the management reduced the rates to a minimum of $3 per day, and when it is remembered that every one of the 220 guest rooms is equipped with a private bath, it will be seen that this is far from exorbitant.

Montreal's social community never abandoned the Ritz-Carlton in its time of need, and never would. In fact, they supported it to the hilt. Local firms, particularly The Bell Telephone Company of Canada, considered the hotel prestigious enough for their most important events, and one of these, on the evening of February 14, 1916, was history making indeed, because it illustrated the far reaching possibilities of telephone communication.

First came a fine feast in the Oval Room:

Cantaloupe
Madrileine in Jelly
Boiled Gaspè Salmon with Cucumber Sauce
Mousseline of Guinea Squab Duchesse

Roast Lamb with Mint Sauce
Salad Victoria
Bombe Canadienne with Maple Sauce
Fancy Cakes
Croûte Ivanhoe
Fruit: Grapes, peaches, pears
Coffee

After dinner, Bell Telephone chairman, Charles Fleetford Sise, Jr.
escorted colleague officials, local businessmen, and civic leaders into the
Grand Ball Room to take part in inauguration ceremonies for the world's
then longest-distance telephone call — 4,227 miles from Montreal to
Vancouver. Their wives and daughters were invited too, but according
to the official invitation, and even though it was St. Valentine's Day,
they were only allowed to watch the black-tie proceedings from the Ball
Room's gallery.

"It was the most wonderful demonstration ever witnessed by any
gathering in this city," said the *Montreal Daily Mail*. "The human voice
actually pulsated along the wires of the wonderful Bell Telephone system,
and it did it from the Ritz-Carlton Hotel."

Another local newspaper, the *Montreal Star*, described the scene:

> Stretching across one end of the large ball room was a table with four
> branches running at right angles. Several telephones stood upon the
> table at the end, while at 250 places upon the branch tables and in the
> galleries, were other phones. After C.F. Sise, Jr., and R.W. Hicks had
> given short explanatory addresses and showed moving pictures of the
> *Imperial Limited* running into Vancouver, various scenes in the coast
> city and other views, the connection starting at Montreal was made.

This was at around 10 p.m. Eastern Standard Time. At the head table,
Charles Sise picked up his telephone. After a few seconds, the audience
heard him tell a local operator, "I am ready, Madam. You may now make
this call." Then Sise said, "Gentlemen, if you will kindly lift up your
head sets I think you will hear Vancouver on the phone, shortly." They
all obliged, and, in stunned silence, heard the fledgling telephone system
go to work.

The call, Sise had said in his opening address, was being made with
the help of the American Telegraph and Telephone Company, whose
officials were there to witness the event. Guests in the Grand Ball Room
that night quickly understood why American help was needed. The
telephone link would "leap-frog" across the continent, clicking as it

Local firms were quick to consider the Ritz prestigious enough for their most important events. On the evening of February 14, 1916, The Bell Telephone Company of Canada made history in the Grand Ball Room. Company officials, local businessmen, and civic leaders took part in inauguration ceremonies for the world's then longest-distance telephone call — 4,227 miles from Montreal to Vancouver. "It was the most wonderful demonstration ever witnessed by any gathering in this city," said the *Montreal Daily Mail.* "The human voice actually pulsated along the wires of the wonderful Bell Telephone system, and it did it from the Ritz-Carlton Hotel."

PHOTO COURTESY OF THE BELL CANADA TELEPHONE HISTORICAL COLLECTION passed from one major exchange to the next — first Troy, then Buffalo, then Chicago, Omaha, Denver, Salt Lake City, Portland, and finally Vancouver.

There, local businessmen and politicians sat before their telephones at the British Columbia Telephone Company headquarters, waiting eagerly but apprehensively to hear Sise's voice. If successful, the telephone call would outdistance by more than 800 miles a transcontinental conversation only a few months earlier between Dr. Alexander Graham Bell, speaking from his New York City office, and his colleague, Thomas Watson, 3,400 miles away in San Francisco.

It was around 10.10 p.m. Eastern Standard Time when Sise heard the final click in the Grand Ball Room as, on the West Coast, the receiver was finally lifted.

"Hello," a voice crackled from afar.

"Hello," shouted Sise. "Is this Vancouver?"

"Yes, Sir," came the reply. "This is Vancouver speaking."

The telephone link had been made and the dressy Ritz-Carlton gathering broke into instantaneous applause. A cluster of nearly thirty waiters and busboys, who had been waiting excitedly in the Grand Ball Room doorway, rushed to distribute bottles of champagne to each table. Corks popped. The champagne flowed and spilled. The conversation continued. Neither the Ritz-Carlton, nor any other Canadian hotel, had never heard anything quite like this.

"I would like to speak to Mr. Peck," Sise said.

In Vancouver, Peck came to the phone.

"What's the weather like out there?" Sise asked him.

"It's been raining all day," Peck said mournfully.

"Well, it's been snowing here," Sise said.

Then Lord Shaughnessy, sitting next to Sise in a head table gathering that also included Sir Edward Osler and Sir Frederick Williams-Taylor, asked to speak to F.W. Peters, the CPR's Vancouver superintendent.

"Hello. Hello. Is that you Peters?" Shaughnessy asked.

"Yes."

"Is the CN train in yet?" Lord Shaughnessy continued with a twinkle.

He was referring to the Canadian Northern line, one of several railway companies that would be incorporated into Canadian National in the 1920s. It made for an amusing moment because everyone in the Ball Room that night knew that as a railwayman, Lord Shaughnessy possessed a keenly competitive and pioneering spirit. Besides, his link with the CPR was legendary.

More laughter rang through the Ball Room when Alderman Leslie Boyd, who said he was "representing the Mayor and citizens of Montreal," asked Vancouver Mayor William McBeath how he had recently managed to defeat a candidate named Joe Martin in the mayoralty race.

"Simple," said McBeath, his voice strong and clear. "I got more votes."

After conversations between Montreal and Vancouver businessmen, most of which consisted of polite, mutual inquiries about each other's health and wives, the line was switched to Portland, then south to San Francisco for what the *Mail* called "the most dramatic moment of the whole evening."

A man, known to most of those Montreal invitees only as "Mr. Heller," answered the phone. "Hello, this is San Francisco," he announced.

"Good," said Sise. "What time is it out there?"

"It's just seven-thirty-one," Heller replied.

Guests in the Ball Room checked their watches. It was 10.31 p.m. Eastern Standard Time, and although they had eaten and drunk well, and would normally have been at home by then, they were enjoying every moment of the illustrious occasion. So were the waiters — more than fifty of them now — who had closed all other hotel restaurants and bars, and converged on the northern wall. Frank Quick had moored himself in the gallery.

"And what is the temperature out there?" Sise persisted.

"It is just sixty-nine degrees here in San Francisco," said Heller.

"You're lucky," said Lord Shaughnessy, butting in. "It's well below zero here, and snowing."

To help illustrate the point that West Coast weather was balmy, Heller flicked a switch in his exchange and connected the phone line to a microphone that had been placed on rocks in San Francisco Harbour. The sound of the Pacific Ocean now rushed into Montreal — while Bell Telephone organizers showed, on a huge screen flanked by two potted plants, moving pictures of a typical seascape. "Those present," said the *Star*, "could hear as distinctly as if they were within a few feet, the roar and rush of the mighty breakers."

The occasion — "remarkable and record-breaking," said the *Gazette* — climaxed when Mr. Heller asked if he could play some recordings over the telephone line, and the Montreal gathering urged him to do so. It was just as well, because Heller would not have needed too much encouragement, anyway. First came Sir Harry Lauder singing his hit song

"I Love a Lassie." Then an American tenor sang "Then You'll Remember Me" from the operetta *The Bohemian Girl*. Finally, Heller played a humorous recording, "Cohen on the Telephone," performed by an American comedian.

It may not have been as spontaneous as guests thought it was, but just as the San Francisco end of the proceedings were winding down, Charles Sise asked Heller, "You don't happen to have a recording of our National Anthem, do you?"

"As a matter of fact," said Heller, "I do. It's right here beside me."

"Good," said Sise. "Will you play it, please?"

Heller placed the record on the turntable of his wind-up phonograph, and lowered the steel needle into the first groove. Behold, the music poured through 3,400 miles of copper telephone wire that weighed almost 3.5 million pounds and was supported by 151,000 telegraph poles, right into the Ritz-Carlton's Grand Ball Room. It was received with patriotic reverence. The *Mail* reported:

> Everyone one rose instantly, and with the individual receivers pressed to their ears, they heard "God Save the King," all three verses of it, played as they had never heard it before. It was an inspiring moment, and the conclusion was the occasion for tremendous applause.

Thus the Ritz-Carlton had hosted a major event, and when news of it was wired around the world it could not help but enhance the hotel's reputation as a major Canadian institution that would be called upon time and time again to help document history.

For the time being, though, the Ritz would have to content itself solely with Montreal's distinguished families. Marcelle Turgeon was nine when it opened and still recalls her parents strewing her bed with the balloons and noisemakers they had brought home from the gala banquet and ball. She then began visiting the hotel for herself. As World War I approached, she recalls, the lobby always seemed to be full of men and women in uniform. As a child, she decided that she was standing in an important place. There was something about the hotel that told a girl so young that the Ritz was at the very centre of Montreal's social life and always would be.

On reaching the "coming out" age of eighteen, Marcelle Turgeon learned to be "seen" in the Oval Room at lunch on Saturday, and that it was a social "must" for her to stay to attend the "dance tea" (*thé dansant*) between 3 p.m. and 6.p.m. "As a special treat," she recalls, "my parents allowed me to take part in events such as these the year *before* I 'came out.'" As she grew older, she was often to be found attending Saturday night dances, as well, especially those organized for debutantes in the Grand Ball Room.

At one of these in 1919, her friend, Pauline Archer, a young hospital worker, met a soldier named Lieutenant Georges Vanier who, wounded on the front line in France, had recently learned to walk on an artificial leg. They married, of course, and Vanier went on to became Canada's first French-Canadian Governor General.

Also in 1919, royalty began to arrive at the Ritz-Carlton Hotel, and Frank Quick put on his best cutaway suit to welcome it into the Vice-Regal Suite with the same outstretched hand that greeted ordinary people who would stay in ordinary sleeping apartments. "The only difference was," remembers Anne Quick, "we had to keep well away and use the rear staircase because when royalty arrived, the second floor was always sealed off from the public and most of the staff."

The young Edward, then Prince of Wales, began the first of a series of visits to the Ritz-Carlton, sometimes alone, and sometimes with his younger brother, George, who was to become King.

By staying at the Ritz, he was breaking with tradition. Until then, royalty had nearly always patronized the Windsor, but the Prince had come to dislike the "ponderous, Victorian atmosphere" there and felt that the Ritz-Carlton was "newer, smarter, and more up-town." Besides this, he liked the ice cream — vanilla, chocolate, and strawberry — that was freshly made by the hotel's Italian-born master pastry chef, Jean Baptiste Pellerino, who joined the Ritz shortly before the Prince's visit and stayed forty-five years.

Pellerino, a wiry, happy man who was barely five feet tall, gave his life to the Ritz, working from 8 a.m. until 10 p.m. every day. He made cakes for his church, his relatives, his friends, and the hotel often at only a moment's notice. All were invariably decorated with spun sugar, and were hailed as culinary masterpieces, earning "The Little Chef," as Pellerino was known, fond recognition. For the Prince, he crafted a spun-sugar horseshoe and trimmed it with violets.

The management, meanwhile, made sure that the Prince lacked for nothing. Frank Quick took careful notes of the Prince's special tastes, and, to acknowledge his passion for jazz, had the Vice-Regal Suite fitted out with the latest wireless set, a gramophone, and two grand pianos. The Prince of Wales could not play the piano but soon began inviting to his suite friends and musicians who could.

His second visit to Montreal, in 1923, was particularly memorable for its idiosyncracy. The moment he had screeched his touring car to a halt outside the hotel, he leapt from the driver's seat and, without reporting to the front desk, and leaving his luggage in the vehicle, raced upstairs to the mezzanine floor — and gatecrashed a women's bridge tournament in the Blue Room.

A theory goes that the Prince was eagerly searching for the men's washroom and had made a mistake. The reason for his unusual behaviour, however, which shocked the lobby staff and sent the bellboys up to see what was going on, remains a mystery. According to an elderly Ritz doorman named Charles "Charlie" Chapman, the women were somewhat taken aback by the intrusion on their solitude and, on their first reaction, were all set to call the management to have the intruder ejected. But then they recognized just who he was. Predictably, they mobbed him, and the bellboys were now required to escort the Prince downstairs to collect his luggage before taking him to the Vice-Regal Suite to begin a two-week stay.

The hotel's worries were frequent when the Prince of Wales checked in. Time and again he would break tradition by walking through the uptown streets, alone and at night. Once, he was "missing" for several hours, and it was left to Quick's secretary to try to find him. Having ascertained that he was not in the kitchen sampling Jean Pellerino's ice cream, which he liked to do, she telephoned those Ritz patrons who were known to be among his friends, to find out where else he was likely to be. She finally tracked him down at the University Club, where he often enjoyed lunch.

"Excuse me, Your Highness," Quick said carefully, "but I have something to ask you. We can't stop you going out, but it would be nice to have some idea where you're going. Not that I want to be nosy, or anything, because I'm not. It's just for your own safety, in case something happens to you. Do you think, Sir, that you could avoid walking the streets alone?"

It appears that the Prince heeded the hint. A few days later, after lunching at the Mount Royal Club, he was seen walking back to the Ritz with lawyers Lieutenant-Colonel Allan Angus Magee of Montreal and Major Alvin L. Chipman of Nova Scotia. A few nights later, however, when he was invited to dine at the home of the prominent merchant Donald Forbes Angus, he abandoned his official car and, to the surprise of his hosts, chose to arrive by himself — in a taxi.

The Ritz-Carlton Hotel still spawns happy memories for Lily Cochrane, now aged eighty-three, a niece of Sir Mortimer Davis, the philanthropic founder of Imperial Tobacco. She lived in the hotel with her parents for fourteen years. She writes from Biarritz, France:

> The Ritz was really wonderful in those days. It was a lovely time — the decor, people, and the clothes the visitors and patrons wore would be regarded as *vieux jeu* today. We had a suite — two bedrooms, sitting room, and a bath — which, I think, cost $5 a day. The bellboy used to walk my dog and he was thrilled with his ten-cent tip.
>
> The Ball Room was wonderful for "coming out" dances, tea dances, and our yearly closing from Miss Edgar's and Miss Cramp's School. During the First World War, our school play for the Khaki League was performed there. I may add that I was leading lady and that Frances Doble, who later became a star actress on the London stage, did a balloon dance.

Over the years, on return visits to Montreal to meet old friends, Lily Cochrane has always stayed a week or two at the Ritz-Carlton. "It's hard to stay away," she says. "People like me, to whom the hotel will always mean so much, will always keep coming back to it." Most always did, which is why the old place survived.

A lot, though, was due to Frank Quick, his advertising and his price cuts. "These are lean times in the hotel business in Montreal as elsewhere," *Hotel and Travel* later reported, "but the Ritz-Carlton has managed to do very nicely when a great many people were predicting that it would be a very bad winter season." Said another trade paper, *Hotelier*, "The management of the Ritz-Carlton Company Ltd., is composed of leading financiers and capitalists of Montreal and they are to be commended upon their adoption of a more liberal policy whose wisdom has been vindicated by an increased patronage of what is generally regarded as one of Canada's premier hotels."

It was, indeed, a premier hotel with a premier clientele. But more strenuous times awaited it.

CHAPTER FIVE

Pickford, Fairbanks, and the Dark, Lean Years

"Montreal's leading families,
who still had the money,
did not desert the Ritz during hard times
and it survived
with its social reputation unimpaired."

MACLEAN'S MAGAZINE

Early in 1924, Frank Quick's health snapped. Incessant smoking had caught up with him and he fell ill with severe bronchitis. He was fatigued, too. "Daddy had worked, oh so hard at the Ritz," Anne Monette, now in her seventies, remembers of her father. "He needed a rest very badly."

Quick got one — seven months in the Royal Victoria Hospital, where doctors said that the rheumatism, from which he had also been suffering in his shoulders and legs, was really arthritis. He finally went home in a wheelchair.

Within months, though, as soon as he was on his feet again, he succumbed to the urge to return to his career. He helped organize, and became the first managing director of the Newfoundland Hotel in St. John's, and took the Ritz-Carlton's housekeeper, Jessie Fox, and its chief accountant, fellow countryman Harry Hales, with him. "Daddy was loved," says daughter Anne. "He and his staff were always inseparable."

Quick's replacement at the Ritz-Carlton Hotel was his assistant manager, Emile Charles Des Baillets, who in many ways was his opposite. Des Baillets was a fearsome-looking Swiss with milky-brown hair and grey-blue eyes, who stood a thin six-foot-two inches tall. He also sported a bushy moustache and shovel-shaped beard which earned him the nickname, "Rasputin," and it was not totally out of place. "The Ritz was

81

To the staff, Emile Charles Des Baillets was a fearsome-looking Swiss with milky-brown hair and grey-blue eyes. He stood a thin six-foot-two inches tall and sported a bushy moustache and shovel-shaped beard which earned him the nickname, "Rasputin." His leadership was disciplined, strict, and relentless, and he protected the Ritz fiercely, putting the fear of God into anyone who thought that he shouldn't.

PHOTO COURTESY OF THE CITY OF MONTREAL ARCHIVES

the Ritz," a cook said, "and to Mr. Des Baillets there was nothing else like it in the world. He protected it fiercely and put the fear of God into anyone who thought he shouldn't."

His leadership was disciplined, strict, and relentless. He absolutely forbade any of the employees — even his eminent executive chef, Charles Schneider — to visit the hotel during their off-duty hours or to be seen standing on the sidewalk outside. "Not that we had much time for that," says Rudy Doseger, a Swiss-German whom Schneider had lured from London's Savoy Hotel as his sous-chef. "Most of us started at eight, finished at two, went home for a break, then went back to work from five till the dining room closed at nine at night, and we did it six days a week!"

The directors felt that Geneva-born Des Baillets, then aged forty-two, was just the manager they needed to rejuvenate their hotel and reinstate some of the pride and dignity it had shed in the previous decade, and to some extent they were right. With his appointment, the hotel moved back into the Continental convention, in which Des Baillets had been so scrupulously schooled. He had started his career in 1909 as an assistant at L'Hôtel Baur-au-Lac in Switzerland before moving on to the famous Hotel Konversationshaus in Baden-Baden, Germany, where he served under none other than César Ritz himself. During World War 1, he managed Hôtel Bonnivard in Montreux then, in 1919, came to Montreal to join his brother, Charles-Jules, who had emigrated to Canada fifteen years before and was then the City of Montreal's chief engineer.

Des Baillets was elegant, dignified, exquisitely mannered, and the epitome of ineffable class and formality. "He even wore a tie on a fishing trip," says his nephew, Jacques Des Baillets. No one ever followed him through a doorway, and he rarely raised his voice. "He was a thoroughly fine person, always so suave and gentle," Anne Monette remembers.

An equally succinct and affectionate sketch of Des Baillets has been passed down from a friend of his son Charles-André, who was to be killed while on a Royal Canadian Air Force flying mission over France in November 1941: "Old E.C. was a man of infinite personal propriety. During his tenure he *was* the Ritz. He set the tone from the start, from the lowest chamber maid to the haughtiest maître d'hôtel or sommelier."

Not surprisingly, especially being the traditionalist he was, Des Baillets vehemently believed that fine sherry, not cocktails as the Americans would have it, should always precede dinner, and that port wine was automatically served with the coffee. Thus he endeared himself to all people who luxuriated in fine dining and comfort, like the elderly woman

The hotel's most celebrated and colourful permanent resident was a Basque painter named Alphonse Jongers who had financed his way through art school as a strongman in a travelling circus. "He was a big, ape-like character with long arms and a bulldog face," a colleague said, but no one would ever suspect it from this flattering self-portrait. Jongers took rooms 901 and 902, where he established himself as Canada's leading society painter.

PHOTO COURTESY OF THE CITY OF MONTREAL ARCHIVES

who arrived at the hotel one day to be greeted deferentially by name, then after signing the leather-bound guest register, escorted by a bellboy to her room, where she was joined by the housekeeper.

In many ways, the woman typified Des Baillets' clientele. She was American, wealthy, important — and intent on staying at the hotel for several weeks. In others, however, she was unique. On being shown her big, sparse suite, she surveyed it with a studied nonchalance, and nodded approvingly with the hauteur that somehow accompanies money.

"This will do nicely, thank you," she said. "Now you may send up my belongings."

Within a few minutes, two porters were trundling half a dozen crates into her room, breaking them open and quickly assembling their contents into a large double bed. From another crate emerged an armchair. "I always bring my own bed and chair," the woman said matter-of-factly. "When I sleep here, in my own bed, I feel perfectly at home."

This incident, however, provoked no surprise on the part of management, or comment by the staff. Des Baillets was the first Ritz manager to impress on employees that they were to accept such eccentricity as an article of faith, just as they did when a permanent guest once called the front desk asking to have a red bedroom chair changed because it did not quite match the rose she was wearing on her dress.

That afternoon, Des Baillets lost no time in sending the Ritz-Carlton's upholsterer to see her. He, in turn, suggested a set of chairs and a *chaise longue* in suitable reds which might, he dared hope, harmonize with her flower. Fortunately for him, they did, and the guest was happy. Such was the extra attention that Des Baillets felt visitors should be afforded and in this case, as in others, it was never mentioned on the bill.

Des Baillets, slavish and submissive, delighted in watching his guests — rich, rare, or retired people with a yearning for comfort — being themselves, and feeling at ease in the elegant surroundings of Canada's foremost luxury hotel. He was heartened to know they felt sufficiently at home to install their own furnishings or change a suite's colour scheme, and he enjoyed their lust for a Ritz-Carlton trait — breakfast in bed.

The hotel's most celebrated permanent resident during Des Baillets' tenure was a Basque painter named Alphonse Jongers who had financed his way through art school as a strongman in a travelling circus. "He was a big, ape-like character with long arms and a bulldog face," a colleague said. "But his looks never impaired his success because he was always so charming." As Jongers' career in art blossomed, he designed furniture and stage settings at the 1889 Paris Exposition and worked with John Singer

Sargent on murals for the Boston Public Library in 1892. Four years later he came to Montreal to open a studio, but then returned to France where he won wide acclaim as a portrait painter.

By the time he began living at the Ritz-Carlton late in 1924, he had already committed Lord Aberdeen and the Duke of Grammont to canvas, and was now looking for more people to paint. With no difficulty at all, he was able to strike a deal with the Ritz directors — that so long as he systematically painted them, then their wives and their children, he could stay in the hotel rent free.

Jongers took rooms 901 as a bedroom and 902 as a studio, where, despite having garnered numerous international prizes and being made a Chevalier of France's Légion d'Honneur, he became better known for a series of amorous pursuits than for his prodigious outpouring of portraits. The chamber maids, it is said, rarely felt safe in his presence. Wherever he went, be it to attend exhibitions of his work in New York, Washington, or London, his reputation — to Des Baillets' displeasure — preceded him. But as a ninth-floor neighbour so often maintained, "At least dear Mr. Jongers is making our lovely hotel better known."

"I like my room for painting," Jongers told Madeleine Rocheleau, now an artist in her own right, who modeled nude for his *Sofa bleu*, "because the red-brick building next door casts a very pleasant glow on all my subjects."

Once when she arrived for a two-hour session, Jongers told her, "I can't paint today. My tailor has come over from England and wants to measure me up for a new suit." Indeed, the happy-go-lucky Jongers kept his goatee beard well trimmed and his wardrobe well stocked, and was always neat in one of many imported tweed suits, crisp shirts, and crocodile skin shoes. It was integral to his image, he maintained, as Montreal' preeminent society painter.

As the hotel's reputation spread even farther afield, so it drew celebrities by the score: Field-Marshal Earl Haig, Laird of Bemersyde; Lord Baden-Powell, the founder of the Boy Scouts; explorer Sir Ernest Shackleton; British Prime Minister James Ramsay MacDonald; United States President Calvin Coolidge; and many more. Royalty continued to arrive, too. The Duke of Kent stopped by, and Prince Edward made two more visits to the Vice-Regal Suite, another with Prince George.

Early on a sparkling Sunday during that visit, in 1923, a squadron of the Royal Canadian Hussars mounted on brown horses, drew up in line outside the Ritz-Carlton Hotel to escort Edward to a civic reception at City Hall. He appeared in the hotel's doorway, waved to the crowd that had gathered eagerly to see him, and entered a waiting car which drove off with the hussars, clad in blue and red uniforms and black-plumed hats, providing an impressive escort and adding glitter to the morning. "It was a touch of glamour and colour, of dignity and discipline," remembers historian Edgar Andrew Collard, "which was so rarely seen in the streets of Montreal, and the Ritz, at such times, was the royal headquarters."

Rumania's Queen Marie stayed at the Ritz-Carlton, as did Prince Takamatsu, the Emperor of Japan's brother. He spent his six-week honeymoon there, and to accommodate him in his customary style the housekeeper went down to Henry Morgan's department store on St. Catherine Street and asked the manager if he would lend her a complete set of Oriental furnishings. Chef Schneider, meanwhile, studied Japanese cooking. Nothing would ever be too much trouble at the Ritz-Carlton. Emile Charles Des Baillets had pledged himself to that.

In the mid-1920s, actress Sarah Bernhardt booked rooms at the Ritz-Carlton just a day or so before the Irish tenor John McCormack, who sang to the staff after dinner one night in "a voice of pure, shimmering gold."

When newspaper reports announced the arrival of Mary Pickford and Douglas Fairbanks — "America's sweethearts" of the silent movies — hundreds of excited people thronged outside the hotel hoping to glimpse their idols together. They never did. They saw Miss Pickford waving from an upstairs window. But where was Mr. Fairbanks? He had gone down the elevator to the mezzanine from where he performed the un-Ritzlike act of climbing onto the hotel's parapet to acknowledge the adulation.

"What on earth are the arts coming to?" a horrified doorman reflected later. "While all that dreadful fuss was going on outside, the great opera soprano, Madame Amelita Galli-Curci, bless her, was standing in the lobby — *completely unnoticed!*"

Fairbanks later thanked Des Baillets for "the customary benevolence" that had earned the hotel the prosperity and reputation it justly deserved, and the Prince of Wales always did the same, usually handing the manager a gift. The Prince was so pleased with Des Baillets' attention, in fact, that he presented him with his silver cufflinks.

While benevolence was ever-present at the Ritz-Carlton, however, prosperity was short-lived. The Depression rocked the hotel to its very foundation. All that remained was the Ritz Idea, now evident only in the manicured little lobby, with its gleaming brass and shining marble. Beyond this, the hotel was dying. One of the *chef de réception*'s first jobs each day was to stuff letters into numbered pigeonholes, one per resident,

Two views of the Ritz-Carlton, looking east and west on Sherbrooke Street.
POSTCARDS COURTESY OF THE MICHEL BAZINET COLLECTION

at the rear of the front office. But all too often, there were no letters at all. Unable to pay their bills as their incomes dwindled following the 1929 stock market crash, many permanent guests moved out, and Des Baillets appeared uncharacteristically despondent.

"Poor 603, one of our very loyal, long standing residents is giving up her room tomorrow and is moving down to Verdun," he lamented. "From the Ritz to Verdun! Can you imagine that? What a terrible tragedy it is!"

Rather than see a drastic lowering of its standards, the Ritz resigned itself to working on a smaller scale. It curtailed maintenance and closed a third of the rooms it had reserved for travellers, turning off the radiators to cut down on heating, and swathing the furniture in dust sheets. On those suites that remained open, it slashed prices from $6 a day to $4.50. It saved more money by cutting its valet services and trimming back menus. These were decisions that had to be made to encourage whatever clientele existed.

Montreal's leading families tried harder than ever to support their hotel in this, its time of direst need. They turned out to eat and drink there regularly and for as long as they could afford to, but not so often in the Oval Room. All too frequently they had little choice but to dine in the less expensive basement Oyster Bar — until it closed, that is, sending home the six waiters and busboys. Then the Oak Room cut back on service, opening only for breakfast during the week and for lunch on Saturdays, and another fourteen men were laid off. In fact, during the Depression, and "with solemn regret," the Ritz-Carlton dismissed more than two-thirds of its 230-person staff; for the first time in their hotel's short but illustrious history, the patrons of Montreal's Golden Square Mile had to wait for service.

Gradually, the majority of the permanent residents stopped taking meals in the dining rooms. It was then discovered that they had covertly converted their suites into efficiency apartments by installing cooking facilities. For the comfort of other guests, one woman had to be asked not to fry liver and onions in her room; another was seen searching the bushes in the Dutch Garden for a plucked chicken that had fallen from her window ledge, where it had been left to keep cool.

Even in hard times like these, however, dignity and aplomb prevailed at the Ritz. All too many of the dowagers who had once dined in long gowns and lace dinner mittens over manicured hands that held lorgnettes, their hair as tight as helmets, became nothing more than ornaments in the lobby. Members of a Ritz breed unto themselves, and by now almost all of them Victorian widows, they kept their upper lips

The hotel's little Dutch Garden, later called the Ritz Garden, and now known as the Duck Garden, was always a popular spot for summer lunches and dinners served beneath fine poplar trees. On warm evenings, patrons walked directly onto the patio from the Oval Room, then the main restaurant, by descending the steps at left. There they asked waiters to serve them their coffee and liqueurs. In later years, various managers enlarged and developed the garden, and made it one of Montreal's most distinguished eating spots.

PHOTO BY THE RICE STUDIO LTD
COURTESY OF THE RITZ-CARLTON COLLECTION

stiff as they viewed depleted bank books.

A bankrupt businessman was much less philosophical. He committed suicide by leaping from his eighth-floor Ritz-Carlton bathroom window — but not, it should be noted, before presenting the cashier with a box of fine, imported chocolates.

As conditions worsened, the directors — particularly Sir Charles Gordon, Sir Herbert Holt, and Sir Montagu Allan — dug deeper and deeper into their pockets to keep the Ritz afloat, at times wondering if their investment was worth it. "We don't always have to *make* money," Sir Montagu had so frequently reminded the board, "but, by God, we don't have to lose it, either!"

Charles Hosmer, meanwhile, who died in 1927 after a stroke that left him paralyzed and deaf, had passed down the bulk of his fortune to his only son, Elwood, who had followed him into Canadian Pacific and become a manager there. Elwood was also a Montreal stockbroker, but there his success in life was stunted. He was a thin, delicate, somewhat brittle man, aptly known as "The Grey Ghost of the Ritz." Although he had inherited his father's majority shares in the Ritz-Carlton Hotel and was now a director, he did not, by any stretch of the imagination, possess a similar desire for commercial prosperity, even when he became the company's president.

A bachelor, and a close friend of Alphonse Jongers, Elwood Bigelow Hosmer lived just a doorman's cry away from the Ritz, up the hill on Drummond Street, where he owned four of the finest Canaletto paintings to be found in an art collection anywhere. But he spent more time in bars and gambling. To the management's deep concern, another of his good friends was a Greek floor waiter named John Feratsos, who delighted in playing the horses and inspiring both patrons and staff to do the same.

A fondly-told Ritz-Carlton story about Elwood finds him sad and disoriented in Monte Carlo one weekend, where, after having lost several thousands of dollars at the blackjack tables, he asks a hotel concierge to direct him to the most lively nearby nightspot, where can sublimate his sorrow.

"Are you from Montreal?" the concierge is said to have asked.

"Yes," Elwood replied.

"We had a man here from Montreal only last week, and he sure found *his* way around."

That visitor from Montreal, it transpired, was none other than Elwood's father who, time and time again, had implored his son to ditch gambling for honest, hard work.

Elwood Hosmer was a thin, brittle man, aptly known as "The Grey Ghost of the Ritz." Although he inherited his father's majority shares in the hotel and became a director, he did not possess similar desires for commercial prosperity. A bachelor, and a close friend of Alphonse Jongers, Hosmer lived just up the hill on Drummond Street but spent considerably more time at the Ritz — drinking and making the guests unwelcome.

PHOTO COURTESY OF THE CITY OF MONTREAL ARCHIVES

But Elwood was born to make his own way in life. Dour, silent, and uncommunicative, mainly, he was usually to be found engrossed in crossword puzzles in a leather chair in the Palm Court, where he drank gin "borrowed" from the hotel's liquor supply, and smoked expensive Corona cigars cadged from the gift shop which now faced bankruptcy.

When he was not doing either, he was generally trying his hardest to deter outsiders — even the most earnest and loyal patrons among them — from enjoying the hotel's facilities. According to one contemporary witness, he "did some of this in a strange, self-flagellating way. He had the dreadful habit of consuming far too much, for he was in the Palm Court from morning till night. And when he had, he routinely relieved his bladder in the nearest plant stand. This practice, I can assure you, was not received at all well down at the Ritz!"

Nor was Elwood's sharp, cynical tongue. During Saturday luncheon, which was a three- or four-hour ritual for those who could still afford to pay 45 cents for eggs benedict served on crumpets, or 50 cents for salmon with a light cream sauce, he would snap his fingers for a bellboy's attention and ask in the loud voice he intended to be heard up the curving staircase and onto the mezzanine, "Would you please be good enough to tell me just how long these wretched women are staying? If you can't, go home!"

Quite often, Elwood would fall asleep, snoring. Or he would reminisce morosely about how his attempt to fly the Atlantic Ocean in the mid-1920s was so abruptly aborted when his plane, the Flying Whale, crashed into the sea only half a mile after take-off from the Azores. He and three companions had spent thirteen hours drifting in the cold, turbulent water before being picked up by the liner Minnewaska.

One account of the rescue says, "Mr. Hosmer was sitting on the wing of the airplane smoking a cigar, and crying."

By the following week, however, Elwood had reinstalled himself in the Palm Court armchair where he had become conspicuous by his absence and, in his own way, missed. Many times, when he could no longer stand up, or if he had become belligerent and insulting, the staff had to send him home. "Being president of the company didn't matter," one worker reflected. "The moment Mr. Hosmer became a bloody nuisance and started swearing at the guests, out the door he went!"

Actually, it was invariably left to the ever-tactful doorman Jamieson, a lanky Englishman with a white waxed moustache, to handle those situations. He would beckon a waiting taxi cab and, the moment it had drawn close to the hotel's steps, take Elwood Hosmer by the arm and lead him toward it with the gentlest of persuasion. "It's such a lovely night, Sir. It really is. Don't you think that you need a little fresh air after inhaling all that cigar smoke, Sir? I think there are times, Sir, when we could all do with a little bit of that. Or a walk, perhaps... and an early night, Sir, to sleep off the trials and tribulations of a *very* tiring day? Good night, Sir."

There were also times when, at only 6 p.m., and after a particularly hard day's drinking, the bellboys had to carry Elwood out. On his departure, the lobby staff sighed with relief.

As sad as it was, though, and perversely, a positive element emerged from all this. During those painfully poor Depression years at the Ritz-Carlton Hotel, and as eminently unsuccessful as he was in dealing with life on a personal plane, Elwood remained a refreshing reminder of good times gone, and a symbol of hope for the future. At half-past ten on nights when he had consumed less liquor, or spent an evening drinking milk and could therefore make his *own* way down the front steps, the lone duty doorman presented himself to the entire lobby and announced loudly, "Mr. Hosmer, Sir. Your *car* is here."

Manager Des Baillets, who so often had to work late, would lope to the Palm Court doorway to watch the president depart. "At least one man can still afford his own chauffeur," he would mutter gloomily. "The Murray Hill bus company people must be very happy these days."

Indeed, during the late 1920s and early 1930s, Emile Charles Des Baillets, the noblest Ritzman of them all, was frequently a forlorn, tragic figure helping the few porters the hotel could afford to pay, carry luggage. "Just think," he was known to complain ruefully. "Not long ago Mr. Harry McLean, the contractor, arrived here with thirty-six pieces of luggage and there were many Americans like him. Now they only come with one club bag because they only plan to stay two days. And they only ever come on business. Not like the old days."

But Des Baillets would not give up. For one unnerving period, the corner of Sherbrooke and Drummond streets threatened to become run-down, and he had to fight to preserve his territory. He thought nothing of depositing the hotel's garbage into the back alleyway, and was a familiar sight plucking litter from the gutter outside the front door.

One night, legend has it, he saw three young women, their faces garish with paint, their eyes bright and appraising, standing beneath the hotel's parapet, and lost no time telling them to move.

"Shoooo! Go on! Get away from here!" he said with agitated flicks of his long, white hands. "You are not welcome here!"

More serious was that by 1936, the Ritz-Carlton's list of permanent guests had dwindled from more than 100 to a mere twenty-seven. Only those people who had managed to survive the Depression with their coupons intact had lasted there, the woman in 709, for example, whose live-in nursemaid took her down to dinner every night.

On one occasion, just before they were about to order, the woman peremptorily declared to the entire restaurant that she did not need assistance, and told her companion to leave. Some time later, however, she saw a woman sitting alone on the other side of the room, beckoned a waiter. "Who *is* that person over there?" she inquired. "She looks familiar. Ask her if she would care to join me." She and her nursemaid were reunited for dessert and coffee.

Drastic staff cuts remained in effect for several years at the Ritz-Carlton. To Des Baillets' utter chagrin, breakfast in bed had to be curbed, and delivered only to "permanents" or to the infirm — such as the elderly Canadian Army major in room 403, who had lost an arm in World War I. Once, it was left to manager Des Baillets to carry the major's breakfast himself! And quite often the night manager, an amusing Russian named Alexander Tchimourine, who is believed to have been a Cossack in the Imperial Guard, and who had emigrated to Canada via Paris, had to take charge of the front desk and room service, too.

There were, however, several bright spots during those long, lean years. In June, 1936, Des Baillets renounced his Swiss citizenship to become a Canadian. And on November 11, 1937, Pierre Demers, a twenty-two-year-old short order cook who was back in his home town after having worked that summer at the CN's Jasper Lodge in Alberta, stopped off at the hotel time keeper's office looking for six months' work as a chef. "I had the impression," Demers recalls, "that if ever you wanted to have a good career in cooking, you had to go to the Ritz because, despite all its problems, all it was going through, it had the reputation of being the very best there was."

Laurent Reymond, the new executive chef, hired him as a $125-a-month night cook, and when spring bloomed offered him a permanent job on the day shift — with Sundays off!

Demers was jubilant. He had started his working life making toast at the Windsor Hotel during school holidays; his first job on joining the CN Hotel chain was to hack meat off chicken bones. "I never thought I'd ever be good enough to make the Ritz-Carlton," he says. But he was, and it was the start of an illustrious, thirty-nine year career at the hotel.

That year, too, Lord Beaverbrook was so impressed with Ritz-Carlton hospitality on his first visit there that he autographed a photograph of himself, and wrote on the back an appreciative note to a chamber maid: "To Lillian, the *very* good Keeper of the House."

Perhaps the most encouraging event for Des Baillets, however, was another that would earn the hotel international press coverage abroad. On the night of January 10, 1939, a group of Montreal businessmen and Bell Company of Canada officials returned to the Ritz-Carlton to help celebrate the official inauguration of the telephone line between Canada and Newfoundland. This time they sat in the Blue Room with telephone earpieces to listen to a conversation between Governor General Lord Tweedsmuir in his office at Government House, Ottawa, and Vice-Admiral Sir Humphrey Walwyn, Governor of Newfoundland, in St. John's.

Later, Charles Sise Jr., who had now become Bell's president, led his invited guests to the lobby telephone booth where each took his turn to speak to a Newfoundland counterpart. The new service was opened to the public at 7.30 a.m. the next day. By then, however, Emile Des Baillets had already been at work for an hour, checking on the steamy kitchen, helping Laurent Reymond draw up that day's menu, and ensuring that his head porter had raised the hotel's Union Jack. There was always plenty to do at the Ritz-Carlton Hotel, even in the worst of times. And the indefatigable Des Baillets was inevitably at the centre of it all, as he had been for more than a decade.

His personal qualities, which permitted few people ever to know him well, shone forth clearly in his performance. He was respectful without being obsequious, dignified yet never self-important, and stoically pragmatic as he steered the Ritz-Carlton Hotel through many years of grave financial embarrassment.

"I am an optimist," he so often said. "I have a feeling that things will get better, that more people will one day want to live here with us permanently."

They did, but the worst at the Ritz-Carlton Hotel was not yet over.

CHAPTER SIX

Hotel For Sale

"The hotel needed a new boss
more than new clients, if you ask me.
It was going downhill so fast
you could hardly keep up with it."

RETIRED RITZ WAITER

Also in 1939, Sir Charles Gordon, who had been the Ritz-Carlton's president for three years, died. He was succeeded by a thirty-eight-year-old lawyer, Frederick Thomas Collins, who, as a member of the Montreal legal firm of Meredith, Holden, Haig, Shaughnessy, and Heward, had been counsel to the hotel since he was first called to the Bar in 1925. Collins freely admitted to having had no experience whatsoever in actual hotelkeeping — he specialized in tax and banking law — but promised, nonetheless, plenty of ideas about how the hotel could be economically run. He needed all of these. The Ritz-Carlton Hotel Company had never really recovered from the Depression and the "slow thirties," as the directors described them, and was tumbling into bankruptcy. It owed $105,956 in unpaid taxes alone, as well as a further $465,275 in bond interest, and appeared to have little hope of ever paying either. "The place was bust and doing no business," one shareholder reflects.

Instead of forcing the Ritz into bankruptcy, its creditors, particularly the Bank of Montreal, which had come to acquire most of the original shares and debentures either in trust or against unpaid mortgage payments, installed Frederick Collins into the director's chair temporarily, as "a corporate caretaker," to help pull the hotel around. "Mr. Collins was put in there," says another investor, "to make sure that no one ran away with the store. Not that anybody really wanted to. The hotel had already seen better days and, quite frankly, was teetering on its last legs."

A superb view of Sherbrooke Street — "Montreal's Fifth Avenue" — with its expensive townhouses and tall trees, cutting eastward through part of the Golden Square Mile. Judging by the cars parked on both sides of the thoroughfare, the picture was taken in the 1940s.

PHOTO COURTESY OF THE RITZ-CARLTON COLLECTION

One sous-chef, Rudy Doseger, recalls frequently arriving at work to find more staff than guests and patrons. Indeed, so grim was the Ritz-Carlton's financial state that Sir Charles Gordon's son, Blair, who inherited his father's shares and directorship, told Collins, "This hotel's going absolutely nowhere at all. We might just as well sell it and get it off our hands — and soon. That way, we'll cut our losses."

Collins agreed that the hotel *should* be sold. "But we can only ever consider this," he told Blair Gordon, "when the time is right."

By his reckoning, the time was nowhere near right when, in 1939, a surprise offer to buy The Ritz-Carlton Hotel Company came from Europe — from a group of French investors headed by a man named François Dupré, but largely and mysteriously backed by money put forward by the Singer Sewing Machine Company. The French wanted to buy the company for only $250,000, but Collins was monumentally unmoved by the idea. "I think we should wait a while," he advised the directors. "One day we will get much more for the Ritz than that."

His immediate concern was that if he and his colleagues accepted the terms of the offer they would be letting the Ritz-Carlton investors down badly. After all liabilities had been met, the deal would have meant that first mortgage bond holders would only have received between five and ten cents on the dollar. Second mortgage bond holders, meanwhile, would have been paid nothing at all, and the company's preferred and common shares would have been rendered absolutely worthless. "We were always prepared to consider selling," Collins later remembered, "but the price just had to be right, that's all."

A financier who knew Collins well, however, viewed the task that lay ahead with pessimism. "Mr. Collins headed a company," he observed, "that had a beautiful building but not nearly enough to put inside it. There was nothing to sell but debts — and a lot of work for whoever took the place over. That beautiful old building was nothing more than a shell."

The French offer, then, was rejected out of hand and, on instructions from the Bank of Montreal — and the Royal Trust, which had come to hold thousands of shares in various private estates — Collins set about devising ways to pull in more business so that the hotel could eventually be sold for a considerably higher price.

"In this business," he told the board, "the top of the hotel should, logically, always support the bottom. If it doesn't, we might all just as well go home."

The low rate of guest arrivals that had dispirited Emile Charles Des

A guest checks in while a disciplined bellboy waits to help him to his room
with his luggage. Note the curving front desk tucked somewhat
inconspicuously into a corner of the old lobby — just as César Ritz wanted it.

PHOTO COURTESY OF THE RITZ-CARLTON COLLECTION

Baillets throughout the previous decade was soon to be solved largely by circumstance. During the early part of World War II, the Ritz-Carlton, like hotels in other parts of Canada and throughout the United States, became exceptionally busy. It was jammed with scores of wealthy refugees, including Lady Duveen, widow of the British art connoisseur, Sir Joseph Duveen, who were escaping Europe.

Generals and policy makers like Herbert Lehman, head of the United Nations Relief and Rehabilitation Administration, stalked through the Ritz-Carlton lobby, and Fedor Gusev, a one-time ambassador to the Court of St. James, rubbed shoulders with Colonel Robert McCormick, publisher of the *Chicago Tribune*, a man he might otherwise not have met. All found the hotel friendly and refined. As a British travel guide put it, "The traveller feels as much at home in the Ritz-Carlton in Montreal as he does in the Carlton in London. Therein lies the ineffable charm of the Ritz system."

Collins, however, was not satisfied. Charm was one thing the hotel had never lacked. Money, though, was something it needed badly, and if he were to realize his plans, money now had to *pour* in, even if it meant spending some to make it.

Due largely to the sudden influx of guests, he could now afford to pay a contractor to paint all the rooms. This, part of a more comprehensive renovation program to come later, had to be carried out piecemeal — one room at a time, rather than floor by floor, he recalled — because cash was not coming in fast enough for it to be done any other way, and probably would not for a long time yet.

Symbolic of the company's decay was a lot of basic maintenance work throughout the hotel that had been left undone. Some corridor ceilings were cracking and crumbling, and a refrigerator unit in the main kitchen was leaking so badly that water dripped down to the cellar floor. "This hotel hasn't been painted or repaired since about 1929," Collins declared, "and it's really not good enough. We could have at least repaired pipes and splashed a bit of paint about."

The plight was best illustrated when shortly afterwards, a maître d'hôtel was seating a party of four at a table in the Oval Room when he saw a hole in the carpet. To ensure it remained unnoticed to his customers he stepped to one side and surreptitiously covered the damage with his foot. "Carpets were frayed or torn everywhere you looked," says John Dominique, who was then an enthusiastic busboy in the Palm Court. "But there wasn't much you could do about it. There wasn't enough merchandise around. You couldn't just do repairs when you

GRANDE SALLE DES FÊTES
HÔTEL RITZ-CARLTON, MONTRÉAL

The Grand Ball Room—or the Grand Salon des Fêtes—set for a concert in the 1930s. Said to have possessed the best acoustics in town, it became the permanent home of the Ladies Morning Musical Club, which engaged the world's finest musicians to perform there.

PHOTO COURTESY OF THE RITZ-CARLTON COLLECTION

wanted to. And carpeting was very hard to get."

The decay around him apart, Collins set about an intensive drive to "popularize" the Ritz-Carlton, as Frank Quick had sought to do, by allowing more local groups to enjoy its public rooms. He made a dapper young desk clerk named James Connolly the hotel's first functions manager, and immediately assigned him the job of launching a coast-to-coast advertising campaign. Connolly, who had been with the Ritz-Carlton for five years and was disturbed by the lack of business it had been drawing, responded by promoting the hotel in several popular business and travel magazines, and in thirty leading newspapers. "That should do the trick," he said. "Nearly all our customers read, I should think."

A social secretary named Helen Montreuil was then hired specifically to spread the word as far afield as possible that the Ritz-Carlton Hotel was not only for the rich, the famous, and the wealthy, but for everyone. Initially, Miss Montreuil, a jolly, buxom, chain-smoking woman, was recruited solely for her encyclopedic memory for Montreal bloodlines which, the management felt, would be useful in moments of crisis. She would function well in this role. She could let it be known among Montreal's "best" families, most of whom she knew intimately, that the Ritz Ball Room, or maybe a small salon, could be ideal for their daughter's Sweet Sixteen Party, her graduation dinner, or her wedding reception.

Miss Montreuil's primary function then, was to book as many private dinner parties and receptions as she could, not just for families in Westmount, Outremont, or the Town of Mount Royal, but for those right across the city. Once, when she complained that the Ritz-Carlton should only concern itself with "old-moneyed people," Collins was swift to call her into his office.

"Several ordinary weddings can be far more profitable than one large society function, Miss Montreuil," he said. "After all, there are *three*-figure sums as well as *four*."

From then on, Miss Montreuil had to broaden the scope of her solicitations and, like all other employees who worked under Collins, did exactly as she was told. The results of her labours were predictable, and quickly evident. The Ritz had been home to such organizations as the Junior League of Montreal and the Ladies' Morning Musical Club since the early 1930s. Now new ones began to hold their major events there: the Westmount Women's Club, the Macdonald College Alumni, the University of Toronto Alumni, the Women's Canadian Club, the Young Railwaymen's Club, the Junior Board of Trade, the Montenegran Club, the Soldiers' Wives, the St. Mary's Hospital Ladies' Auxiliary, the Montreal Convalescent Associates, the Zonta Club, and the RCAF Women's Auxiliary. Many of these actually established headquarters at the Ritz-Carlton Hotel.

There was never a more majestic sight at the Ritz-Carlton, it is said, than that of Miss Maysie MacSporran, head mistress of Miss Edgar's and Miss Cramp's School, leading her pupils through the Grand Ball Room and onto the stage on their graduation day, to the music of Wagner's *Die Meistersinger*. An audience of 400 usually turned out on such occasions, to listen to speeches, sing hymns and patriotic songs, and to watch the girls, all of them clad in long white dresses, receive their certificates. The school, and Miss MacSporran, was also to remain faithful to the Ritz for several years from 1940 on.

About this time, the Canadian Club began to meet regularly at the Ritz, too, and Holt Renfrew launched big, twice-yearly fashion shows there, each of which drew audiences of several hundred women. Many of these women eagerly awaited the arrival of numerous smaller shows given in the early afternoon throughout spring and fall in the Palm Court, where they took their daughters to be "seen."

"The Ritz-Carlton hotel is today as it was in the era when the motor car was a novelty," the *Gazette* reported, "a hostelry of elegance and distinction offering a fitting background for the city's social life. It was at the Ritz that Montreal was introduced to its first fashion luncheon. It was at the Ritz that today's leaders of the city's social life made their debuts as their daughters have done since."

Another important attraction was a series of lectures, each followed by luncheon, given by some of France's more successful writers. Organized by La Conférence de l'Alliance Française and sponsored by the French Consulate, these lectures were invariably well attended. But Collins' greatest *coup*, he always said, was attracting the 250-member Saint-Laurent Kiwanis Club, which has an office on the hotel's first floor to this day.

From his arrival, Frederick Collins was perceived as a tough, unyielding businessman who knew exactly what he wanted and was determined, at all costs, to get it. He was also kind, fair, and quick to acknowledge work well done. He boosted his workers' morale by organizing dances for them as well as an annual bowling tournament, and a summer outing to Belmont Park for their children. "If you could spend your life working for one man like this," Pierre Demers says, "you would be very fortunate, indeed." The results of Collins' drive were quickly apparent. "More and more social functions, club meetings, banquets dances and concerts are being held at the Ritz-Carlton than ever before," the *Gazette* reported. Noted *Montreal Star* headlines: "Steady Campaign Increases Ritz Business 100 Per Cent." James Connolly's advertising program had not been in vain.

Much of the additional business, however, could be directly attributed to another of Collins' ideas. He made it considerably more attractive for outsiders to enjoy the hotel by slashing meal prices. Dinner in the Oak Room now cost 90 cents instead of $1.20; Sunday brunch in the Oval Room was $1.50 instead of $1.85. Group meals could be even cheaper, particularly when they were organized by the hotel's new Banquets Department of which Connolly was soon to be head.

By March, 1940, only four months after becoming its president, Frederick Collins could honestly report to his colleague directors that the Ritz-Carlton was actually starting to make money again — and that it was probably financially better off than it had ever been. It had a year's bookings for as many as 100 receptions and nearly 200 private banquets, with promises of numerous more. To the disappointment of a lot of the dedicated waiters, however, Collins had saved money by ordering a stop to the swank Ritz flatware and crested china, replacing it with less costly place settings.

Emile Charles Des Baillets looked on through all of this with some disdain. From the outset, Collins had not impressed him in the slightest. "He is a lawyer who should be making laws," he grumbled, "and not trying to make hotels. He knows absolutely nothing about them! He thinks more about money than people."

Already fearing that allowing too many local organizations at the Ritz-Carlton would mean having to compromise standards, Des Baillets now had to grapple with another of Collins' ideas — "If we relax this silly custom of expecting men to put on a black tie and jacket for dinner, more and more ordinary people will enjoy the hotel, too. Doesn't that make sense?"

Des Baillets reluctantly agreed that it probably did, but he contended fervently that not being suitably and formally attired in the Oval Room contravened one of César Ritz's basic philosophies, an integral part of his original Ritz Plan. Just how guests should appear at meal times, was something true to the manager's heart. "The table," he had recently told a *Gazette* reporter "could be looked upon as one of the greatest pleasures of civilization. Dinner is a rite, and everyone should dress for it."

But Collins disagreed — vehemently. On too many occasions, "this outdated tradition," as he called it, had inhibited dining room custom to a scant two dozen patrons, the rest preferring to dine informally after a hard day in their clubs.

"We have no choice in the matter, Mr. Des Baillets," Collins said.

"If I may say so, Sir," Des Baillets retorted, "Monsieur Ritz wouldn't like what you are suggesting at all!"

"César Ritz is dead," Collins countered quickly, "and times must now begin to change."

This, he made clear, did not mean that men would be allowed into hotel restaurants without a jacket or a tie. On the contrary, the hotel would build up a collection of these so that if patrons should arrive "improperly attired," they could be "duly accommodated."

His manager was not in the slightest appeased. In fact, he was angered. That night, in November, 1940, Emile Charles Des Baillets went to his suite, packed, left, and checked into the Mount Royal Hotel. The following day he found another job managing a new inn, Hôtel l'Estérel — then called Domaine Estérel — in Sainte-Marguerite, Quebec, where he stayed three years before accepting a teaching position at L'Ecole Hôtelière du Rivière-du-Loup, Quebec. "There is no future for me at the Ritz," he said in a letter to the directors.

They, in turn, told Des Baillets they were sorry to see him go, and that if he should one day want to return, "a position would always await" him. Then they promptly replaced him with another Swiss — Albert Frossard who for nearly ten years had been maître d'hôtel in the Oval Room, where, to capture patrons' imagination, he had billed himself "Albert of the Ritz." He ensured that his efforts never betrayed the hotel's idea of what a good restaurant administrator really should be, according to this somewhat cynical description:

> If in the course of his many years' practice of the rudiments of the business he manages to acquire the manners of an ambassador, the palate of a *cordon-bleu*, the wine knowledge of an expert wine-dealer, the cheerfulness and the graces of a society hostess, and the long-suffering endurance of both Ulysses and Job for bores, wealthy maniacs, fribbles, hotel cranks and restaurant faddists, he is then — and only then — ready to become a *maître d'hôtel*.

Like all three Ritz-Carlton managers before or after him, Frossard was European-trained. He had served variously as either captain of waiters or as an assistant manager many of the best hotels — for example, the Palace in Montreux, Zurich's Baur en Ville, the Kulm Hotel in St. Moritz, and the Grand Hotel in Sandford, Holland. Most impressive, perhaps, was that he had learned to administer the big, busy desk staffs at both the Copocabana in Rio de Janeiro and the eminent Savoy Hotel in London.

He, too, needed all the know-how he could muster, for while business was, indeed, beginning to boom, war-time shortages again made it difficult to maintain the graceful living standards set by the original founders, and which visitors had come to expect. According to the directors, the hotel was "once again at a terrible disadvantage because too many fine young men have been called to the colours." Hence, Frossard fought relentlessly to help the new president boost business with a staff that was predominantly local.

"For a busboy, the work was the same as it always had been," says John Dominique, "but there was a lot more of it and it was harder. There weren't enough of us to look after all those wealthy refugees — boat loads of them — who settled in as permanent guests. But it was good to see the hotel picking up because it had been down for so long. If you ask me, it had been more like a club because that's the way Mr. Hosmer had wanted it. Now, suddenly it was a hotel again."

To make Collins' renovation program complete, Frossard sold some of the bedroom furniture that was now beginning to wear, tear, and break, and systematically installed more luxurious replacements. Better beds and dressers, and more comfortable chairs, he felt, were absolutely needed to modernize the Ritz-Carlton and preserve its place among North America's best hotels. Some patrons were aghast, however, when they heard that he had sold the big, solid-brass bedsteads for a mere $1.50 each.

The first part of the hotel to suffer as war raged, Frossard had already found out before his promotion, was the kitchen. Certain items became so scarce that they could no longer be served, and this saw the end of several of the guests' favourite, fancy dishes. Until then, the hotel's menus contained a Russian dish or two almost every day, particularly borscht, for which the spices were too costly to import. So was caviar. Its scarcity prohibited chefs from making an Oval Room specialty — a sandwich of griddle cakes spread with caviar and topped with sour cream.

The problem was further compounded when Italy joined the war and numerous patriotic patrons shunned spaghetti and ravioli. "Due to international complications," the Ritz explained tactfully, "certain items must be removed from our menus." It was not long, though, before many patrons decided that they missed their pasta and began asking to have it reinstated, which it was. But it was a long time before borscht or caviar could be served again at the Ritz-Carlton Hotel.

Despite his lack of knowledge of the hotel business, Collins recognized the uncanny ability of his young chef, Pierre Demers, and despatched him to work at "21," the famous New York City club, to gain more experience and to ferret out some new recipes. Demers obliged and promptly returned with a dish he called *Le poulet 21* — boiled chicken sauteed in butter, flavoured with brandy, and served with a cream sauce in a border of wild rice — which remains on the menu to this day.

One man who developed a propensity for Demers' new-found dish, by the way, also had an odd way of ordering it. He silently handed the waiter a little piece of paper on which he had drawn the picture of a little chicken, nude except for a bow-tie. "There was never any accounting for what some diners did when they dropped in to eat in a good mood," Demers recalls. "But if they were in a bad mood you had to watch out."

On subsequent visits to New York City, he tasted recipes he didn't like — even at the Ritz — and told Collins so. "I'm not paying you and sending you on trips to find out what's bad," Collins replied. "I want you only to come back with what's good. Don't forget that."

Demers didn't. The outcome was that in 1942, when Laurent Reymond joined Emile Charles Des Baillets at Hôtel l'Estérel, Demers became the Ritz-Carlton's executive chef. He was twenty-seven, the youngest man ever to hold the position in the entire Ritz chain, and more inventive than he ever thought he would need to be. On days when the hotel could not buy meat — "Hotels weren't allowed to in those days," Demers says — he cooked baked beans which he laced with rum, serving them on Boston-steamed bread. All too frequently there was insufficient shortening for his pastry, and rarely any butter. So he had to use margarine, making it tastier by mixing it with milk or cream.

He made mayonnaise, in fifteen-gallon batches, by boiling ten gallons of water, thickening it with flour, and adding two gallons of cooking oil and five dozen eggs. "You had to make do with what you had, sometimes little, and all too often nothing but a few vegetables," Demers remembers. "But we did it, and well, I think."

The customers thought so. From the moment Demers took over the kitchen, the Oval Room was often packed. "It is at the Ritz today," reported the *Herald*, "that smart Montrealers congregate for luncheons on Saturday, and it is here that Sunday high noon dinners are becoming increasingly popular. Beginning again this autumn, Sunday evening buffet suppers will be served, affording Montrealers the opportunity of entertaining their friends in a delightful and informal manner."

As the years rolled on, though, manager Frossard's problems stretched far beyond food. He was dismayed to discover that a large part of the hotel's poor financial state lay in the previous management's laxness in collecting its money. The books had not been properly kept; bills had not been made up and delivered regularly enough to too many of the permanent residents. They, in turn, had been only too happy to live in the hotel without paying. Some owed several months' rent.

One of the debtors, Frossard was saddened to find out, was none other than Alphonse Jongers who, having painted all the directors' portraits, was now expected to pay for his studio and room. Despite spending a lot of money on gin while keeping Elwood Hosmer company in the Palm Court night after night, and treating his models to chocolate sundaes and liqueurs, he was also an Oval Room "regular," usually with a different woman, and it was a luxury he obviously could not afford. He owed the hotel nearly $1,500 in meals and rent.

Jongers' excuse was that as his name as a society painter had grown and his work had become more popular, so fellow artists had convinced him that he should charge no less than $5,000 per portrait. He had recently exhibited his work at London's Tate Gallery and New York's Metropolitan Museum, after all, and piled up more honours. But while the hotel's directors and aristocrats like Lord Aberdeen and the Duke of Grammont had been able to afford his fees, most Montrealers could not. Poor Jongers, now approaching his seventies, had priced himself out of the business and, consequently, had fallen on hard times.

The Ritz-Carlton directors, which then included Elwood Hosmer and the aging Sir Herbert Holt, immediately took compassion, as they so often had before. After discussing the dilemma for many weeks during regular board meetings, they graciously allowed the struggling artist to liquidate his debt by paying an extra $50 weekly. This, Jongers said, he was happy to do. He finally paid the Ritz-Carlton Hotel in full, in fact, only three weeks before dying in his bed there on October 2, 1945, just a few days before his seventy-third birthday. Shareholders by the dozen sent flowers to his funeral, and the directors attended it.

When the ubiquitous Elwood Hosmer died six years later, an era at the Ritz-Carlton Hotel that had been highlighted by triumphs, but fraught with troubles, had drawn sadly to a close.

Frederick Collins studied the Ritz-Carlton's books stretching back to its inception and reflected on the ebb and flow of the hotel's fortunes. Business during the early years was slow, he said, and the moment it showed signs of quickening, the hotel faced World War I. Thereafter, from about 1919 — an exceptional year — until 1923, both room occupancy and restaurant patronage were high. One thing that never ceased to trouble him was the thought that Frank Quick had been blatantly extravagant by allowing the lights to remain on in unoccupied rooms.

During the mid-1920s, Collins saw from the books, the hotel suffered a mild recession that worsened during the Depression and from which it took many years to recover. Sure it had good seasons, but they were outnumbered by the bad. One bleak night in 1940, shortly after he had become president, he would frequently tell colleagues, he had taken his wife to the Ritz-Carlton for dinner to find that only fourteen visitors had checked in. Room occupancy, he maintained over and over again, was "the staple diet of *any* hotel."

It probably is. But down in the bars and restaurants, where the tipping was done, the men had slightly different ideas. John Dominique, soon to become a Palm Court waiter, had come to know and genuinely like the patrons, especially such "regulars" as Major Andrew Holt, Sir Herbert's stockbroker son, another permanent guest and a Ritz director. "No matter what our hotel looked like," Dominique says with the fervour of a true Ritzman, "it was still the finest in Montreal, and you were there to look after these people, and they were satisfied with whatever you did for them. Every move you made, every bit of service you gave them, was appreciated. They never looked at you as if you were nothing. Time and time again I told myself we were catering to the best kind of people in Canada, or North America come to that."

Maybe the world?

"Yes, the world. That's why our hotel was the best — even in the worst of times."

CHAPTER SEVEN

A New Life —
in the Old Ritz Style

"Cary Grant might have been disappointed
when he stayed at the Ritz-Carlton
a few years back. The local hotel didn't
iron the laces of his tennis shoes.
But never mind. They sure made up for it."

MONTREAL BROADCASTER BETTY SHAPIRO

In the six years that Frederick Collins was the Ritz-Carlton's president, his cost-cutting measures and promotional ideas paid handsome dividends. By May 1, 1946, when he was forced to leave the board on being appointed Mr. Justice Frederick Collins of the Quebec Superior Court, the hotel had no debts at all and $250,000 in the bank — "very favourable results," said a letter to shareholders from the board.

Now the company was indeed eminently more saleable, and for a considerably better price. Thus, it was not totally surprising that world peace should be accompanied by a second attempt by François Dupré to buy the hotel. This time he made an offer the directors could not afford to turn back. Influenced by "the uncertainty of the longer term prospects" of the Ritz-Carlton, despite its "extensive patronage" and "the remarkable improvement which has taken place in its financial position and physical condition during the past seven years," they recommended that the shareholders accept Dupré's terms.

To both media and patrons, details of the deal remained genteelly obscure. All that was made public was that Greenshields & Company, a Montreal brokerage firm, had combined with "foreign interests" to buy the hotel. But there was considerably more to it than that. There unfolded a story of one man's yearning to broaden a little empire.

François Louis Jules Dupré was a tall, urbane Parisian who had orig-

François Dupré (left) and Jean Contat (right) welcome a visitor. Dupré entered
both finance and hoteliery with vitality, force, and success
and, by the mid-1940s, was clearly Paris' most accomplished hotelier, owning
l'Hôtel Georges V, the Plaza Athénée, and l'Hôtel La Tremoille. He had met
Contat at the Ritz in New York, and sent him to Montreal to give the
Ritz-Carlton a new life.

PHOTO COURTESY OF THE RITZ-CARLTON COLLECTION

inally set out to become a financier. In 1912, while the Ritz-Carlton was being built, he was sent by the Paris bank for which he worked to train as a manager for a year at Barclay's Bank in London, England. While there he met Melville Greenshields, one of the Greenshields partners, who was managing his firm's tiny London office.

The two men struck up a friendship and instead of rejoining the bank when his London assignment was over, Dupré opened a Paris office for Greenshields which functioned until it was razed during World War I. He later married the Duke of Polignac's widow, Daisy Singer of the Singer Sewing Machine Company; with her family's backing, and with wisely invested money of his own, he entered both finance and hoteliery with vitality, force, and success.

By the mid-1940s, he was clearly Paris' most accomplished hotelier, owning l'Hôtel Georges V, the Plaza Athénée, and l'Hôtel La Tremoille, all of which were doing well. Upon deciding that he wanted a fourth such establishment, Dupré approached Greenshields in Montreal, where he had ready-made business contacts. After a lot of shrewd bargaining with the senior partners he was able to organize a syndicate to buy the Ritz-Carlton, with himself at the head.

Initially, the Greenshields men found Dupré intimidating. He had an astute mind but was austere, with an annoying arrogance and an overpowering sense of superiority. Eventually, though, they broke down some of this. They began to tease the aloof Parisian — whom they called "Le Comte" or "Le Baron" — about his supercilious French attitude to big business. When Dupré chuckled, it made for a friendly, relaxed atmosphere in which the financial future of the hotel could be negotiated.

"Those guys," remembers Peter Kilburn, one of the original mediators, who is now chairman of the Ritz-Carlton board, "were the only friends Dupré had in Canada. In time, they probably became his only friends, anywhere."

François Dupré bought nearly two-thirds of the original 20,000 shares in the Ritz-Carlton Hotel and, in so doing, succeeded in gaining complete control of it. Three members of the Greenshields board, Richard Johnson, Russell Bell, and Charles Greenshields, emerged as major shareholders, too, and this ensured that Dupré's new company was well represented locally.

No one, however, not even the Bank of Montreal and Royal Trust, the transfer agent, both of which had come to hold most of the original shares in private estates, ever knew exactly how much Dupré paid for

General manager Jean Contat was considered "a charming tyrant" who played as hard as he worked. He was an honour student of the world's best school for hoteliers—the chain of Ritz hotels—and had worked his way up from being a waiter at the Ritz both in Paris and in London, to become manager of the Ritz in New York City. "Maybe, with the years, some of the little things guests like have become lost or forgotten," he said when he first set foot at the Ritz-Carlton. "Maybe, just maybe, I can bring them back."

PHOTO COURTESY OF THE RITZ-CARLTON COLLECTION

the Ritz-Carlton. He had entered into numerous private transactions in which he bought first, second, and third shares, and many different types of debentures, all for widely varying prices. To further complicate matters, none of them was acquired in his own name; all were bought by several of his many companies, or by his associates. One estimate, based on the number and the value of the shares and debentures that changed hands said the deal cost Dupré slightly more than $2.7 million; another said that to acquire control of the Ritz-Carlton he wrote a cheque for $3.1 million.

Of overriding importance to the company, and the other shareholders, was that Dupré had the reputation of buying run-down establishments and transforming them into superb ones. "My philosophy when I buy a hotel," he said, "is to put as much money into it as I pay for it." He pledged to make the Ritz-Carlton as good, if not better, than the hotels he owned and ran in Paris. In essence, he was promising to give the Ritz-Carlton a second life — and he did.

Concluded in the fall of 1947, the sale installed François Dupré at the head of the Ritz-Carlton for eighteen years as its first foreign president. With him, as he set about administering the hotel by telephone from his Paris office, came some of César Ritz's panache, an endless stream of ideas, a lot of imagination — and a *general* manager and fellow countryman named Jean Contat, who would oversee the daily operations of the hotel, even the work of Albert Frossard.

Trim, ebullient, and bespectacled, Contat was instantly regarded as "a charming tyrant" who played as hard as he worked. He liked horseback riding (he had once served with a French cavalry division), became a member of the Montreal Hunt Club, and tended cattle on a farm he bought in Brigham, near Cowansville, Quebec, within weeks of his arrival. In his new position his experience soon became apparent. He had been an honour student of the world's best school for hoteliers — the chain of Ritz hotels. In fact, he had worked his way up from being a waiter at the Ritz both in Paris and in London, to become manager of the Ritz in New York City, where Dupré had first met him.

On the way, Contat had become a rigid believer in giving the clients "better quality than they had ever known," and he would reinforce this conviction at the Ritz-Carlton. "Maybe, with the years, some of the little things guests like have become lost or forgotten," he said when he first set foot there. "Maybe, just maybe, I can bring them back."

Under Dupré's instruction, he undertook an immediate and comprehensive modernization of the Ritz-Carlton, and this meant making it

Helen Montreuil (right) enjoys a glass of wine in the new Maritime Bar with Jerri Sullivan, one of the Ritz Café at Night performers. Miss Montreuil rose from her job as social secretary to become the hotel's first public relations officer.

PHOTO COURTESY OF THE RITZ-CARLTON COLLECTION

more accessible than it had ever been to a wide spectrum of travellers on the one hand, and to Montrealers wanting to drop in for drinks and a meal on the other. Only days after his arrival, old storage space was cleared from the mezzanine to make way for new offices and extra staff.

In a matter of weeks Helen Montreuil, now an old Ritz hand, was promoted. She became the hotel's first public relations officer, and was told in no uncertain manner to attract even more outside organizations than she already had. This time she did not complain. The banquet manager was ordered to prepare himself to cater to an influx of weddings, private parties, business functions, and group dinners — anything that would make money.

One of the first groups to accept the invitation was La Ligue de la jeunesse féminine de Montréal, the French equivalent of the Junior League, which began organizing an annual revue at the Ritz in aid of paraplegics and blind children. It was to stay around for years.

Overnight, newspaper social columns were littered with notes that enhanced the hotel's dignity, and elevated its credibility as an elegant place to stay for several days at a time. Said the *Gazette*'s social column, typically:

> Lady Williams-Taylor of Nassau, the Bahamas, who spent the summer at the Manoir Richelieu, Murray Bay, is at the Ritz-Carlton until September 24.

And:

> Lady Davis has arrived from St. Andrews-by-the-Sea, NB, to spend a week in town and is at the Ritz.

Once again, the Ritz-Carlton was bustling with socialites. It was their special home-away-from-home. Fortunate guests who matched up to Ritz requirements could honestly say that when they stayed there, they did so in surroundings which combined the classic good taste of a magnificent hotel with the informal ease of a rich townhouse. They could eat better than ever in the chaste splendour of the Oval Room under a ceiling which was already being hailed as an antique — and "the most perfect in the Adam style on this continent."

In either the quiet elegance of the Palm Court or the formal air of the Oak Room, they could see — and be seen by — the pillars of old Montreal society, many of them now visibly aging. Or they could meet the world's most distinguished businessmen. They could be recognized themselves, or simply sit by and watch others being recognized, instead. A favourite pastime at the Ritz was to sink into a lobby sofa and watch personalties arrive and depart by the dozens, and observe the polished, affable way they were pampered by the staff.

Anyone might have walked in through the big front doors during the early 1950s — from singer Gracie Fields and the British speedboat racer Sir Malcolm Campbell, to actress Loretta Young and the Italian opera tenor, Beniamino Gigli. François Dupré and Jean Contat were, indeed, giving the Ritz-Carlton another life.

During long staff meetings that stretched well into the night, new activities were contemplated to boost business in the dining and banquet rooms, and to beef up reservations. To pave the way, a new job was created in the lobby office. James Connolly, who was always so finely groomed from his carefully brushed blond hair to his shiny black pumps, was promoted again. Quiet, assured, and arduous, he became the Ritz-Carlton's first executive assistant — a perfect foil to the flamboyant, sometimes erratic Contat — charged with "capturing" major events from other hotels.

Take the Montreal Hunt Ball, for instance, which had previously been held in various private homes. The decorating arrangements for one of these included life-sized papier maché horses polka-dotted in various Hunt colours and festooned with ropes of flowers, a fox's head sculpted in ice for the buffet table centerpiece, and the sounding of hunting horns to announce dinner.

A passageway between the Grand Ball Room and the dining room was hung with draperies and lined with paintings of hunting scenes. To the consternation of the dozens of Ritzers who had been involved in the organizing, the brass plaques beneath several of the pictures were entirely inappropriate. They identified portraits of Vernon Cardy, a well known horseman who also happened to be a rival hotelkeeper. No one would admit responsibility, of course, but the lack of discernment was remedied only minutes before the guests arrived. The tags — not the pictures of Cardy — were hurriedly removed.

James Connolly's new job also meant he had to pull in better-paying bookings, so he began to contact airlines and large corporations, many of them as far away as Mississippi, New York City, and Vancouver, just to let them know that the Ritz-Carlton was available for small conventions.

"Perhaps a third of our guests are still permanent residents," Connolly once explained, "and, if we wanted them, there could be many more. But we must keep about one hundred and thirty suites vacant for people from out of town. We must always look after them, you know."

Like Helen Montreuil — and to the delight of both Dupré and Contat — Connolly set a fine example in the art of mastering another Ritz requirement: remembering guests' names so that they always felt wanted, cared for, and important.

Occasionally there were lapses. When the great Austrian actress Elisabeth Bergner checked into the hotel, for example, a bellman escorted her to her suite with a welcoming smile and efficient dispatch. On his return to the ground floor, though, the elevator boy was met by a verbal onslaught from the duty clerk, a youth about his own age at the front desk.

"Why, why, why?" he hissed. "Why didn't you greet Miss Bergner by name? She *has* been here before, you know!"

The elevator operator bowed his head in shame.

Just how well the staff did recall guests by name was aptly illustrated when the hotel received a letter announcing the impending visit of a British businessman:

> You will recall that the Colonel is six feet seven inches and a half tall and weighs 350 pounds. I trust you will keep this in mind.

When the note landed on Connolly's desk, he was completely unruffled by it. He read it slowly, then put it in his in-tray to await a response. "It's a very nice thought. It really is," he said. "But writing to us really wasn't necessary. The Colonel was here once before. We remember him very well. We had to extend his bed."

Similarly, waiters and desk staff were trained to be discreet and to know, intuitively, when a person wanted absolute privacy and should *never*, therefore, be addressed by name — the protocol-conscious Russians who were "regulars" at the Ritz, for example. They always insisted on anonymity, and to ensure that they got it, the management suggested that they register in groups under the Russian equivalent of "Smith."

That was not all. One stocky, grey-haired man spent all his Sunday evenings chatting with friends in the Palm Court. Yet not by the blink of an eye did waiters ever betray their knowledge that he was Quebec Premier Maurice Duplessis — only that Monsieur Duplessis, whom the staff generally regarded as a devoted Ritz patron and a bon vivant, preferred others in the room not to disturb him. Waiters even aided the Premier in breaking one of his own laws by serving him a drink without a meal on Sundays, usually a glass of champagne in a Palm Court fireside chair. To keep him from view as he drank, they placed a screen around

The Montreal Hunt Ball, an annual Ritz event. The decorating arrangements
were invariably lavish. This one had life-sized papier mâché horses
polka-dotted in various Hunt colours and festooned with ropes of flowers, an
abundance of flags protruding from the Grand Ball Room balconies, a fox's
head sculpted in ice for the buffet table centerpiece, and the sounding of
hunting horns to announce dinner.

PHOTO BY GERALDINE CARPENTER
COURTESY OF THE RITZ-CARLTON COLLECTION

him, and this tended to arouse suspicion. But that kind of attention was what Duplessis came to relish.

"I knew all that," says John Dominique, whom Jean Contat promoted to become the Palm Court's maître d'hôtel. "I even recall times when Mr. Duplessis came in and shocked everyone by ordering a glass of milk before dinner, instead of his usual."

Nor did the staff bat an eye when they discovered that Captain Gordon H. Murray, who had begun to preside over the lobby and the Oval Room, actually had a wife who lived in Arizona and who joined her husband at the Ritz for a couple of weeks each year. The floor waiters always knew what was going on, but never spoke about it.

It was noticed by other patrons, for example, that each time Mrs. Murray arrived, her husband bought her a new Buick or a fur coat. The hotel was much more alive with gossip, however, when Mrs. Murray moved into the room next door to her husband's, then into a suite at the end of the corridor, and then took another on an entirely different floor before moving back to Arizona. Such strange goings-on never fazed the floor waiters or the desk staff, and they certainly evaded all questions about them.

Under Contat and Frossard, the hotel again became more widely known for its a unique attention to rooms, or, in Ritzese, "floor service." Snug in her tenth-floor aerie, amid a profusion of lost-and-found objects like umbrellas, gloves, and spectacles, Marcelle Gohier, one of the first French Canadians to head a Ritz-Carlton department, kept strict order.

As head housekeeper, she was charged with directing a staff of thirty-six maids, seven housemen, four seamstresses, four linen helpers, and a woman who was available to sew lingerie, pack clothes, or run shopping errands for busy guests.

Well into her second decade in the job, Miss Gohier emerged as a benign authoritarian who aptly defined the Ritz concept of fine service, and followed it to the letter. "We prefer to employ only those maids who have worked in private service," she said. "We teach them three things — and if they don't master them all, and quickly, they are dismissed."

The maids, she insisted, *had* to learn to understand each guest's individual tastes, to respect his or her privacy at all times, and to be ready to do any extra service even when it was well beyond the boundaries of the job. To uphold the hotel's reputation, they began tidying rooms three times each day. This meant that when the hotel was full, they, or the part-time helpers Contat hired at peak periods to ease the workload, often had to work overtime to get the job done. But the maids never complained.

Just as routine to them was Contat's insistence that they remember not merely to turn back the bedclothes, but to memorize just *how* each guest preferred this simple chore to be done.

Doing things exactly as the guests preferred them invited a barrage of requests that would have been regarded as eccentric by most large hotels. At the Ritz, however, coping was invariably a part of the maids' daily routine. Housekeeper Gohier insisted on it. She was a woman of immense tolerance where guests were concerned, and she saw nothing peculiar at all in their solicitations.

Some women, for instance, liked to sleep with their feet up. When they saw Albert Frossard lunching in the Oval Room, or on the little Dutch Garden patio, they told him so. Raised feet, they said, acted as a check against varicose veins. Frossard, who knew most of the hotel's most loyal patrons from his restaurant days, understood perfectly. From then on, maids on each floor were told to keep a running list of all people with leg ailments and ensure that the moment they arrived at the Ritz-Carlton for their next visit, they found special wedges had been inserted under their mattresses. "If we have made people comfortable," Miss Gohier said, "then we have done our job."

The hotel's elaborate mnemonics came firmly into full play in all such matters. The widow of a Chicago industrialist complained that the Ritz-Carlton had "got carried away in its new-found affluence by buying new bedding when the older stuff was better." Oddly, she told all this to a waiter one morning, and he took her complaint seriously, and relayed it quickly to Housekeeping.

"If there's anything I hate next to my skin," the woman said, "it's percale. It's too hard. It has been known, you know, to make me itch quite considerably!"

Swiftly, a set of softer, linen sheets was put aside especially for her. The next time the woman checked in, they were on her bed waiting — and a chair had been placed in the centre of the bedroom facing the window. Once, several years before, she had said she wanted her room set that way so she could spend a few minutes enjoying the view of Mount Royal before unpacking her suitcases and going down to the Palm Court for a cocktail and the Oval Room for dinner.

Now that another war was over, the staff, which Contat had increased from 275 to 325 as business improved, was predominantly European again. The corridors were filled with gracious gestures and polite, refined accents. Every night waiters — a thirty-five-man corps of them scattered throughout the hotel — moved lithely between tables and kitchens. On good days, the tips they received were as high as their morale, which manifested itself in an unyielding allegiance by all members of the staff. This, in general, was due to the hotel's renewed stability, and the joy the workers experienced in serving celebrated people in such a celebrated place — either that, or their fear of the dynamic Contat or the stone-faced Dupré, whom they had come to know as "les enfants terrible."

Whatever the reason, employees continued to be intensely proud to have a job at the Ritz-Carlton Hotel. Denis Laganière is a perfect example. He joined in 1946 as a young, slim man of twenty charged with operating the night elevators and running errands. Swept up in the bustle of people and faces, he had his sights firmly fixed on shedding his pill-box hat for a more senior Ritz uniform. Meanwhile, though, he was intensely grateful for the job he had, and indulged in its daily adventure.

When Edward, Duke of Windsor, returned to the hotel in the late 1940s with his wife, Wallace Simpson, it left a lasting impression on Denis Laganière. "They came through the lobby and into my elevator with so much grace," he recalls, "that it is still in my head. Their social status was so different from yours and mine, so they learned how to hold themselves up with this special grace. They'd learned how to walk, smile, and say all the right things at the right time — how to greet people, how to make the little night elevator guy feel so good about pulling down this big lever to take them up to the Vice-Regal Suite. I felt so good about my job, in fact, that I worked at it six days a week and never even thought of asking for time off."

Nor did Frossard's Danish-born successor in the Oval Room. He *really* shuffled his life around for the hotel. By ennobling the Ritz, he felt, he was ennobling himself, and he did this in style. He felt that his name — Sven Rasmussen — was both inappropriate and a hindrance to an ambitious maître d'hôtel, so he billed himself as "Charles of the Ritz," and spent his entire working life bowing and scraping to patrons as though they were the last things on earth. "He was so dedicated," said a colleague who called himself "Gaston of the Ritz," and was another of several staffers who were happy to "change" both their lives and their names to hold their jobs, "that it drove you to the edge of insanity just to watch him."

A highly strung, fastidious man with wire spectacles and a thatch of brown hair meticulously plastered to one side, Charles would stop in mid-stride to reorganize someone else's flower arrangement if he disliked it. He would readjust the curtains and re-set a table if he thought it needed it. With his handkerchief he was constantly flicking specks of dust the normal human eye could never hope to discern from his podium-like desk inside the Oval Room entrance.

To Charles, the customers always came first and he vowed never to let them down. This was an unimpeachable benediction. Thus, while supervising a Law Society banquet, he was horrified to spy a busboy sneaking an hors d'oeuvre. "The housekeeping department has interfered," he explained to his diners, with precious courtesy — then sent the entire tray of food back to the kitchen to be tossed into the garbage.

Dinner was a more important affair than ever at the Ritz-Carlton during the late 1940s and, with the surge of visitors, waiters and busboys quickly formulated ideas of their perfect customer. Or, at least, the diner they most enjoyed serving. "Charles of the Ritz," whose opinion counted throughout the hotel, based his conception on the Norwegian pulp and paper tycoon, C.B. Thorn, whom he regarded as the absolute paragon he would have liked all guests to emulate. Albert Frossard declared without any reservation that Mr. Thorn's knowledge of wines and specialty dishes far exceeded that of most good headwaiters and chefs. Charles, though, it was said, knew more about Mr. Thorn than anyone, except Mr. Thorn's wife.

He also developed a talent for putting names to faces, even those he had only seen once, and automatically associated them with their favourite dishes. "Mr. Little, president of Anglo Pulp and Paper, is here for his usual," he would tell Pierre Demers. Mr. Little came so often that Pierre Demers would go to the butcher to have the steak cut especially for him, and he ensured that a stock of it was always on hand.

After having commanded the corps of waiters and been a maître d'hôtel for thirty of his forty-two Ritz-Carlton years, Charles claimed to know more famous people by name than anyone else in Canada, and he probably did. He not only associated celebrities with the meals they liked, but with where they preferred to sit — "Mr. Rubinstein, the pianist," he said, "likes a table in the north-east corner, and Lord Beaverbrook a place near the French windows that open onto our lovely garden. In summer, His Lordship prefers to sit out there with his coffee and brandy."

As for Mr. Thorn, he cared little about where he sat — only that the food was good. Charles agreed wholeheartedly with Frossard's assessment of the shy, lumbering tycoon as "the last of the great connoisseurs," and he once said exactly why.

"Mr. Thorn's dinner," he explained, "usually lasted for three hours, and nearly always between seven sharp and ten-fifteen. First, he would talk over the entire menu with the chef, arranging every detail of what he wanted to eat. He would start with a cocktail and follow this with hors d'oeuvres, aquavit, and beer. With his consommé, he'd take a Bristol Cream sherry, then he would pause for a smoke.

"A fish course came next. With it, Mr. Thorn drank red wine, a Norwegian custom. Then he would pause for another smoke.

"Following this was a meat dish. One of his favourites was a mixture of lamb and goose livers with *sauce Périgueux*. This he ate with red wine, of course, and he would pause after it for a third smoke.

"Often, for dessert, he ordered *bombe Nesselrode* with chestnuts and vanilla, accompanying this with a dryish champagne. Then came his coffee, a good cigar, and a fine liqueur."

After that, said "Charles of the Ritz," Mr. Thorn called for his scotch and soda, and when he had drunk that, he thanked the chef and retired until morning to the seventh-floor suite he always rented overlooking Sherbrooke Street.

No one was more delighted with Thorn's dining room performance than the captain of waiters, a somewhat choleric-faced Austrian named Joseph Riedl. "Too many patrons," he complained, "have succumbed to the awful American urge to rush lunch or dinner. Unfortunately, some eat in less than an hour and, just when they think we are not looking, they have actually been known to wipe their plates clean with the last of their bread rolls."

The first Ritzmen to hear from Mr. Thorn in the morning were those who worked in room service. During this period, about ninety percent of all guests expected breakfast in bed, and Thorn was no exception. Thanks to hundreds of Ritz-Carlton guests like him, the hotel found it profitable to oblige, and took on extra staff — more than twenty extra floor maids and a dozen part-time helpers — to revitalize the service with a vengeance.

It was work made considerably easier by the advent of ingenious electrical appliances. A floor waiter not only had his own pantry, but one which was equipped with a brand new refrigerator, oven, toaster and all manner of other gadgets that ensured that meals could be delivered fresher and hotter than ever.

No matter how much the management honed service and tended guests, however, the dignity of the old place was all too frequently disrupted. Shortly after Victor the doorman replaced the retired Jamieson on the lobby staff and was working nights, Sir James Dunn, founder and owner of Algoma Steel, burst into the lobby and belligerently demanded a bowl of cereal and a large glass of milk.

"I'm sorry, Sir," Victor said apologetically, "but we don't serve cereal at night. Besides, Sir, our kitchen is open only for snacks served in rooms."

Sir James went away only to return an hour or so later with a large box of cornflakes, which he systematically scattered in the foyer, across the lobby, and around the front desk. "Now," he screamed, "the Ritz-Carlton has finally got cereal!"

Ritz veterans' eyes still roll whenever Sir James is mentioned. "He made Mr. Frossard work very hard and drove him crazy," a maître d'hôtel recalls. "He'd order a bottle of the best champagne and get Mr. Frossard to pour it. He'd taste it, then kick the bucket halfway across the Oval Room, shouting and screaming his head off." Sir James Dunn was known, too, to spread his paper on the breakfast table, knocking everything onto the floor — then laugh as he watched waiters and busboys pick it up. "Thankfully," says the maître d'hôtel, "we've only ever had one patron as bad as he was."

There were other breaches of dignity with which to contend. One night in 1947, a gunman held up a Verdun grocery store, then drove up to the Ritz-Carlton and demanded money from the night desk clerk. Fortunately, the cashier had dropped that day's takings into the Bank of Montreal's night depository on his way home, so the gunman received only $400 before fleeing into the darkness. The incident, however, unnerved the staff for days, even though the thief was finally apprehended.

Not long afterwards, a happy millionaire walked into the frigidly correct atmosphere of the Palm Court where some of Montreal's most formidable dowagers had assembled for tea, their little fingers crooked just so. The women were clad in silver fox fur stoles, the prevailing fashion of the day.

"Pussycats!" the man shouted. "Look at all the pussycats!"

Lorgnettes were raised, but the intruder was pointedly ignored. He accepted this icy challenge, though. "Pussycats!" he cried again, and darted among the group, snatching as many furs as he could, and dragging some of the women from their wicker chairs with them. Draped in his acquisitions, he then ran upstairs toward the Oval Room.

Money and its appurtenances have always been respected at the Ritz, but millions will never save a guest if he fails to match up to the high standards of behaviour expected of him, particularly when it comes to annoying other guests. This is never supposed to occur. Hence a manager quickly appeared to resolve the problem, announcing stiffly that the police had been called. The furs were retrieved and returned to their owners with apologies, and the millionaire left the hotel quietly.

A few months later, however, he returned, having sent thirty-six pieces of luggage ahead of him. Even though he scattered tips around the lobby, the front desk told him — politely, but firmly — that no suite was available for him at the Ritz-Carlton that day, and that there would probably not be one for him in the future.

A young woman appeared on the garden terrace one day in a cotton skirt and bolero, made her way down to the grass, and spread her towel. She then began to peel off her outer garments to reveal herself in a polka-dot swimsuit. The busboy was scandalized. He called the maître d'hôtel who approached the woman with cautious solemnity.

"Excuse me, Madame," he said. "But you can't do that!"

"Why not?" she responded with composure. "I *am* a guest here."

Her excuse was unacceptable. "You may well be staying with us, Madame," the maître d'hôtel said. "But this area is reserved for our diners."

The girl was bundled back to her room.

Considerably more of a nuisance was the young Englishman who registered in the hotel in 1949 as "Lord Harrington." He had an impeccable Eton accent, a slightly arrogant air, and a fund of authentic data about Britain's aristocracy, with which he fascinated the staff. Always mindful of titles and ranks, the managers called him "My Lord," just as they had addressed Lord Shaughnessy. And in return, "His Lordship" tipped with the abandon that was expected of him.

Although he boasted that he had recently spent $600 on haberdashery, and had penetrated some of Montreal's best-known families — selling one of them his 1948 Pontiac sedan for $1,300 — "Lord Harrington" had not paid his hotel bill. "I'm having awful difficulty getting my funds out of England," he told the cashier repeatedly. "Can you wait a couple of days?"

The cashier could, and did. Finally, after having been at the Ritz-Carlton for three weeks, the guest wrote a bad cheque — just about the time Montreal police had begun to make inquiries about a 1948 Pontiac sedan reported stolen in Vancouver.

A few days later, the bad cheque in his hand, Frossard and a house detective went to talk to his delinquent guest. Alas, he found luggage in the room, but "Lord Harrington" was nowhere to be seen. He had fled. The man was eventually jailed in Georgia for a similar fraud. Police there successfully unmasked him as one of Lord Milford Haven's former stableboys, who had been dismissed from his job for stealing.

"But what's so odd about that?" Victor the doorman used to say between doffing his hat, opening the doors of cabs and limousines, and helping aging patrons up the front steps. "After you've been here as long as me and Jamieson have, you will have met 'em all — the rich, the famous, the good, and the naughty, if you get what I'm trying to say. Even rich people, and especially those who pretend to be rich, can be very naughty sometimes."

CHAPTER EIGHT

"Grime Doesn't Pay," and Putting the House in Order

"The very rich are not like you and me."

F. SCOTT FITZGERALD

Jean Contat prided himself on reinstating at the Ritz-Carlton some of the old-fashioned protocol and punctilio that had been lost over time. On a typical day in the late 1940s, about twenty guests checked in or out; on a heavy one, there were fifty. The turnover — small compared to today's front desk business — enabled the hotel to elevate standards throughout the entire building and afford more personalized attention in the authentic, Continental style.

Single rooms were now costing $8.50 a night, double rooms $10, and suites up to $30, depending on what floor they were on and whether they had a rear or front view. Meals and other services, however, boosted the amount considerably, and most people who stayed at the hotel spent an average of $35 a day. Not everyone, of course, was able to afford this. But Contat and Frossard, who looked back jointly across more than sixty years at the highest echelon of hoteliery, knew exactly who could. They devised a stereotype of who their typical guest was, and toiled ardently to meet that person's needs so that he or she would always come back.

They welcomed first-time guests obsequiously; when a visitor arrived at the Ritz-Carlton for a second time, he or she could count on being recognized instantly. If she was distinguished, famous, or just plain wealthy, she would be met at the door by Frossard or Connolly and, once taken to her room, find flowers there. If the guest happened to be a distinguished, famous, or wealthy man, an open bottle of scotch awaited him, and sometimes a cigar.

If, however, the visitor was François Dupré, making one of his five annual calls to the Ritz while en route from his home in Paris to his villa in Reading, near Montego Bay, Jamaica, he would be paid the kind of attention that was only ever accorded monarchs. Surprisingly, Dupré never slept in his hotel. Whenever he came to Montreal, he stayed in a house on Summerhill Terrace that he maintained expressly for his visits, and these lasted only a matter of days. Nonetheless, he was met at the Ritz-Carlton door by general manager Contat or manager Frossard; James Connolly, the executive assistant, was invariably assigned to escort him to his office, and a bellman would carry his briefcase and his porkpie hat.

Ironically, the attention lavished upon him proved something of an embarrassment, particularly when Dupré ate at whichever Ritz restaurant happened to take his fancy. "Always," Contat wailed, "always, no matter what I tell the waiters, they insist on serving him the big double portion. Then Monsieur Dupré asks me why the hotel is being so wasteful!"

François Dupré's ideal dinner, which, without exception he ate alone at a left-side balcony table in the Oval Room, included an entrée, soup, a main dish which was quite often a veal chop, and two glasses of wine. For supper, he was usually content with tomato juice, an omelette, one order of carrots, a little dish of spinach, and a glass of champagne, and he would take nearly two hours to consume all this in leisurely succession. While he ate he made copious notes of those things in the hotel that bothered him, and which he felt could be improved: the lighting, perhaps, the speed of service, or the length of the waiters' hair.

"Excuse me, Contat," he once said, coldly surveying some small variation in the way the chefs de réception were dressed, "but I thought I insisted all the men were to wear dark suits."

"Yes, Sir, you did," Contat responded quickly, and with rare timidity. "I'll see to it that the matter is taken care of at once."

"And what about the ice water?"

"What about it, Sir?"

"Well, if you *must* follow this awful North American tradition of serving water with all meals, will you *please*, please make sure that the ice cubes aren't so awfully large?"

"Absolutely, Sir."

Dupré was quiet and pleasant, but was perfection personified. "People who dropped trays in the dining room," says Pierre Demers, "trembled in their shoes in case he ever found out what they had done. It got so bad sometimes when he was around that the waiters and kitchen staff never spoke, and sometimes not for a week after he'd gone."

Such an accident, some former staffers recall, occurred when Maurice Duplessis, famished and impatient, signalled a veteran Russian-born waiter in the Oval Room to bring the hors d'oeuvres tray — immediately.

In his eagerness to oblige, the waiter tripped over a protruding foot and drove the hors d'oeuvres trolley into Duplessis' table, spreading its contents around for several feet and knocking over a bottle of wine.

"What the hell do you think you're doing!" Duplessis roared, rising from his chair and wiping his suit. "Look what you've done to me!" Then, more quietly, he added, "I think, waiter, that you were a little too fast."

Luckily for the waiter, it was an incident about which François Dupré never got to hear, and he kept his job for fifteen years afterwards.

Besides being tough, critical, and wealthy, Dupré also happened to be experienced, unshakable, determined, and talented. He was a grandson of Jules Dupré, a leading French painter from whom he derived enormous savoir-faire, which he never failed to put to good use.

His hotels were only one part of his business life. He also owned and administered one of France's leading stud farms in Ouilly, Normandy, and a stable in Gouvieux, near Chantilly. His horses, which he bred himself as a hobby, were remarkable. Over the years those like "Bella Paola" and "Tantième" won many of the world's most prestigious racing events, including the English Oaks. Dupré became one of the few men ever to own winners of both the English and the French Derbys.

Like his earliest predecessors at the Ritz-Carlton, he secured exactly what he wanted, and when — his secretary Denyse Papineau, for instance. She had been working for a firm that provided lighting and scenery for movies, and which had offices at the Ritz-Carlton. When Twentieth-Century Fox arrived in Montreal to make *The Scarlet Letter*, directed by Otto Preminger and starring Charles Boyer and Linda Darnell, all of whom rented Ritz-Carlton suites, it lured Denyse Papineau onto its staff. Two months later, Jean Contat decided that he wanted her to join the hotel as secretary to James Connolly. Miss Papineau did not reach Connolly's office, however. Recognizing her bilingual abilities, Dupré immediately swept her into his, where she remained for nearly fifteen years.

This unquestionably bespeaks Dupré's business prowess, which soon set new criteria at the Ritz-Carlton. Under his tight rein — and with the assistance of Richard Johnson and Russell Bell, both estimable administrators in his absence — the hotel would not only have a second life, but would never be, or look, the same.

Had you walked past the Ritz in June, 1949, you would have seen a placard announcing, "Grime Doesn't Pay," and, above it, balanced on scaffolding, a man in blue overalls named Gaston Rocheleau. He wielded

Yvonne Contat in the Ritz Garden with her two pet poodles. A smart Parisienne, she mingled so freely with the socialites that she was eventually considered one of them. "I was sociable, *very* sociable," she says. "It was part of my job as the general manager's wife, to be nice to the right kind of people, and make them all part of a happy Ritz family."

PHOTO BY RICHARD ARLESS ASSOCIATES
COURTESY OF THE RITZ-CARLTON COLLECTION

a 100-pound pressure hose which pumped a mixture of silica sand and water onto the limestone, and watched the hotel's grime of thirty-six years flood down onto the sidewalk below.

The Ritz-Carlton's 750,000 square-foot frontage was being cleaned by Allied Building Services, the firm regularly called upon to remove the soot, grime, acid rain, and deposits left by pigeons from Nelson's Column in Trafalgar Square, London, and from a giant silo in Montreal's harbour. It would soon clean Windsor Station, among dozens of other Montreal buildings. "Grime doesn't Pay" was its slogan, which it proudly displayed wherever it went to work, even outside the Ritz-Carlton Hotel.

Rocheleau, was twenty-seven, married, but in love with his work. "Every stone, like every lady's face," he said, "needs a different kind of cleaning."

"Yes," said his boss, stocky Harry Tannenbaum, "and when it's done properly it makes people think you've built a new place."

Accordingly, the hotel's exterior was soon beginning to sparkle like it had on its opening in 1913. But so was the inside, as decorators busied themselves with transforming the Ritz-Carlton into François Dupré's conception of what it should be — a cross between his Paris hotels and the prestigious Hôtel de Paris in Monte Carlo.

No one understood his vision better than yet another figure so integral to the development and preservation of the Ritz Idea, or most certainly the Montreal interpretation of it — Jean Contat's wife, Yvonne. She was a smart, throaty-voiced Parisienne who mingled so freely with the socialites, that she was eventually considered one of them. "I was sociable, *very* sociable," she says. "I got friendly with anyone who was anybody in Montreal — the Van Hornes, the Stewarts, the Drummonds. They liked me. I liked them. That was all part of my job as the general manager's wife, to be nice to the right kind of people, and make them all part of a happy Ritz family."

There were times, though, when Yvonne Contat's vitality and presence about the hotel were so obvious that staff and patrons alike began to wonder whether she was managing the Ritz-Carlton Hotel instead of her husband. When Jean Contat established his office on the first floor, he also built one for Dupré. But when Dupré was absent, it was used by Yvonne Contat instead. She became more than a silent partner. She was part of a team that comprised the directors, the managers, and her husband, who had earned himself the sobriquet "Le petit Napoléon."

"The staff," Contat used to grumble with an overriding splash of paranoia, "tries to keep things from me. They really do. They know how I can flare up. I lose my temper fifty times a day because things go wrong and I am last to hear about them. So my wife keeps up with everyday events for me, thanks to God."

Madame Contat reflects, "Jean was extremely fair and correct. He flared up, yes, but *never* in front of an employee or a guest. If you were called into his office, well, something awful might happen. He really made demands when it came to running a hotel." She was generally perceived as being kinder than her husband, more tolerant with people, yet unyieldingly firm.

She certainly handled Maurice Duplessis well. One day she entered the lobby just as he was telling the head porter to move the Quebec flag. Duplessis wanted it to replace the Union Jack which had always flown in the centre of the three flags that fluttered from poles protruding from the hotel's facade, a little way above the parapet.

"I'm terribly sorry, Mr. Premier," Yvonne Contat said, "but the Union Jack is staying right where it is. The flag of our guest of honour's country always flies on its right, and the Quebec flag flies on its left. That, Mr. Duplessis, is protocol."

"You are in Quebec," Duplessis countered. "Quebec's flag should be in the middle."

"You are in the Ritz-Carlton Hotel, Mr. Premier, and the Union Jack is staying exactly where it is!"

Around the hotel, Yvonne Contat was dignified, articulate, polished, and respected — not only as the manager's wife, but as a person who had strong ideas and was committed to the Ritz cause. She quickly displayed a magnificent talent for decor, and this instilled unprecedented passion into the Ritz-Carlton. Both her father and brother, she points out, were architects, and she learned from them at a time when a young woman's role was defined for her. Yvonne had been told to learn to play the piano and to stay at home sewing. She did both well, but longed for the chance to develop a career of her own.

On marrying Jean Contat while he was a manager at the Ritz Hotel in New York City, she began to carve a profession out of being the wife of a celebrated hotelkeeper, whom she aided and abetted in numerous causes, and enjoyed every moment of it. The Ritz, then, gave Yvonne Contat the chance she had always yearned for, to exercise a keenly astute interest in buildings, art, and decorating, and her exquisite taste for antiques.

Those who saw her early work accused her of having an obvious taste for a flat, angry Pompeian red. Suddenly, they said, all the chairs in almost every room were reupholstered in that colour and the walls in the narrow, gleaming lobby were painted a similar shade. This assessment, however, was far too superficial. Even though Madame Contat was self-taught, as a decorator her talent was considerable. In fact, even professionals asked for, and took, her advice. "I just loved the challenge of making the Ritz a better place," she says now.

Dupré recognized her ability, too. He had originally started to refurbish the Ritz-Carlton using Muller and Barringer, a New York City firm of interior decorators, to "put it back in order." Six months later, however, he declared, "These people live in New York. They don't know what's going on up here, for goodness sake." And he told Yvonne Contat that she was now free to take over. He gave her a free hand.

She accepted it gladly. "I knew," she says, "that any effort and energy I spent wouldn't be wasted — not in the slightest. The Ritz-Carlton was one of those gorgeous buildings that are presented to a North American city only once, maybe twice, in its lifetime. It was, and still is, a magnificent place to be."

It quickly became apparent that the Ritz-Carlton guest rooms had lasted well because they had been constructed by and for Montreal's most wealthy men, with a wonderful disregard for cost. By the standards of most other hotels, Contat and his wife discovered, they were large, airy, and solid. "The men who built the Ritz evidently believed that wives should retire to bed early," *Mayfair* magazine once reported. "Sitting rooms could be shut off from bedrooms, and once the door was closed, a guest could sleep while a party was raging next door."

Happily, the closets, or cupboards, had remained integral to the Ritz decor, too, having been left untouched during previous renovations. Huge, three-door affairs, they provided an abundance of useful storage space. A young *Vogue* photographer assigned to photograph the hotel discerned their worth the hard way. She stepped inside one of these cupboards to change her film in darkness, forgetting that its doors could not be opened from the inside. She stayed imprisoned until she was finally released by housekeeper Gohier, two hours later.

The Ritz-Carlton's furniture, however — even that ordered by Frossard shortly before the Contats' arrival — was already showing signs of wear. "We couldn't replace everything," Madame Contat says. "We had to do what we could within a budget." She concentrated on painting rooms and suites, and organizing widespread refurbishing of all the hotel's furniture.

The sanding, staining, and French polishing of solid mahogany chests, dressers, and night tables was the least of her problems, though. Far more serious was that virtually all the sofas and armchairs in the rooms, suites, and salons were worn, grubby, or faded. They were fine pieces of furniture, however, that deserved to be recovered long before being discarded; Yvonne Contat announced that she could save the hotel money by smartening up existing furniture or, as she said, "making it live again."

For this, she bought hundreds of yards of tapestry, linen, cotton, and various kinds of brocade — anything that could be used to make new curtains, recover or reupholster — from a friend, a Manhattan wholesaler of high quality materials. Then, entirely on her own initiative, she organized a workshop on the tenth floor where carpenters, upholsterers, painters, seamstresses, and plumbers could set about putting all the rooms in order, one by one.

The workshop was an ingenious idea. It meant that all the work — from stripping and staining to sanding and stitching — could be coordinated and administered from one place. Schedules could be devised and maintained; colour schemes could be harmonized. For example, the woman who made cushions and slip covers could match her work with that of another who made curtains. Both could then see that their materials suited the paint workmen were using.

Whatever the changes of this initial refurbishing, Yvonne Contat wisely ensured that the hotel's stately qualities were enhanced, and that nothing detracted from or spoiled the original shell itself. Certain fixtures, she recognized, had to stay because, after all, they *were* the Ritz: the white marble fireplaces, some of which still worked well, for instance, the embossed ceilings, and the heavy doors. Initially, then, she brought new life to the rooms with rejuvenated furniture, bright curtains that often matched the upholstery, modern mirrors, and Martha Wild prints on newly painted walls, but left the building's character firmly intact.

Not every guest room was decorated in the same way. "It depended on which direction it faced," says Yvonne Contat, "and whether we felt we wanted it light or dark." She and her workers mixed and matched materials, paint and wallpaper — all to redecorate the hotel in such a way that it also looked unique, luxurious, and unmistakably Continental.

While decorating was underway, Frossard and Contat had to ask permanent guests to move temporarily into alternative suites. Most did so willingly, but some refused. For the most part, the residents were particular about decorations and several, already having furnished their rooms to their own tastes, did not want them altered. Some had grown accustomed to their surroundings, and one of them was dear Captain Murray. When he saw his newly refurbished room, he gruffly declared, "I liked it the way it was!" So, to keep him happy, the management reinstalled the old curtains and original pieces of unrepaired furniture.

One wealthy resident, Ritzmen remember, went to the other extreme. While on a vacation in France, he had fallen in love with French Moderne. He returned to his Ritz suite and promptly hired European artists and decorators to transform it into a shrine for his new-found art love. Ritz managers made neither demands nor comments — not even when they saw that the man's ceilings had been painted blue and dotted with silver stars.

Abstract objects followed in profusion, they noted; free-form, stilt-like furniture was imported, and a cubist carpet laid. Even the inside door knobs of the suite were changed to match the new motif. This work was finished in late fall, just in time for the Ritz to turn on its radiators for the winter. The art lover then threw up his hands in despair. Unaccustomed to Canadian temperature changes, the furniture warped, wilted, and crumbled, and the new paint cracked and peeled. The task of redecorating and refurnishing his quarters was left to the Ritz.

The management also cleared old storage space in the south-west corner of the top basement floor and, on Dupré's instructions, adapted it to earn money. The earliest renovations included the addition of the Ritz Café, a restaurant which Contat opened in the spring of 1949. It was a large room panelled in oak, with indirect lighting in a cove ceiling and square pillars covered with mirrors. Yvonne Contat immediately set about decorating it to resemble a Paris bistro, draping the little tables with blue-and-white checkered table cloths and installing on each a copy of an antique gold lamp she had bought in Florence.

Every afternoon, after high tea had been served, the off-white patterned carpet was rolled back to reveal a dance floor, and the little "bistro" was suddenly transformed into the Ritz Café at Night, a glamorous supper club which served drinks, dinner, or both.

Facing the entrance was a small stage which was subsequently, and exquisitely, designed by George Campbell Tinning, the Montreal painter who found himself the resident Ritz decorator and scenic artist. Saskatoon-born Tinning, who had been an official army war artist and was a member of the Royal Canadian Academy of Art, gave the stage a red-and-white striped canopy and a Venetian motif for a backdrop, and partitioned it from the rest of the room by long poles topped by Venetian

Every afternoon, after high tea, the carpet in the Ritz Café was rolled back to
reveal a dance floor, and the little "bistro" was suddenly transformed into the
Ritz Café at Night, a glamorous supper club which served drinks, dinner, or
both. It was also a showcase for the world's finest cabaret acts.

PHOTO COURTESY OF THE RITZ-CARLTON COLLECTION

lanterns. Tall gold spears held up a voluminous swag of red and white satin damask which was gathered at the middle by a large white shell.

Besides her taste for decor, Yvonne Contat had developed shrewd insights into showbusiness and began to book the "class acts" for the stage. All of them were women she felt patrons would enjoy. The Café's entertainment opened with a blonde, husky-voiced French singer, Suzy Solidor, who owned a Paris night club called Chez Suzy. She stayed at the Ritz-Carlton for six weeks, delighting crowds night after night with such songs as "La Seine" and "Le Petit Rat de l'Opéra." Then came Anne Francine, whom the hotel billed the "socialite singing star." Miss Francine was said to have had a special way with the blues, which she sang in either French or English. She, too, enjoyed success. The same could not be said for most of the entertainers who followed during that first season, though, and the Ritz Café at Night closed down for the summer with mixed prospects.

Contat launched the Café's fall season with a supper dance, which drew members of the Montreal social world by the dozen. Among the patrons who flew up from New York City for the occasion was Brenda Simms Kelly, Sir Frederick Williams-Taylor's granddaughter. Yvonne Contat later engaged a procession of singers who so endeared themselves to the clientele that they were invited back year after year: Geneviève, Jane Morgan, Fernanda Montel, Celeste Holm, and a woman with the somewhat imposing name of Hildegarde Monique Van Vooren. "The gilded goddesses came and went," once critic wrote, "varying in name, artistry, material, and style, but each was part of a genre so well suited to the Ritz-Carlton's expectations — sophisticated, seductive, and invariably low-key."

Low key? Well, most of the time — until Josephine Premice, a young Haitian calypso singer and friend of Russell Bell turned up, that is. She had already been drawing heavily at a nightspot on St. Lawrence Boulevard; she would do the same at the Ritz Café with such favourites as "Yellow Bird" and "Me grandmother's coming, it's nearly twelve o'clock. Get up!"

Swaying gently before the microphone, her face a blend of mischief and child-like innocence, Miss Premice, by far the city's top cabaret artist, transformed the usually decorous nightclub into a somewhat raucous and certainly most unRitz-like house of bawdy fun and laughter. With recommendations like that, the Café became one of Montreal's most sought-after nightspots, especially on Thursdays, "Cook's Night Out." Without telephoning ahead for a reservation, it was impossible to

Johnny Gallant (right), the Café's outstanding accompanist. He was installed
on the little stage at a grand piano—beside the double bass, guitar, and
accordion that comprised the Joseph Settano Trio, also shown here.

PHOTO BY VARKONS STUDIO
COURTESY OF THE RITZ-CARLTON COLLECTION

get a table. And this Ritz advertisement explains why:

THE RITZ CAFÉ AT NIGHT. This is an ideal place to come for Lunch or Dinner. On "Cook's Night Out" you will be surprised and pleased at our fast and efficient service as well as the delightful meal at a very moderate price. Lunch, 75 cents, Dinner, 85 cents.

The maître d'hôtel during the Café's early days was affable Ernie Ireland — from England, no less — who, having been a waiter in the Palm Court, had come to know a lot of the regular patrons personally, and visited them at their homes and attended their parties. Generally conceded as being Contat's "spy," he kept a running night-by-night record of what went on in the Café. "Mr. Daniel Doheny and his friends misbehaved very badly last night," he once reported. "They were throwing sugar."

"Were you, Mr. Doheny?" Contat asked, suspiciously.

"Yes," Dan Doheny admitted. "We were trying to attract the attention of friends a few tables over."

"Please don't let it happen again."

"No, Sir. We will try not to."

The incident, it should be recorded, did absolutely nothing to impair either Daniel Doheny's career, or his association with the Ritz-Carlton. He blazed on to distinguish himself as a prominent Montreal lawyer, and Queen's Counsel, and simultaneously become vice-chairman of the Ritz-Carlton board, the hotel's solicitor, and its secretary.

Ernie Ireland, meanwhile, a favourite among patrons for his repertoire of jokes and "mean" martinis, was succeeded in the Café's early years by a good-looking Spaniard named Corbillon Corby who recruited half a dozen fine Spanish waiters to help him, some of whom worked in the hotel for many years thereafter. A Swiss maître d'hôtel, Jean Vallouz, came next and he was followed by Alex Majourcan, a finicky Frenchman.

To do his job well, Majourcan once said, he really needed to know as much about ministering to showbusiness personnel as he did about serving food and wines. As they ran the Café, though, he and Yvonne Contat could always count on stalwart help from the resident pianist and master of ceremonies, Winnipeg-born Johnny Gallant.

An accompanist of outstanding skill, Gallant, who was once married to writer Mavis Gallant, was installed at a grand piano beside the double bass, guitar, and accordion that comprised the Joseph Settano Trio. Originally, Gallant's piano was black, but one day it was wheeled through the kitchen to the freight elevator and taken up to the top-floor workshop

A somewhat "staged" publicity photograph that marked the 1948 opening
of the Maritime Bar in what had once been the barbershop reserved for
permanent guests' servants. A more modern version of the defunct Oyster Bar,
the new public room provided a relaxed, leather-and-copper setting in which
the social set could enjoy a quiet, informal drink.

PHOTO COURTESY OF THE RITZ-CARLTON COLLECTION

where it was stripped, painted, set out to dry on the roof, then returned to the Café for that night's show, glossy white! Some time later, when the stage was redesigned in black and gold under a ceiling dripping with 200 gold-and-crystal "drop" lights, the instrument made a return visit to the painters to regain its original colour. "But it was all the same to Johnny," Yvonne Contat says. "He could play anything, anywhere."

Gallant was so admired by the customers as he supported the singers or played dazzling solos, his fingers cavorting up and down the keyboard like tireless squirels, that he became a Ritz-Carlton fixture for fifteen years in its Café at Night, and saw it become a showcase for some of the very best the world of cabaret had to offer, anywhere.

The Café attracted the public and hotel guests alike, and some in its audiences were highly distinguished. French screen actor Charles Boyer and fellow countryman Maurice Chevalier, both friends of Suzy Solidor, were to be seen relaxing there regularly after delighting their own Montreal fans. In the twilight of his life, British actor Charles Laughton spent long evenings there, once with American film star Tyrone Power. Every night, following their performances at Her Majesty's Theatre, Marlene Dietrich and a young Montreal composer-pianist named Burt Bacharach dined in the Café; the illustrious German maestro Otto Klemperer, in town to conduct the Montreal Symphony Orchestra, found what he heard there a refreshing musical contrast to Beethoven and Brahms

Usually, when he was in town, François Dupré made a point of auditioning new singers himself, and attending the afternoon rehearsals of those who were already established in the Café. In this, his admiration for attractive young women could not go unnoticed. More than once he dropped in during the evening, too, just to sip mineral water and watch the waiters glide about their business. His shrewdly critical eyes would narrow on the minutest *faux pas*, but widen considerably at the sight of a singer's seductive low-cut, off-the-shoulder dress.

During Dupré's large-scale renovations, the one-time servants' barbershop became the Maritime Bar, a more modern version of the defunct Oyster Bar, and this provided a relaxed, leather-and-copper setting for a quiet after-work drink. Thereafter, Jean Contat usually enjoyed long lunches in the Maritime Bar while his wife ate alone in the Oval Room. "That way," he explained, "we will know better than ever just what is going on here."

Inevitably, the new bar was frequented by stockbrokers, bankers, and advertising executives, all of whom cherished the idea that the waiter

The Maritime Bar was frequented by stockbrokers, bankers, and advertising executives, all of whom cherished the idea that the waiter could bring the telephone to their tables. But it was about three years before this new public room became popular. "If we served ten lunches there," said the Irish barman Danny Flynn, "we were very lucky."

PHOTO COURTESY OF THE RITZ-CARLTON COLLECTION

could bring the telephone to their tables. But it was about three years before the new public room became popular. "If we served ten lunches there," said waiter Danny Flynn, a portly, white-haired Irishman who greeted customers with a broad silver brogue, a big golden heart, and a lot of stories about how he had tried his fortune on an Alberta farm before travelling east on a freight train, "we were very lucky. And if we served that many dinners, we were extremely lucky."

From the outset, one Maritime Bar "regular" was a retired British army major and former Ritz-Carlton director who drank too much, too often. The management got so tired of helping him into his bed after a long, hard night that Contat — as anxious as he was to ensure that the hotel kept its patrons — distributed a memo which said, "Please take note. Under no circumstances is the Major to be served any more alcoholic beverages in this hotel." Later that very day, however, he and the Major seated themselves together at the bar counter, and Contat beckoned Danny Flynn.

"What will you have, Major?" Contat asked. "Your usual?"

Flynn stood silently, raising his eyebrows as the Major ordered a triple gin. The drink was served, of course, and later that afternoon, poor Flynn faced Contat in his office.

"What could I do?" he pleaded. "I couldn't refuse to serve the man with *you* there, could I?"

The knack for dealing with awkward situations, Contat told him, was integral to keeping a position at the Ritz, and he suspended the hapless employee for a week without pay.

Two days later, though, Flynn was back at work. Contat had acceded to patrons' demands. The Maritime Bar, they said, was not the same without Danny Flynn, and never would be. His stories were far too good. Besides, they said, he was the only man they had ever met who could pour drinks and carry on eight different conversations all at the same time.

One of Flynn's fondest yarns was about how he returned to Montreal from Alberta fully intending to catch the first cattle boat back to Ireland — until he joined the long queue of job hunters that assembled daily outside the Ritz timekeeper's office. "You were dead lucky to have work, let alone find it in a tremendous hotel," Flynn used to say.

"That's right," says John Dominique. "And if you weren't any good, they showed you the door. There were lots of people who went crazy to work at the Ritz, even though they knew they'd only get thirty-six cents an hour!"

Prime Minister Louis St. Laurent welcomes a debutante to
Le Bal des Petits Souliers. The ball, which raised money to buy shoes for
underpriviledged children, became an institution unto itself, launching
Montreal's social season for many years.

PHOTO BY METRO PHOTOS
COURTESY OF THE RITZ-CARLTON COLLECTION

The Grand Ball Room was redecorated, too, in time for a gala ball, on September 14, 1949, in aid of the Montreal Symphony Orchestra. The nearly 400 who turned out saw that the duresco plaster walls, with their white wood trim and gilded metal, were now pale pink; the heavy grey silk curtains which once matched the upholstery of the balcony rail, were a deep pink with splashes of Yvonne Contat's favourite shade of red.

All approved.

"Terrific!" said Air Vice-Marshall F.S. McGill.

"Delightful!" said Brenda Simms Kelly.

"Simply lovely!" added Gloria Just, who attended the ball with her sister, Pauline.

Gloria, by the way, wore a full gown of pink net; Pauline was attired in gold lace with a matching stole. Yvonne Contat, who spent much of the evening with the Ball Room's decorator, Isabelle Barringer of New York City, was bare-shouldered in a pale green dress which sported a spray of white orchids.

The following month the Ritz-Carlton hosted Le Bal des Petits Souliers, which was attended by Prime Minister Louis St. Laurent and his wife who wore a silver and turquoise lamé gown with silver accessories and the corsage of white orchids that Frossard had given her on her arrival. The event, organized by La Ligue de la jeunesse feminine, which raised money to buy shoes for underprivileged children, became an institution unto itself as it launched Montreal's social season for many years to come.

Ah, those society galas! "It was worth working at the Ritz in that era," says John Dominique, "just to see the dresses and know all the people. That's what made me stay around so long. The customers were so civil and good. They were people you couldn't find anywhere else, and the dresses and the fancy costumes the women wore were something to behold — an array of absolute splendour!"

Just as Le Bal des Petits Souliers became a hotel appendage, so did the new Ritz Beauty Salon on the mezzanine, under the management of the renowned coiffure-artist Monsieur Francis. "As modern as tomorrow," said the *Gazette* on the salon's opening on December 17, 1949:

> It has the latest, most comfort-giving and scientifically-exact equipment — dryers that do the job with the greatest rapidity, permanent wave machinery that is the last word, leather upholstered chairs that invite complete relaxation, a facials room that has plenty of daylight and indirect lighting that both reveals and flatters. Air-conditioning is a feature but not as unusual as the air-freshening system.

One corner of the hotel was designed to harken back to old Quebec—a two-room suite Jean Contat and his wife decorated in authentic French Canadian style and called L'Appartement Canadien. "We just felt like having a little bit of old Quebec in the building," he explained. "After all, we *are* a Quebec hotel." The suite rented for $29 a night.

PHOTO BY RICHARD ARLESS ASSOCIATES
COURTESY OF THE RITZ-CARLTON COLLECTION

Appropriately, a new men's barbershop would follow, as would a penthouse for the Contats. Madame Contat looked at the roof, then phoned Dupré and told him, "There's storage space there doing nothing, yet we are using an apartment that could earn money. Why don't we make that space our living quarters?"

"Draw up the plans," Dupré said.

In only weeks Jean and Yvonne Contat had a penthouse with a bedroom, livingroom, den, kitchenette — and a little roof garden where they could walk their two black French poodles, "Mlle Bébé" and "Mr. Bonny." Another manager later enlarged the apartment considerably, but when the Contats lived in it, it was small and cozy, with a magnificent view of Montreal.

While the salon and penthouse were modern, one little corner of the hotel was specifically designed to harken back to old Quebec — a two-room suite which Contat elected to decorate in the authentic French Canadian style and call L'Appartement Canadien, to rent for $29 a night. "We just felt like having a little bit of old Quebec in the building," he explained. "After all, we are a Quebec hotel."

Wooden floors were laid, then painted, and heavy wooden beams were attached to the ceiling. The livingroom had an abundance of old pine furniture including a huge, two-door armoire, a rough-hewn table that had once adorned a farmer's kitchen, a bench-bed scattered with cushions and which served as a couch, a sofa, a spinning wheel adapted to become a standing lamp, a church window which was now a mirror, various large pieces of earthenware, a cast iron clock dating back to 1870, and the grandfather clock that had once adorned the Ritz lobby. A pine mantlepiece was installed above the fireplace, and the room fairly littered with framed prints of Montreal scenes, many of them more than eighty years old.

To the utter surprise of the more than 100 guests who attended the suite's opening, including Governor General Lord Alexander of Tunis, who had driven down from Ottawa to inaugurate it, the bedroom floor was bright red. It was partially covered by Quebec-loomed carpeting which matched the upholstery of the chairs. A washstand served as a dressing table, and a converted oil lamp hung above two twin sleigh beds.

Montreal Mayor Camillien Houde understood the decor perfectly — "Magnifique!" he said. Maurice Duplessis, however, who asked to see the suite several days later, was jokingly cynical. "Why have old furniture like this?" he mused with a chuckle. "My mother used all that stuff every day of her life and after she died we threw it all away."

During Contat's tenure, the Ritz-Carlton's wine cellar came to be regarded as one of the finest and most complete in the country. The management had discovered that Ritz room guests, more than half of them wealthy Europeans like Mr. Thorn, really knew what good wines were, how they should be chilled and served, and with what kinds of dishes. So, accordingly, did Ritz waiters, particularly Josef Riedl. "Wine," he said, "does more than spark digestion." He also knew that in luxury restaurants it was — and still is — the cornerstone of profits.

"What shall I eat today, waiter?" a customer asked Riedl.

"Wine," he said quickly. "A light, fruity wine with a good bouquet."

By this method, and with the help of manager Frossard, who was himself widely regarded as a formidable wine authority, the hotel sold more bottles, particularly of the finest vintages, than any other Canadian hotel — about 300 on a good day, and no fewer than sixty on a bad one. Albert Frossard, the picture of sartorial elegance in a tuxedo, was often to be seen back in the Oval Room, admiring bottles of Clos Vougeot 1937, Richebourg 1934, or even Haut Brion 1926.

"What do *you* suggest I eat, Monsieur Frossard?" patrons asked him.

"Wine, of course. What else?" the manager reiterated with a twinkle. "And these are exquisite! They cost a few dollars more, perhaps, but that should not be *too* important."

To most patrons it wasn't, so the Ritz-Carlton felt comfortable stocking up with the world's finest wines. On any given day it could boast more than 5,000 bottles of 150 of the very best vintages to be found anywhere, some of them kept in stock exclusively for the odd visitor who only asked for them occasionally. Other sections of the cellar were given over to nearly 100 different types of liqueurs; among its collection of 280 spirits, the hotel listed more than sixty brands of scotch alone, and a dozen of gin. The oldest of its twenty-odd brandies dated back to 1815, the year of the Battle of Waterloo.

Complementing the promotion of the hotel's best wines and encouraging patrons to drink well, was the custom of serving fine Continental food. A few months after buying the hotel, Dupré went into the main kitchen on a routine inspection and stood for a moment watching Pierre Demers work. "They tell me you are the executive chef," he said after a while. "Is this so?"

"Yes," said Demers. "I'm afraid it is."

He remembers, "Mr. Dupré almost fell on his back because I was so young. Most executive chefs he'd met were already in their sixties, and French. I was then in my thirties, and was French Canadian."

Dupré felt that if Demers enlarged his repertoire of recipes and further refined his cooking skills, the Ritz-Carlton would get many years of exquisite meals from him, and called him into his office to say so. Pierre Demers, he thought, would not be merely a good chef, but a great one. "I haven't asked you here to tell you I'm not pleased you are with us," he began. "On the contrary, we are very lucky to have you. But you can't be so young and be in charge of all that luxury business. You have got to get more experience."

Demers remembers, "I was always interested in learning. The moment you stop learning as a chef, you're finished."

He was delighted, then, when Dupré sent him back to New York, this time to study at the Ritz under the great chef Louis Diat. Three months later Demers returned to Montreal to head a staff of forty cooks, including ten chefs, who worked shifts in the hotel's gleaming kitchens.

Pierre Demers was a gourmet's chef, and he regularly pitched in himself when a special dish was required. "The wonderful thing about cooking at the Ritz," he often said, "is that it never gets boring. With our foreign guests, we are continually getting requests for meals that have never been prepared here before."

To keep abreast of an ever-growing array of international dishes, Demers and his assistants would regularly prepare national meals for members of Montreal's consular corps, who had banded together to form a diplomatic gourmet's club. Each month, the dishes of a different country were featured. The Ritz was also the meeting place for the famous Club 55, a group of gourmets who regularly planned epic feasts there, and wrote about them for their magazine, *Gastronomie*. They bestowed their top accolades on the hotel and chose its main restaurant above all others in food-conscious Montreal as the rendezvous for their annual Champagne Dinner.

Pierre Demers was particularly proud of his *coulibiac de saumon*, which he made from an old Russian recipe said to have been donated by a New York banking family. Besides the Baltimore businessman, a California executive telephoned him regularly to find out when the salmon would next appear on Ritz menus. When it did, and when he knew that Demers had cooked it, he flew to Montreal for a few days especially to taste it.

Demers believed that while recipes could indeed be "traditional," the taste should always be memorable. "Making them so is the mark of a true chef," he said.

Contat and Dupré expected chefs, like all other Ritz employees, to be long on memory, too. They were. In addition to his encyclopedic

Part of the Ritz lobby, as guests would have seen it in the late 1940s, with its shining marble walls and smart elevator attendants who were proud of the hotel, and showed it. The brass mail box remains to this day, but the decor has been drastically changed.

PHOTO BY ASSOCIATED SCREEN NEWS LTD.
COURTESY OF THE RITZ-CARLTON COLLECTION

knowledge of cooking, Demers had to remember that special guests had special tastes and make a note of them. First, there was the co-invention of Demers and Contat to appease a "regular" who complained persistently that the proper savour of fresh meat was missing from Ritz-Carlton steaks because they were too thick. The two men retired to the kitchen and returned shortly afterwards with their "Steak Charles," a paper-thin filet with a sprinkling of finely ground pepper, fried for a moment in butter. Aptly named after that fragile head waiter, who was the first to deliver it to the customer's table, it remains a staple of Ritz-Carlton menus to this very day.

Lord Beaverbrook, meanwhile, a regular Ritz-Carlton visitor throughout the 1940s, always liked what he called "a man's meal" of steak or chops — or both — "without the trimmings." Another illustrious visitor, one of Canada's leading industrial millionaires, insisted that no food be served to him on silver. He would only accept those meals that were brought to the table on china. "Rich men don't very often say *why* they don't like certain things," Demers used to tell his staff. "They simply say that they *don't* like something. Our job is to see that they don't get it."

Some of the top chefs to be found anywhere backed Pierre Demers in his views, and they were similarly meticulous in their work. Fernand Bigras, a young Ritz chef, was one. He was an authority on the delicate job of ice carving. Another, of course, was the little master pastry chef Jean Baptiste Pellerino who, trained by Auguste Escoffier, had come to be rated one of the greatest sugar-work cooks in the world. These men were artists. They had the temperament of artists. They would lay out vegetables like a painter meticulously applying paint with a palette knife, or construct a raspberry tart like Michelangelo creating a great mosaic, and they were intensely proud of their work.

Ask the South African golfer Bobby Locke, or the entertainer Liberace. When Locke celebrated a birthday at the hotel Pellerino produced — on the spot — a replica putting iron from spun sugar, and set it out on a long silver dish; Liberace's first visit prompted the cooks to craft a grand piano out of sponge cake, which was laid on a silver platter and presented to him as he dined in the Oval Room.

To oblige a customer or to induce a smile, Pierre Demers' kitchen staff made cakes to resemble hockey sticks, footballs, traffic signs, even earphones. To satisfy one faithful customer at his daughter's wedding, they made a four-foot high Dream Cake depicting a huge swan opening its wings. The cake had to be made in sections so it could pass through the kitchen doorway, and be assembled at the table.

The Oval Room is set for a Ritz-Carlton smorgasbord, splendidly
laid out on tables made to stretch to fifty feet. Guests came in droves to eat
the finest food in Montreal—suckling pig, lobster, game, various hams and
roasts, hors d'oeuvres, and a score of desserts ranging from fruits steeped in
liqueurs to all manner of cakes, tarts, and pastries. Despite its low price of $3,
the all-you-can-eat buffet made money.

PHOTO BY DAVID BIER
COURTESY OF THE RITZ-CARLTON COLLECTION

The Ritz-Carlton's mighty mass of culinary talent was put on view, unabashedly, every day of the week. Said another advertisement:

Give Your Morale a Lift!
Dine Today
At the Ritz-Carlton

THE BEAUTIFULLY APPOINTED MAIN RESTAURANT OF THE RITZ, "THE OVAL ROOM," oval in shape, of lovely proportions with a high-domed Adam ceiling. This room, sometimes called the Adam Room, is cleverly lit by a soft glow of a lights attractively concealed in a beautiful cornice. Club Breakfast, 50 cents, 75 cents, 95 cents. Lunch, $1, $1.25 cents, $1.50 cents. Dinner, $1.50 cents, $1.75 cents, $2. Afternoon tea, 50 cents.

The cooks' talents was displayed with particular drama, however, when the Ritz staged its traditional Saturday lunches and Sunday buffet suppers, both splendid smorgasbord affairs set out in the Oval Room on tables that were often made to stretch to fifty feet. Guests came in droves to eat the finest food in Montreal. "We had everyone there — the Prices, the Pitfields, and Judge Collins would come back and see us," says John Dominique. "We had to squeeze extra chairs into the restaurant otherwise you couldn't have gotten all the people in."

The evening smorgasbord was especially lavish and was launched to entice "the younger social set" home earlier than usual from a Laurentian skiing weekend. It was always a money-maker in spite of its low price. A high turnover of guests allowed the hotel to hold this at $3 — for suckling pig, lobster, game, various hams and roasts, hors d'oeuvres, and a score of desserts ranging from fruits steeped in liqueurs to all manner of cakes, tarts, and pastries. It was a lesson in psychology to watch who went back for fifth helpings.

One of the hungriest patrons of all was a certain Baron Rothschild. He not only visited the table several times, but before leaving the restaurant was seen to stuff his pockets with cheese and rolls. "We understood," Dominique reflects, wistfully. "We understood that poor man perfectly. He'd been having terrible difficulty getting his money out of France and, in Canada, he was damn near broke."

The gastronomic supremacy that the hotel enjoyed as it rolled into the 1950s is, perhaps, best illustrated by the time Jean Contat was sitting in the hotel's lounge with a bluff, pukka Englishman named Caryl Hardinge, or Viscount Hardinge of Jahore, to be correct, whose uncle had been

Viceroy of India. He was the archetypical Ritz-Carlton patron if ever there was one — wealthy, distinguished, discriminating, and free-spending. Like the earliest patrons and several since, he sat on the hotel's board of directors.

His Lordship was drinking a double whisky on the rocks; Contat was sitting idly in front of him, watching, waiting, thinking. As usual, the atmosphere in the Ritz's public rooms, was pleasantly mulled. Contat broke the silence.

"You know what, Caryl!" he said, leaning forward with innocent enthusiasm. "We should start a restaurant. No, wait. I mean it. Somewhere near here. With fine food. Not too big, but very nice. It would be a good thing — good for the Ritz!"

Lord Hardinge put down his glass and straight-armed himself erect, palms on his knees. "A restaurant, eh? Good idea, that. We could use a good restaurant, eh? Eh? No place to go but the Ritz-Carlton now, and I'm getting bloody sick of it."

Both men laughed.

This rapport between the hotelkeeper and the peer reflects in no uncertain way the two men's complementary roles as manager and director in the ongoing struggle to preserve an idea — the Ritz Idea, with all that it had come to mean. "This hotel is still a club," Contat so often said at the outset of his tenure, "and I want to transform it into a grand hotel of the very finest quality. You watch me do it."

"You'd bloody better, by George!" said Lord Hardinge with a ringing guffaw that was heard in the lobby, "or you don't bloody get paid next week." And he ordered another stiff drink.

CHAPTER NINE

Ducks and Howard Hughes in the Nifty Fifties

*"Room 818 was a suite with a beautiful sitting room and
an equally lovely bedroom — just right for my honeymoon.
We had breakfast there before leaving for England.
The prices, however, seem to have changed a trifle.
It is quite astonishing to contemplate
what one could buy for $16 in 1950."*

BERNARD J. FINESTONE,
CHARTERED INSURANCE BROKER

The 1950s were frenetic at the Ritz. It was a decade totally preoccupied with giving the hotel a face, a heart, and a soul that was quite different from the one Jean Contat had inherited. While his wife supervised decorators in virtually every corner of the building and did a lot of their work herself, the staff hurried about their jobs with renewed vigour. Pierre Demers, meanwhile, cooked with unprecedented zeal as his staff began supplying meals to Air France's trans-Atlantic passengers.

The project started when French President Vincent Auriol stayed at the Ritz in April, 1951, and asked the hotel to prepare a meal that could be served on the way back to France to him and his thirty-five-person entourage of advisors and secretaries. "It wasn't a question of if we could provide the President with a gourmet meal," Demers recalls, "but of how we'd pack it so that it could be served hot during the flight."

His concerns were not without foundation. In the early 1950s, a Montreal-Paris flight in a Constellation 749 took about eleven hours.

French Embassy officials immediately suggested that before cooking the meal, Demers should go to New York City to see how Air France prepared in-flight food in its kitchens there; Demers, in turn, proposed that Air France might like to send its New York City chef to the Ritz-

Chef Pierre Demers—on rare table assignment in the Duck Garden. He started his career making toast at the Windsor Hotel during school holidays, then joined the CN Hotel chain where his first job was to carve meat off chicken bones. His Ritz days began in November, 1937, as a short order cook. Demers later became a $125-a-month night chef, and, during an illustrious thirty-nine year Ritz-Carlton career, was hailed as a world class executive chef.

PHOTO BY CANADA WIDE
COURTESY OF THE RITZ-CARLTON COLLECTION

Carlton Hotel to see how some of the world's finest gourmet dishes were cooked every day of the week. That, for the French president's flight, is exactly what happened. Air France's senior chef, Raymond Veaudor ("golden veal"), checked into the Ritz so that he and Demers could work together. The meal, which comprised hors d'oeuvres of smoked salmon and a main dish of breast of chicken in a champagne sauce, so delighted Auriol that, on his recommendation, Air France asked the hotel to cater all its Montreal-Paris flights.

The "Ritz-Paris Affair," as the association came to be called, lasted twenty-five years — until all overseas flights began arriving at or departing from Mirabel Airport. This made the catering job more costly for the airline, and more risky for the Ritz, particularly insofar as its reputation was concerned. "There was a big chance," Demers says, "that our food would get spoiled before it even reached the airplane, and rotten food has never been served by the Ritz."

During most of the "affair," Air France's catering manager, René Bonnet, worked at the hotel. He occupied a glassed-in control desk behind the Ritz-Carlton's main kitchen, from where he coordinated meal packing with transportation, and watched Demers and his staff of sixty dramatically increase their production. At the outset only about 300 airline meals a day were prepared, but when Air France wanted Ritz-Carlton food on their military and chartered flights, the number grew to 3,000.

"We always had to bear in mind," Demers says, "that the air crew had to be able to serve a meal in forty-five minutes. We also needed to consider that we couldn't serve food that would stink up the plane."

They didn't. Nonetheless, Pierre Demers ran headfirst into problems with the International Air Transport Association (IATA) on another matter. Officials there had said that while first class passengers were to receive hot meals, economy class travellers were only entitled to sandwiches. Demers decided for himself that first class passengers would have roast beef, freshly carved in front of them, and that all others on the plane would have "open face" sandwiches — cold cuts on French bread, with an assortment of fine pickles and a choice of mustards on the side.

Demers' idea of a sandwich, IATA contended, wasn't theirs. According to official regulations, they pointed out, a sandwich was "meat, eggs, or vegetables, or a combination thereof, placed between two slices of bread." The Ritz-Carlton's happy-go-lucky executive chef agreed that an ordinary sandwich did indeed look like this, his idea of one to

A view through the Palm Court to the entrance of the Oval Room, decorated by George Campbell Tinning for the Coronation of Queen Elizabeth II on June 4, 1953. Gold and red ribbons streamed from banisters and balconies throughout the rest of the building and a six-foot replica of the Royal Coat of Arms, like the one pictured here, adorned the lobby. Tinning also hung flags and bunting from the front of the hotel.

PHOTO BY DAVID BIER
COURTESY OF THE RITZ-CARLTON COLLECTION

be enjoyed during a long flight differed. With both the quality of Ritz service and the comfort of economy class passengers always uppermost in his mind, he went on serving his open face sandwiches anyway until, a few years later, IATA allowed hot meals for all air travellers.

While work raged on in the kitchen, Yvonne Contat referred daily to a running record of which guest rooms still had to be refurbished, and how. Now though, with this work well underway, she could inflict her inimitable magic touch upon the public rooms. She flew regularly between Montreal and New York City to buy fabrics and accessories. While there she also hunted out, auditioned, and engaged night club performers she thought would please audiences in the Ritz Café at Night. It was a quest that often had her flying off to Chicago, London, and Paris at a moment's notice.

"I was always looking," she says, "for acts that would fit our clientele — class acts, relaxing, elegant, in good taste, and with no bad jokes."

In her travels she picked up antiques, bric-à-brac, little pieces of sculpture, and paintings — anything she felt might give a certain room a personality of its own. "When I look back, as I often do," she adds, "not all the rooms were the same at the Ritz. They might have all looked the same at a quick glance, but they were really quite different. I had tried to give to each its own special character, with a little collection of paintings, maybe, a special colour, a piece of handiwork on the coffee table, even the way I got the decorators to draw the curtains around the windows. You don't have to have lots and lots of money to make a beautiful place more attractive."

Onlookers were in awe of Yvonne Contat's taste and originality. They felt, as Dupré did, that whereas decorators did fine work in the hotel because they were expert and professional, Madame Contat accomplished infinitely more because she brought to bear a natural talent that was fuelled by her love for the hotel and its staff, and her admiration for all that was being done to further the Ritz Idea.

Yvonne Contat hired good people to help her, from the most ardent seamstresses and artisans, to the most meticulous plasterers and wallpaper hangers. She brought George Campbell Tinning back into the hotel, and from then on he became a Ritz-Carlton legend. Tinning's first job now was to produce a series of watercolours for some of the rooms. That done, he painted adventurous murals on walls, ceilings, and in alcoves — beautiful work which, in too many cases, has since been covered up or torn away. Nonetheless, some of his finest pieces can still be seen at the hotel today.

The intersection of Mountain and Sherbrooke streets before the Ritz was extended in the late 1950s. The hotel's existing steel structure, architect Ernest Barott explained, was not strong enough for a vertical extension. So he suggested the building be enlarged laterally. But could a new wing be added in the Adam style and thus remain faithfull to the original façade? The finished job, Barott promised, would look as if it had been constructed in 1912.

PHOTO BY ABC NEWS PICTURES
COURTESY OF THE RITZ-CARLTON COLLECTION

"Working with a woman like Yvonne Contat," Tinning said, "was a privilege. I enjoyed every single moment of her energy and ideas, not to mention her infectious laughter and friendship."

They achieved a lot together. When Dupré ordered the barbershop replaced by the Maritime Bar, he envisioned an atmosphere in which "gentlemen would be transported while enjoying their food." No one quite knew what this meant until, a little later, Madame Contat was in Jamaica. While there, she took a ride in a glass-bottomed boat, and when she saw beautiful fish darting above the turquoise coral below, she said, "That's it! That's the Maritime Bar!" But it was Campbell Tinning who was assigned to make the idea a reality — on the bar's ceiling. As time went on, many of the families Yvonne Contat had got to know so well hounded her for advice. "Yvonne, please help me," they pleaded. Usually, they were organizing a private dinner or a debutante's ball and wanted her to pledge her encouragement and lavish her flair upon the decorations.

Madame Contat, in turn, often suggested that they speak to Campbell Tinning, a master in the art of giving rooms a special look for a special event. When Mr. and Mrs. John Sharp's daughter "came out," he hung silver and rose streamers from the ceiling to the floor in the foyer and decorated the pillars in the Ball Room itself with six-foot silver and rose sprays and pink and white balloons. The boxes under the balconies sported white and pink lilies, roses, and stephanotis, a climbing hothouse plant with fragrant, wax-like blooms. The stage on which the orchestra would play was banked with fresh flowers.

To mark the Coronation of Queen Elizabeth II in 1953, Tinning hung flags and bunting from the front of the hotel and festooned the Oval Room entrance with enormous gold and red crowns. Throughout the rest of the building, gold and red ribbons streamed from banisters and balconies; a six-foot replica of the Royal Coat of Arms adorned the lobby, not far from where the management had installed a cluster of television sets so that the public could watch the Coronation as it was taking place.

While decorating was underway, the directors and their managers were preoccupied with devising ways to enlarge the hotel to meet a huge increase in business, and they sought, eagerly, to see how this could be done with the minimum of inconvenience and expense. In 1950, Barott, Marshall, Montgomery and Merrett, a firm of Montreal architects, was contracted to find out whether the hotel could support three additional floors. After examining the building for several weeks, Ernest Barott, the firm's big, ruddy-faced senior partner who hailed from Michigan, Ohio, was doubtful. The existing steel structure, he explained, was not nearly strong enough for a vertical extension because the Ritz-Carlton had not been designed to carry any extra weight. So, if additional floors were to be added, all existing columns and beams supporting the entire hotel, would have to be considerably reinforced.

From the aesthetic point of view, which was of major concern to both directors and local preservationists alike, Barott was confident that the Adam style could be faithfully reproduced and incorporated into any extension the hotel contemplated then or later. The finished job, he promised, would look as if it were part of the original building that had risen up in 1912. To prove it he and a junior colleague, Lorne Marshall, went to New Jersey to meet representatives of Federal Seaboard Terra Cotta Inc., which had retained the moulds of the building's original terra cotta trim.

Back in Montreal, Barott drew up complex drawings that showed how the extension would look. He was, however, continually advising the directors that from an economic standpoint, the job might not be feasible. In the first place, the hotel would lose a tremendous amount of money during the many months it would have to be closed while work was being done. In the second, the cost of materials and labour to reinforce the columns and install some new beams and bracing, not to mention a new roof, would be prohibitive; done properly, he said, the completed job was almost certain to cost more than the building's current market value.

If the hotel were to be extended at all, Ernest Barott also advocated, it should be done laterally: westward along Sherbrooke Street to Mountain Street. The directors agreed that this would be a good idea, and gave the general impression that they wanted the work to start soon. They assigned Barott to design a new cornice to replace the one which protruded from the top of the existing building (repair work, the architect had advised, that was absolutely imperative if this part of the original structure was to be prevented from crashing onto the sidewalk), and oversee its installation.

Barott undertook this work — and "ridded the lower basement of rats," he wrote — and waited eagerly to be assigned the major contract. The directors, meanwhile, had second thoughts about it and, in the winter of 1950, assigned the consulting firm of Harris, Kerr, Forster & Co., "to make a thorough study of, and review of, all the financial factors involved."

That report, read to the directors on January 19, 1951, reiterated all that Barott had been saying — that the job could be done, but at an exorbitant cost. It also pointed up other problems: that if the hotel were extended for the remainder of the entire block, as Barott had suggested it should be, guests living at the new wing's most westerly point would have too long a walk to the elevators. Since other important amenities, like the reception desk, room service kitchens, and housekeeping departments were all at the eastern end of the hotel, such a long extension would inconvenience the staff as well, particularly those involved in providing floor service.

Additionally, the Ritz-Carlton directors felt that a new wing would create upheaval they could do without, and incur expenses they preferred not to afford. At least, not yet. They shelved all plans to enlarge the hotel in any way, vertically or laterally, for five years. In 1956, however, when they finally decided that they were ready for the work to begin, Ernest Barott was not asked to oversee it.

One theory put forward — and it was not without some justification — was that Contat and Dupré found Barott "too aggressive." Generally recognized as one of the truly great North American architects, he also happened to be volatile, brittle, and short-tempered. It was not unusual, for example, for him and his clients to engage in stand up arguments that stopped little short of fist fights. The other side of the story is that Barott had grown to dislike Contat and Dupré. He found them "unusually bombastic and silly, and unable to grasp the full magnitude of what they were asking to be done." Yvonne Contat recalls, "Mr. Dupré was the most wonderful man, but he always wanted things done his way and wouldn't listen to anyone else. He didn't want anybody to interfere with his thoughts. In this case, he didn't want Mr. Barott to influence him, even though he'd hired him. He didn't much like Mr. Barott, and Mr. Barott didn't like him."

Yet another reason given was that while the directors acknowledged Ernest Barott's talent, they felt secretly that he was foisting upon them an extension to the Ritz that was too expensive and too modern for their tastes. So his ability was ignored, his services dropped. The next thing the Ritz-Carlton's senior staffers and shareholders knew was that the all-powerful Dupré and Contat had given the job to another architect: Gratton D. Thompson, designer of the big Roddick Gates to McGill University. Thompson, and Pierre d'Allemagne, a well known Montreal consulting engineer, oversaw the construction of the new wing. They used Ernest Barott's original drawings, which faithfully honoured the Adam style he had always admired.

Work on the extension has started. Two townhouses have been torn down,
providing residents living across the road on Mountain Street with their first
view of the Ritz Garden (top right hand corner) from second-storey windows.

PHOTO BY GERALDINE CARPENTER
COURTESY OF THE RITZ-CARLTON COLLECTION

The building itself was constructed by the Montreal firm of A. Janin & Company, and decorated with Federal Seaboard's terra cotta made by its Montreal agent, W. & F. B. Currie of Ville St. Laurent. Controlled by seven Bastien brothers, Currie was forced to close its doors twenty years later when the demand for terra cotta diminished. "We were always so proud," says Freddy Bastien, the firm's former vice-president, "to welcome even the chance to work at the Ritz. Everyone wanted to do a job there." Completed in April, 1957, the work cost nearly $1.9 million. This sum included the price of a second sand blasting of the parent building to make its addition less conspicuous. The consultants made one major modification to the earlier plans, however, to both save and make money. Construction did indeed stretch to Mountain Street, but the extreme westward section comprised an office block and ground-floor commercial space to be rented out to the Canadian Imperial Bank of Commerce. The new hotel wing itself stretched only halfway along the block and was large enough to add sixty-seven extra rooms, suites, and offices.

The Ritz-Carlton immediately put the extension to good use by creating a larger Royal Suite on the eighth floor. The Vice-Regal Suite would remain on the second floor of the original building and be used as a salon that was ideal for luncheon meetings or small banquets. The Royal Suite, however, would be twice as large as its predecessor and command a higher, wider, northward view of Mount Royal.

A sizeable parade of notables were quick to rent the new suite. They included Rose Kennedy, Otto Preminger, who was back for a second visit, actor Cary Grant, and British Columbia's Lieutenant-Governor Frank Ross, who spent hundreds of dollars just on caviar for a seemingly endless stream of small dinner parties in the suite's dining room. Then followed Harry Belafonte, who complemented his love of watercress sandwiches with a craving for soda water, and Artur Rubinstein, who told the staff that before each concert he wanted merely an omelette and a pot of tea delivered to his room.

On any given day in the late 1950s, numerous celebrities like these could conceivably have met each other in any one of the bars or restaurants. Some, however, gave the distinct impression that they were not particularly interested in meeting anyone, as Contat and his wife witnessed one night in 1957 when they arrived back at the hotel from a party. They were dismayed to see a tall, scruffy, bespectacled man in worn-out clothes and maroon carpet slippers standing indolently by the elevator.

The Ritz-Carlton's new wing is finally in place, adding sixty-seven extra rooms.
Completed in April, 1957, the work cost nearly $1.9 million, which included
the cost of a second sand blasting of the parent building—carried out after this
picture was taken—to make the addition less conspicuous. Construction
stretched to Mountain Street, but the extreme westward section comprises an
office block and ground-floor commercial space that is rented out to the
Canadian Imperial Bank of Commerce.

PHOTO BY ARTISTE STUDIO
COURTESY OF THE RITZ-CARLTON COLLECTION

I want to see around here again!"

"Yes, Mr. Contat," the clerk said.

"Do you understand me?" Contat hissed, pointing an accusing finger.

"Yes, and I agree," the clerk added. "But you are talking about a guest."

"A guest?" Contat said taken aback. "Who?"

"Mr. Howard Hughes."

The reclusive, elusive billionaire was just returning to the hotel from an extremely rare walk alone. That day he had checked into not just a suite or two, but more than half of the Ritz-Carlton's entire eighth floor — space he said he needed to house a retinue comprising six body guards, three private detectives, two secretaries, eight financial advisors, two valets, three butlers, and a barber.

Hughes' reputation as an eccentric guest had preceded him, and as soon as word spread that he was arriving to stay at the hotel for a month, the staff braced itself for a slew of demands, many of them extraordinary if not downright bizarre. Several times daily, most often late at night or in the early hours of the morning, the phantom financier needed plenty of sustenance to fuel his work. One of the dozen or so people Contat had assigned to serve Hughes was Paulin Bergeron, the assistant executive chef. To properly cope with his assignment, Bergeron had to actually move into an eighth-floor room for as long as Hughes was there; so did a maid and a floor waiter.

Hughes invariably wanted two twelve-ounce steaks, served with Boston lettuce and fresh vegetables boiled without seasoning, and for dessert, crêpes suzettes flambéed in the usual sauce. In this, his menu was reasonable. If, however, he decided on a whim that he wanted Bergeron to cook him crêpes at three or four o'clock in the morning, he asked that they be as thick as Aunt Jemima pancakes. And there had to be at least three scoops of chocolate ice cream on the side.

On many nights Bergeron was told to prepare for Hughes six different meals, complete with hors d'oeuvres, entrées, and desserts, and send them to his room simultaneously — "anything that sprang into his mind," says Alfred Hirmke, the hotel's food and beverage director. "It might already have been on the menu, or it might not have been. Whatever Mr. Hughes wanted, he had to get."

To the uninitiated, this doubtless appeared to have been the extravagance of a man who was rich enough to afford it. In one sense it was. When his staff had set the meals out on the table, he then chose the one that, at that moment, took his fancy. Beneath this excessiveness, however, was reflected a more tragic side of Howard Hughes — his growing paranoia that whatever food was served to him would surely be contaminated. Thus, day or night, he ordered two other members of his entourage, his travelling dietician and physician, who occupied the adjoining rooms, to meticulously inspect everything that Bergeron had cooked especially for him, just in case it had been laced with poison. At the Ritz, this was a Howard Hughes ritual, just as it had been in other hotels in which he had stayed.

Few people ever saw or spoke to Hughes, not even Contat and other senior management, and that is the way the billionaire wanted it. But they were constantly aware that he was a guest. He refused to allow the maid to make his bed or clean his room, insisting that she only prepare the table for his meals; the floor waiter was told to wheel the food to his door on a trolley, knock four times, then leave. Hughes spent so long on the telephone that to prevent him from monopolizing the switch-board, the hotel had to have an extra line installed for his sole personal use.

When he left the hotel by day, surrounded by as many as eight assistants and guards, Hughes preferred to use the staff staircase so that he would not meet the public. Sometimes he took the service elevator, walked a rear corridor, and left the hotel through a side entrance. On those few occasions when he used the guests' elevator, he ordered the operator to descend directly to the lobby without stopping. Once there, he strode quickly to a waiting car.

Such devoted Ritzmen as German-born Hirmke like to think that Hughes was well satisfied with all that the hotel did for him, and he doubtless was. Upon leaving — his final bill included more than $20,000-worth of long distance telephone calls — he lured the floor waiter who had been assigned to look after him onto his staff because, he said, he admired the way the man carved fish! The waiter stayed with Hughes' organization in Las Vegas for several months before departing in frustration to work in a restaurant.

A further notable change to the hotel under Jean Contat was the expansion of the Dutch Garden into the Ritz Garden, where more and more patrons could lunch and dine during summer. That was in June, 1959. He took it upon himself to engage landscaper T. M. Gillespie to enlarge the seating area from thirty to sixty, install beautiful terraces of shrubs, and put a shallow, kidney-shaped pond in the centre of the lawn and fringe it with flowers, principally coral and pink geraniums.

When Dupré first heard that the Ritz now had a pond, he exclaimed, "Marvelous! We will make it very Canadian and stock it with beavers!"

"Beavers?" Madame Contat queried. "You really mean beavers?"

"I mean beavers," Dupré insisted by telephone from Paris. "Get me beavers for the pond."

"But it won't work, Monsieur Dupré," Madame Contat explained. "Beavers are for the wild."

Some time later, and to prove her point, she drove Dupré to a beaver farm near Hudson, Quebec, where he could see for himself the dams the animals had built and the damage they had done to the trees.

"You are right, Yvonne," he conceded. "We certainly don't want beavers building dams in the middle of the Ritz Garden."

Not long afterwards, while visiting friends in Knowlton, in Quebec's Eastern Townships, the Contats saw recently born ducklings paddling in a little lake behind their farmhouse. "Don't you think it would be wonderful to have little birds like that at the Ritz?" Yvonne Contat asked her husband.

"That is a very good idea," he replied and, without consulting Dupré, promptly ordered two dozen of them to be delivered that weekend. "Every three or four weeks you can bring us another batch and take the other ones back," he told the farmer. "Our pond has no room for big ducks."

So the Ritz Garden pond was stocked with twenty-four white Brome Lake ducklings but not, it must be said, without several initial difficulties. As a César Ritz disciple, Jean Contat had been encouraged to appreciate exquisite breeding, and he did. When it came to ducks, however, he was markedly uninformed. The species of bird he had ordered had been bred for the table and, once placed in the new pond, turned out to be extremely poor swimmers. On their first day there, in fact, most keeled over, sank like stones, and drowned. "They were doubtless succulent but not seaworthy," one patron observed.

Those that stayed buoyant were rescued — as witnessed by another patron, Marlee Dohan. On a hot day in July, she escaped from a Junior League committee meeting and, while taking in fresh air on a balcony above the garden, was bewildered to see Jean Contat and a group of waiters and busboys rescuing the birds. To do so, they had taken off their shoes, rolled their trousers up to their knees, and paddled into the water.

The survivors were rushed to the kitchen and revived. "It's wonderful what a drop of hot bouillon laced with rye whisky can do," Pierre Demers says, "even for ducklings." The whisky further proved to be a useful medication when some of the birds reacted adversely to the chemicals the maintenance staff had sprinkled into the water to keep it clean.

Determined that the pond should have ducklings, Contat told Albert

The Duck Garden photographed shortly after its opening in June, 1959.
Jean Contat engaged a landscaper to enlarge the seating area from thirty to
sixty, install beautiful terraces of shrubs, put a pond in the centre of the lawn,
and fringe it with flowers, principally coral and pink geraniums.
An architect designed the duckhouse.

PHOTO BY RICHARD ARLESS ASSOCIATES
COURTESY OF THE RITZ-CARLTON COLLECTION

Frossard to order a batch of a white barnyard species, and those birds were all right. Well, most of the time. First, Ritz diners found them so beguiling that they couldn't resist feeding them with table scraps. The result was almost predictable. The ducklings became so fat that they quickly resembled Strasbourg geese, and died of indigestion. Second, the Garden plan did not immediately provide for shelter for the birds, and on one colder than usual August night "Charles of the Ritz" took pity on them. He gathered them up and crammed them into a plate warmer in the main kitchen.

It was late on a Saturday and, tired after a long day's work, he forgot to tell his colleagues what he had done. The next day, Sunday dinner had barely been served in the Oval Room when a busboy opened the plate warmer door. Out, in a flurry of feathers, tumbled two dozen hungry, lively, frightened little ducklings, and it was left to amused guests to help waiters and busboys round them up and return them to the Garden.

The problem of accommodating the birds when the weather changed was soon solved. A duckhouse, heated by internal lights, was installed in the centre of the pond. The designer? Ernest Barott's junior partner, Lorne Marshall. "Yes, I remember that," Marshall says with a twinkle. "I remember it like yesterday. Contat had decided to get these ducks and asked if we could make plans for a nice place for them to stay. We thought he was crazy, but we designed the duckhouse anyway." Remembering what the Ritz was like under Contat and Dupré, a former busboy recalls, "It's a wonder they didn't expect those birds to wear white shirts and black bow ties! It was always a very formal place, and what the hotel said went unchallenged. Any one who didn't appreciate it, with its stiffness, rules, and aloofness, shouldn't even have been there."

No one, it seems, ever argued at the Ritz-Carlton, and no one lost his temper. Not even on days when fifty people had checked in, stretching desk staff resources to capacity. One memorable episode, with a less happy conclusion, involved three businessmen who arrived late one night to find that the three rooms they had reserved had been assigned to other guests. The hotel was overbooked.

Michel Bourda, then the assistant reservations manager, conceded that a desk clerk had erred, and offered the men the hotel's one available room. It contained a single bed, and a double bed which two of the late arriving guests would have to share. But would they?

"No," one of them insisted. "We absolutely want the three rooms we asked for!"

The Ritz Garden pond was stocked with twenty-four white Brome Lake ducklings. Patrons found them so beguiling that they couldn't resist feeding them table scraps. The result was almost predictable. The birds became fat, resembled Strasbourg geese, and died of indigestion. All that is changed now. Patrons admire the ducks, but leave them alone.

PHOTO BY RICHARD ARLESS ASSOCIATES
COURTESY OF THE RITZ-CARLTON COLLECTION

Bourda checked the register pensively, wondering how he could arrive at a compromise. This done, he looked up to address the visitors only to discover that the one who had stood in the middle was no longer there. Looking over the counter, Bourda saw him lying on the floor. On checking further, he discovered that the man was dead.

True to Ritz style, a beautiful Japanese screen was brought from an upstairs salon to hide the corpse until the police arrived to remove it, and the two remaining men settled amicably on the lone unoccupied room, where they could now, at least, each have a bed to himself.

Overbooking led to acute embarrassment at the Ritz-Carlton, and excessive demands upon the hotel's limited accommodation were worrisome — particularly when they came on short notice. Bourda picked up the telephone at his home late one night to hear a desk clerk pleading, "Please get down here straight away." A New York flight to London, England, Bourda was informed, had been diverted to Montreal International Airport because of bad weather and the airline wanted its 120 passengers to be billeted overnight at the Ritz.

Bourda and his staff explained with a mixture of satisfaction and regret that the hotel was fully booked, and they spent several hours calling others nearby — and even some loyal patrons — to ask if they could help out.

One patron who responded was the concert pianist Ellen Ballon, who was said to have been one of the hotel's more "difficult" permanent guests. "We shivered every time she rang for us," said a retired floor waiter. "She complained at every opportunity — about the food, the heating, the people in the next room, anything you can think of. There was nothing we could *ever* do to make this woman happy, so some of us gave up trying." Now, staff and patrons alike would see a more tender side to Miss Ballon.

On hearing that the aircraft had been delayed and that the hotel was faced with an unusual dilemma, she offered to spend the night with friends so that the airline's most celebrated passenger, film actor James Stewart, could stay in her suite until morning. It was an offer Stewart said he appreciated, but had to decline. He was happy to sleep that night on a Palm Court sofa instead.

A similar challenge loomed, though no one would have known it by the way Ritz staffers rose stalwartly to the occasion, when the front desk received word that the President of Pakistan, General M. Ziaulsaq, was on his way to the hotel from Montreal International Airport. His request for the Royal Suite was easy to satisfy. His preference for dinner, however, was not. The general wanted a full-course Indian meal of roast lamb, complete with hors d'oeuvres and a dessert, to be served that night to 120 guests who were waiting 100 miles away in a little community in the Eastern Townships.

The duty chef sent busboys out for the ingredients, and the dinner was cooked, delivered by van, and served on time. "If you can't rise to occasions such as these," says Pierre Demers, "you might just as well get out of the kitchen."

For that there was never any need, for rising to *any* occasion made the hotel unique, even at its busiest times. "The fifties at the Ritz-Carlton," says Madame Contat, "were lovely — full of life and constant movement. There was always so much going on."

This was reflected in those long lineups that stretched down Drummond Street from the timekeeper's office. Montreal abounded in men and women who longed to work at the hotel as waiters, maids, clerks, or busboys — or fill any other vacancy that might have sprung up. So the queues grew longer by the day. "Those were the times," remembers one senior waiter, "when you were lucky to find a job at the Ritz, and the Ritz was lucky to find the people it wanted, with all the qualifications it expected. It only ever hired the best, after all, and if the best wasn't good enough, it was turned away. They'd rather be short staffed than take on the wrong people. So you could always feel pretty proud about having as job at the Ritz-Carlton Hotel."

No one knew this better than Denis Laganière who, by the 1960s, had become the night cloakroom attendant, entrusted with a thousand coats a week, and almost as many parcels, handbags, and umbrellas. "The same people," he says, "would come in night after night, week after week for lunch, cocktails, and dinner, and you didn't even give them a claim ticket because you'd insult them if you did. They'd immediately think you didn't know who they were, and that would have been terrible. You just took their hats and coats — 'Yes, Mr. Saint-Pierre,' or, 'Yes, Mr. Duplessis' — and hung them up."

At Christmas, Denis Laganière was inundated with the same prestigious customers, often all at one time, and for the same parties and dinners. "Then," he says, "I was taking their hats and coats and when they'd gone off for their cocktails and dinner, and when I could sneak a little chance, I would try to judge by the shape of the hats or the kind of coats, who they belonged to — 'This is Mr. Price's and that belongs to Mr. Saunders.' Mr. Duplessis was easy because of his walking stick, which I always put right under his hat. I got to know nearly all the people's names by the sizes and shapes of their clothes, and it made my job easier when they came to pick them up."

But then, recognizing each patron's character and temperament, Denis Laganière has always maintained, is as essential to holding down a Ritz-Carlton job as remembering what he likes to eat and drink, and feeling intuitively when the time has come for him to be left alone.

Jean Contat would have been the first to agree.

CHAPTER TEN

Foibles à la Ritz,
and a Very Special Wedding

"Little surprises like this make
a hotel employee's life go round.
You bet they do."

MONTREAL SCENE, 1974

In its unyielding quest for perfection, the Ritz had already housed its complement of the rich, the famous, and the notorious, not to mention the annoying, the mad, and the eccentric, and many more would come. Some of these people just had to be naughty into the bargain. Room service waiter Axel Glasow, whose daily concerns included a permanent guest's preference for "buttered toast with the crusts left on, but crushed," summed it all up quite differently from Victor the doorman. He used to say, and his colleagues agreed, that when Shakespeare declared that the whole world was a stage, he was really talking about the Ritz-Carlton Hotel.

"Who needs to go to the theatre when you're in this kind of work?" Glasow shrugged. "Everything, but everything, always happens right here. And if it hasn't yet, it will tomorrow."

He has never been proven wrong. Just as there had been formidable connoisseurs like C.B. Thorn at the Ritz-Carlton, so there were formidable imbibers other than Elwood Hosmer. None, perhaps, was more spectacular than a British Petroleum executive who used to consume ten double martinis and six Pernods over lunch. He was as atypical as he was unforgettable.

While it was not unusual for him to take a taxi home to bed in a mild stupor at 3 p.m., he would be back as soon as the bar opened at 6 p.m., never faltering, and invariably greeting the waiters as if he had not seen them for a hundred years. Not only were his digestive powers extraordinarily acute, but the more he drank the sharper his mind became. Waiters like big, outgoing Gratton Maloney, who served him with reverence in the Ritz Bar, trembled with terror as they handed him the bill — just in case they had erred in their calculations.

Female imbibers, like the one who "borrowed" coat racks, were conspicuous, too, but usually for an entirely different set of reasons. One woman in particular absolutely insisted that the long succession of martinis she enjoyed on her daily visits to the Maritime Bar was to relieve her arthritis. It may well have, but the same patron would quite frequently shamble off home leaving her dentures on the counter. It usually fell to the discreet barman, Giovanni Bitetto, to tactfully hand them back on her next visit, without so much as cracking a smile — "I do believe, Madam, that you left these. Nothing unusual in this, I can assure you. A lot of people leave their false teeth behind. Would you like your usual? How is your arthritis, Madam?"

One distinguished dowager unwittingly enhanced the hotel's reputation for eccentricity by peeling off her panties when she had drunk too much in the Ritz Café at Night, and putting them in a brown paper bag which she deposited under a corner chair. Considerably more to the staff's preference, though, was the socially active young lawyer who arrived with a different woman every Tuesday night because he approved of Yvonne Contat's taste in nightclub acts. Throughout the entire evening he would spend a mere $6 on soda water, but he never failed to hand the maître d'hôtel a $50 tip for reserving him a corner table.

But good things in the Ritz Café had to come to an end. Jean Contat sensed that musical tastes were changing drastically and he refused to accede to them. It was no longer fashionable, he found, to listen to French chansonniers singing with a white grand piano or a little quartet, and artists good enough to entertain at the Ritz were becoming increasingly hard to find. This became clearly evident in 1961 when he and his wife went to New York City to scout talent. "We could no longer hear the type of performers who would appeal to our clients," Madame Contat says. "All we heard, first in New York, and later in London and Paris, was rock 'n roll, and our guests and patrons certainly would not have liked that!"

Dan Doheny reflects, "The nightclub circuit had dried up. It had fallen victim to television and a tidal wave of changing tastes. Besides being few and far between, all the good acts were too expensive for us."

Jean Contat put it differently. "We are between two generations, unfortunately," he said. "We might as well close the Café at Night." In early 1962, when the winter season was over, that is exactly what he did. For a brief period shortly afterwards, the management tried to lure the younger set into a discotheque — until hotel guests complained that the music was too loud. The Café remained a supper club for another three years, however, attracting regular patrons every evening to listen to cocktail music; on Friday and Saturday nights they turned out in force to dance to the Paul Notar and Johnny Gallant trios.

Music has always been synonymous with the Ritz. Upstairs in the Grand Ball Room, audiences of 400 and more attended concerts by such internationally acclaimed ensembles as the New York Brass and Woodwind Quintet, or weekly recitals by local singers and pianists. The flourishing Ladies' Morning Musical Club, already able to look back over seventy-five years, was bringing the world's finest artists into the Ritz-Carlton's Ball Room, and the list was endless: Dame Clara Butt, the violinist Jascha Heifetz, pianist Glenn Gould, contralto Maureen Forrester, the Amadeus Quartet, cellist Pierre Fournier, flautist Jean-Pierre Rampal, and the baritone Gérard Souzay, to name just a few. The hotel's sounds were eclectic indeed, but rock music would never find a place there.

Between generations or not, the genial old Ritz would continue to remain true to its mandate and faithful to its customers, especially those who had helped sustain it through its impoverished years — but without François Dupré now. In September, 1961, his maid had found him slumped in a chair at his Montreal home. He had suffered a massive stroke which left him partially paralyzed. From then on, he never visited the Ritz-Carlton Hotel again, but administered it from afar with the help of his wife, Anna ("Anci"), a pert, bird-like Czechoslovakian-born Hungarian with strong ideas about cooking and investment. As best as she could, she saw that the hotel did not suffer by her husband's incapacity, and the consensus was that it did not. Both the board and the management shared Dupré's yearning for high standards and had now inherited his ways of effecting them. On December 18, 1963, Bell Telephone Company executives of a new era filed back to the hotel, this time to celebrate the board of directors' 1,000th regular monthly meeting with a luncheon in the Canadian Suite. It was a sedate affair. Other corners of the Ritz, meanwhile, continued to be a hothouse of human foible, some of it humorous, much of it downright tragic. That, the staff knew, was the nature of their business.

"It stands to reason, doesn't it?" Denis Laganière says philosophically, "that when you get a busy place like this and you serve liquor to lots of different kinds of people with different personalities, odd things are bound to happen."

No one knew this better than the nimble, Austrian-born Peter Ryles. Once a busboy in the cavernous main kitchen at London's Savoy Hotel, he became a restaurant waiter there, then emigrated to Canada to be a room service waiter earning thirty-six cents an hour on the Ritz-Carlton's sixth floor. "At one time," he says with unbridled pride, "I served as many as forty breakfasts a day, and hot."

In those days, Ryles says, Ritz guests could call for service by operating a three-light system: a white light over a room door meant that a maid was wanted, a red light a valet, and a green light room service. Since the latter was accompanied by a siren which sounded throughout all the sixth-floor corridors, the waiter was obliged to answer it immediately. "If you didn't," Ryles says, shaking his head, "the entire floor was up in arms. All these heads peeped from behind half closed doors to ask what the hell was going on!"

Ryles loved his job, and he mastered it to the very last letter with keen dispatch and dedicated precision. Like other room service waiters at the Ritz, he wrote each guest's order on a slip of paper which he stuffed into a suction chute that reached down to the kitchen. Here the order was collected by a busboy and placed before a chef, who began to fill it. In minutes, another busboy would phone to say that he was placing the meal in the next ascending service elevator. "And while that was happening," Ryles says, "three more bells could be sounding. A woman in 607 couldn't close a window. A man in 617 wanted a double rye on shaved ice — now! And a group of chamber musicians in 611 felt like a pile of lettuce sandwiches and a crate of Perrier water. Some days it was crazy. If people had just wanted toast and coffee, the job would've been one helluva lot easier."

Some guests, however, were relatively easy to please. Pierre Trudeau's usual breakfast at the Ritz-Carlton, for instance, was half a grapefruit, a boiled egg, dry toast, and milk. Ryles saw that he got it as he liked it, with the egg boiled for no more than four-and-a-half minutes so that the yoke was still soft. Edgar Bronfman was equally as accommodating. He simply ordered a pot of coffee, some toast, and porridge "the way the Scots eat it."

From his working experience in England, Ryles knew exactly what this meant, and he was appalled one morning to discover that the Greek waiter who had been sent up to the sixth floor to help him did not. In his eagerness to please, the waiter was cooking the porridge with cream instead of water!

"What on earth do you think you're doing?" Ryles asked quizzically. "How do you know that Mr. Bronfman wants cream in his porridge? Did he ask for his porridge to be served with cream?"

"No, but that's how we do it Greece," the waiter replied.

"But we're not in Greece," Ryles said. "We are in the Ritz-Carlton. Now cook the porridge with water, the way Mr. Bronfman always has it, and let *him* add cream, or milk, as he so desires!"

By far Peter Ryles' biggest worry was to try to satisfy the big spending Frank Ross, who was fastidiously fussy, excessively critical, and oftentimes blatantly unreasonable. He always asked for a sixth-floor suite so that Peter Ryles would serve him; if for some reason his favourite room service waiter was unavailable, he threatened continually to remedy the matter by checking into another hotel.

The management took these threats so seriously that if Ryles had planned his day off when Ross was arriving, he was told, "You'd better hang around. You know how awkward this man can be. He won't let just anyone pour his drinks."

"You're telling *me?*" Ryles would respond, rolling his eyes. Yet each time Ross arrived, Ryles had to wear the same welcoming smile, offer the same friendly handshake, and perform the same opening line — "Hello, Sir. It is truly a pleasure to welcome you back to the Ritz-Carlton Hotel. Can I get you something?"

Frank Ross could be inordinately selfish, too. "When I am here," he often told Ryles, "I want you to forget about the other guests. I need your undivided attention, and if I don't get it I shall leave, that's all." He persistently rang for service — more often than not to ask to have a drink poured from a bottle already in his room — tipped badly, and never failed to bring his own bar, which consisted of several bottles of scotch, brandy, and champagne.

Shortly after one arrival, he summoned Ryles to his suite and told him accusingly, "Someone has taken my liquor."

"What do you mean, Sir?" Ryles asked.

"I mean what I say," Ross said. "When I was here last time, I left a bottle with you and made a mark on it. The level has fallen. Someone's been drinking my scotch!"

Ryles was rivetted to the floor in muted astonishment. "Not here, Sir," he said eventually. "All the people here are honest. Why would they want to take your scotch? If they want to steal scotch they can get it from the bar. We've got plenty of it down there."

"Well, somebody's taken it."

"Impossible, Mr. Ross. "When you checked out last time you were here I locked your scotch in a cupboard. I can assure you that *I* haven't drunk it."

"Well it must have been some of your staff. I made a mark on the bottle."

"I can vouch for the staff, Sir. They would *not* touch your liquor."

The next time Frank Ross came, he apologized to Peter Ryles. "The mystery of the missing scotch has been solved," he said, cheerfully. "I found out that my chauffeur had been drinking it, and I fired him, of course."

"I'm glad you discovered that, Mr. Ross," Ryles said. "I trust the Ritz-Carlton staff implicitly, and so should you."

He remembers, "You did so much to try to make a man welcome, and all he could ever do was complain. There were times when I would've been very happy if he'd never come back."

Fortunately, Frank Ross was an exception, a far cry from most visitors to the hotel. Almost all, Ryles says with consolation, have treasured the service they have been afforded, on his floor and others, and have rarely abused it or considered it lacking.

By 1963, Peter Ryles had risen to become the hotel's room service manager and was assigned to look after Elizabeth Taylor and Richard Burton when, late on the morning of Sunday, March 15, 1964, they arrived at the Ritz to marry — on only two hours notice. "At one moment the hotel could be quiet with very little happening," he reflects, "then, at the next, and without much warning, everyone would be hopping around like crazy to get things done. This meant that someone famous had just arrived."

Because Contat and his wife were vacationing in Nassau, Taylor and Burton were met in a flurry of handshakes by Albert Frossard and Ryles, who escorted them to suite 810, the Royal Suite, which then cost $600 a day. Ryles opened the door and ushered the couple in. He found them agreeably sociable and predicted, correctly, that they would be easy to please.

Miss Taylor surveyed the suite solicitously, even though she and Burton would only be staying there one night. "This is very, very nice," she observed. "Very nice indeed."

Ryles smiled. "Welcome to the Ritz-Carlton, Madam," he said. "If there is anything I can do to make your stay a pleasant, comfortable one, please don't hesitate to ask for it."

He was almost through the door when Richard Burton called him back.

"Yes, Mr. Ryles," he said, "there is something we would like. Could you please send us up two crates of champagne and two dozen glasses?"

"Certainly, Sir," Ryles said. "Right away."

"And there is one other thing."

"Yes, Sir?"

"We'd like you, if you will, to be at our wedding. Here. Today."

"Yes," Taylor confirmed.   "We are going to be married in this suite. This afternoon."

"In this suite?" Ryles queried, not quite believing what he had heard. "And this afternoon?"

"Yes," Burton said. "In this suite. And we'd like you to be there."

"Absolutely, Sir," said Ryles. "Anything, as I said, to make your stay a pleasant one."

Time was running out, though. It was already 1 p.m., and the wedding ceremony had been scheduled for 2.30 p.m. Ryles ordered the champagne from the cellar and instructed a busboy to deliver it to the eighth floor. This the busboy did by loading the two twelve-bottle crates onto a trolley and using the service elevator. Once the cargo had arrived, Ryles set it neatly onto a white cloth on a service table with the appropriate glasses and two dozen serviettes, and wheeled it into the Royal Suite where Burton had sunk himself into an armchair and was smoking a cigarette.

"I think a nice little drink would do us all good," Burton said, stirring. And he leapt up and uncorked one of the bottles of champagne, watching the foam spill onto the table.

The first Montrealers to hear about the impending marriage were lawyers Edward and Max Bernfeld. They had been contacted four days previously by attorneys Elizabeth Taylor had hired in Toronto. She had originally planned to marry Burton there, while he was playing *Hamlet* at the O'Keefe Centre, but encountered a serious legal problem. Ontario would not recognize Taylor's divorce from singer Eddie Fisher, nor Burton's from Sybil Williams, because they had both been granted in Mexico City. Quebec, the Toronto lawyers knew, had more relaxed laws and might therefore accept Mexican justice. They asked the Bernfelds to handle the case.

Max Bernfeld called in notary Lionel Segal to ask if he would issue a marriage licence. "Yes," Segal said, "as long as you are prepared to write a legal opinion on the validity of both decrees absolute, stating that they are valid and binding according to established international legal standards." That opinion was eventually rendered by Edward Bernfeld after copies of the decrees, written in Spanish but with certified English translations, had been sent by a private courier from Mexico City via lawyers in Nevada and New York City. It was perfectly legal, Bernfeld said, for the Burton-Taylor marriage to take place in Montreal, and he suggested the best hotel in town for the ceremony — the Ritz-Carlton.

Next, since civil marriages in Quebec needed to have "religious authority," Segal set out to search for a clergyman. He found one in his friend, the Rev. Leonard Mason, the English-born pastor of the Unitarian Church of the Messiah. "Keep it under your hat," Segal said, "because it must remain a secret. Elizabeth Taylor and Richard Burton want to get married here and I need you to officiate."

Mason agreed, and he, Segal, and Max Bernfeld went to the Royal Suite to tell the couple the marriage could proceed, that nearly all of the paperwork had been completed. Segal and Bernfeld needed their dates of birth, their full names and those of their parents, and their signatures, and Mason wanted to discuss the final details of the ceremony.

The formalities now complete, the three men spent much of that early afternoon talking Shakespeare with Richard Burton. "We played a game," Segal remembers. "We gave him the first line of a passage from Shakespeare that we knew, and amazingly, and as obscure as it was, he completed the entire speech. All that, and a lot of champagne, too!"

Taylor meanwhile, had retreated behind closed doors to ready herself. Her hair was being done by her travelling hair stylist, an ex-Montrealer, while her travelling butler pressed her clothes. "There was so much going on when I went back to the suite, and all of it in a hurry," Ryles reminisces, "that you could feel the tension in your bones."

That afternoon twenty guests — mostly friends, but also the butler, hairdresser, secretary, and two public relations men — attended the wedding. Taylor made her appearance after the gathering had been seated for ten minutes. She wore a yellow formal dress and her long hair had been braided with yellow roses. "She looked absolutely stunning," Segal remembers. "She was slim in those days, and her eyes shone like purple grapes."

Elizabeth Rossamund Taylor and Richard Burton faced Mason and Segal, their backs to the Royal Suite fireplace. The ceremony lasted a mere seven minutes. Peter Ryles looked on in the tuxedo he kept in his office closet for emergencies such as these. "Afterwards," he recalls, "the rest of that champagne flowed forth and hardly stopped. I know. I had to pour it. I'd never seen so much champagne consumed so quickly and at one gathering! Never!"

Outside the Royal Suite, security guards who had been hurriedly engaged by the hotel fended off the anticipated rush of wellwishers wanting to reach the Burtons' suite. News of the couple's arrival had brought scores of fans and reporters to the hotel, and many of them had forced their way into the basement, jamming both the rear staircase and the service elevator, hoping to reach the eighth floor without being noticed by police stationed in the lobby. "We can't have this," Ryles told the two security guards keeping vigil over the eighth floor. "Mr. and Mrs. Burton want to be left alone now."

All manner of stories evolved from the Burton-Taylor visit, nearly all of them false. The couple did not, for example, escape from the Ritz through a secret passageway behind the kitchen so that they could spend that Sunday evening in a rival hotel. There is no such passageway, and they did not leave the Ritz. Nor did they erroneously leave the elevator at a wrong floor and enter a wrong room and stay to converse with the people they met there.

Montreal is alive with newspaper and radio journalists who claim to have attended a party Taylor and Burton threw for the media. There was no such party. After the wedding ceremony, a small reception was confined entirely to a few close friends. When their guests had departed, at around 6 p.m., the couple ordered dinner in their suite — sirloin steaks, salad, and more champagne — and Ryles was called in to serve this, too. "We don't want any waiters around," Taylor had said. "Just you, Mr. Ryles."

After dinner, the couple watched television, then went to bed.

In the morning, as news of the wedding became even more widely known, fans tried to shoulder their way into the Ritz-Carlton Hotel to glimpse their idols as they departed, and Frossard ordered more extra guards to be brought in to keep them at bay.

Upstairs in the Royal Suite, Taylor was asking Ryles, "How can we get away from here quietly, without any fuss?"

"Are there lots of people out there?" Burton inquired.

"Yes, I'm afraid there are, Sir," said Ryles. "Lots."

"Then we must find another way out," said Taylor. "I don't feel like meeting the public today."

Peter Ryles had already plotted a quick escape route for them. The hotel, particularly the lobby, would be cleared, and the public elevators inactivated by turning off the power supply. Burton and Taylor would then take the service elevator to the second basement, walk through a little maze of passages, mount a short staircase, and leave through the staff entrance that opened out onto Drummond Street. Or they could take the service elevator to the first basement floor and exit the hotel through the kitchen.

One quick phone call to the lobby, Ryles had surmised, would be all that was needed to relay the plan to the waiting chauffeur. He could pick up the couple just around the corner to prevent them from being either seen or mobbed. He could then make a hasty escape to Montreal International Airport.

"So, Madam," Ryles said, "I can escort you down the service elevator myself. I can actually take you to the side door, and I'd be very happy to make all necessary arrangements for the limousine to join you there. Will that be of any help?"

"That would be wonderful," Taylor said.

Richard Burton, though, was uncomfortable with this arrangement. He had sat listening to Ryles explain it with an occasional glance at his watch. He had to be back in Toronto in good time to relax before that night's performance. Suddenly, he rose from a Royal Suite chair and looked down from a window to see the crowd, now numbering hundreds, milling below, and turned to address his bride and her entourage.

"The people have come to see us," he said in his mellifluous Shakespearean voice. "So they should, and so they will. C'mon Liz. Let's go down and meet them."

Thus the Burtons were mobbed on Sherbrooke Street. A few days later, Ryles received autographed photographs from Elizabeth Taylor and Richard Burton. "With best wishes," they each wrote, "and thanks for all your help."

Mementos like these, he says, make a room service manager feel that his work has really been appreciated. Lionel Segal will always remember the occasion for different reasons. The excitement and the stress of his efforts to issue the marriage certificate was enough to send his pregnant wife into labour. On the day of the wedding she gave birth to a son.

In 1965, the year pastry cook Jean Pellerino came out of retirement at the age of eighty-three to help Ritz-Carlton chefs prepare their entries for the 29th Culinary Salon, Jean Contat replaced François Dupré, whose condition was worsening. According to some Ritzmen, even those who admired Contat, his promotion to president was something of a foible in itself. "He now threw his weight around more than he ever did," one director said, "and there were times when we all wished we could've restrained him."

Contat's authority continued to be felt with undiminished force throughout the Ritz each day, however, because he remained the tyrannical general manager as well. As Expo '67 approached, he and his wife supervised more renovations to meet the expected influx of visitors. All the 247 guest rooms and suites, as well as twelve banquet and conference rooms, were refurbished floor by floor in the style and grandeur of Louis XIV.

Long before this work started, François Dupré had called Yvonne Contat to Paris, as he had on more than two dozen occasions, and often on only twenty-four hours notice, to meet him in his office at l'Hôtel Georges V. There, he introduced her to Henri Samuel of Maison Avaloine, the internationally acclaimed French interior designer who had sumptuously redecorated Monte Carlo's Hôtel de Paris, the Hôtel Georges V, New York City's Carlyle Hotel, the Château Versailles, and the homes of the Aga Khan and the Barons de Rothschild.

Dupré told Yvonne Contat that she and Samuel were to undertake the work at the Ritz-Carlton together, and they did. There was no need for the decorators to be reminded to preserve as much as they could of the hotel's original interior. They knew its features only too well — the big fireplaces, the high, embossed ceilings, and the abundance of brass fittings that have remained essential features to this day. Madame Contat and Henri Samuel were aware, too, that the Ritz-Carlton Hotel, now barely fifty years old, was being acclaimed as an architectural masterpiece which they would never want to spoil.

During these renovations the Grand Ball Room was converted into the plush new main dining room — the Café de Paris — and the adjoining Ritz Bar. By installing a new, lower ceiling in the Café, the decorators made the upper part of the former two-storey Grand Ball Room another public salon, the Gold and Grey Room, to be used for receptions.

From then on, the Oval Room became a banquet hall, with plenty of seating for diners placed around an oak dance floor. The room would be used mostly for smaller, less frequent dinner dances. "The world had changed," Madame Contat reflects ruefully. "The day of the big ball was gone. Younger people weren't interested anymore in celebrating with extravagant, dressy functions like they did in generations gone by. That's why we had no more use for our big, Grand Ball Room. We were sorry to see it go."

The public, however, did not immediately understand the management's intentions and scores of people, patrons and historians alike, wrote to the Ritz-Carlton alarmed. They feared that it might be about to change for the worse and lose the character that had distinguished it from other establishments of its age. To allay these concerns, Madame

An artist's impression of how decorators could refurbish the Oval Room
as a busy banquet hall while keeping its beautiful windows
and glorious Adam ceiling firmly intact.

COURTESY OF THE RITZ-CARLTON COLLECTION

Contat called a press conference in May, 1965, and, in her best English, read a statement:

> Since word got around that we are doing extensive renovation work at the Ritz, the curiosity of our guests has been aroused and they comment on the news with great interest, as well as speculate on the nature of this transformation. Contradictory rumours circulate. Guesses are ventured. Letters are addressed to us — all with the view to ascertaining what are the exact changes contemplated at the hotel.
>
> We are extremely happy to note how deeply our clientele is attached to the Ritz, and we are delighted to welcome you here today in order to enlighten you on the subject.
>
> Our intention, in somewhat renovating our establishment, is to retain the tradition of elegance and distinction which always prevailed at the Ritz but, at the same time, to comply with the necessities of modern times. We shall not demolish our Oval Room, as many disappointed guests believed at first; however, without any alteration whatsoever to its beautiful Adam style, we will use same as a function room for all the renowned social events taking place at the Ritz.
>
> Our present ballroom, beginning this summer, will be transformed into a lovely restaurant, the cozy atmosphere of which will certainly appeal to everyone, and where we will continue to serve our guests in the best tradition of the past. We feel that this smaller dining room will provide more pleasant and intimate surroundings. It will be called "Café de Paris"; in the attractive, adjoining lounge, our guests will be able to enjoy their favourite cocktail while reminiscing of the "belle époque," which the interior decorating will revive.
>
> We shall not divulge any more for the time being. The official inauguration will reveal all our secrets.
>
> In closing, we would also like to draw your attention to the fact that our renovation works include the installation of air-conditioning in all our banquet rooms, to add to the convenience of our distinguished clientele. In fact, we shall have the pleasure of welcoming you all to a cool, renovated Ritz!

Madame Contat wasted no time in helping to transform the rooms herself. During a visit to Paris, for example, she bought a Louis XIV chandelier with a matching lamp and wall bracket, and spent six months trying to find a Montreal artisan who could copy each piece to make two sets, one to be installed in the Café de Paris, the other in the Ritz Bar. While these were being made, she was a familiar figure in a hard hat and overalls, assisting workmen as they tore down walls and ripped out electrical fixtures. "It was hard, dirty work," she says, "but it was

The Palm Court photographed from the landing outside the Oval Room shortly
before being completely refurbished. The glass partition (background) was
removed so that the Palm Court open into the lobby, as it does today.
COURTESY OF THE RITZ-CARLTON COLLECTION

tremendous fun. It had the excitement of birth."

Sadly, it was work François Dupré never lived to see completed. He had spent the last two years of his life immobilized and unable to speak or feed himself. He died at his Jamaica villa on Sunday, June 26, 1966, aged seventy-eight — the very day his horse "Danseur" won the Grand Prix de Paris, which carried a $150,000 purse. He was buried in France. The job of preparing the Ritz for Expo, however, went on in Dupré's honour and according to his last wishes.

While drawing up the general design and colour scheme which transformed the old ballroom into a fine, intimate, blue and beige dining room in the true European style, Madame Contat stumbled on the idea of hiding the new air conditioning ducts behind cornices, which she ordered especially made by two Italian Montrealers.

Meanwhile, the hotel placed advertisements in local newspapers:

> The Ritz-Carlton Hotel
> begs the indulgence of its faithful patrons
> for the
> inconvenience caused due to the
> Oval Room and Lounge
> being closed on Saturday, January 24th
> in the Late Afternoon
> It will be our pleasure to serve Dinner
> in the Maritime Bar and Café

As the Grand Ball Room disappeared, and the Café de Paris began to emerge in its place from dust and rubble that reached through the lobby and into the Palm Court, Albert Frossard left the hotel. After nearly thirty years' service he resigned to manage the restaurant in the Swiss Pavilion at Expo '67, and the stalwart James Connolly, now one of the most seasoned, longest serving Ritzmen, took his place. But there were more changes in store. As the Ritz-Carlton approached the 1970s, more financially stable than it had ever been, and somewhat redesigned to meet the tastes of a new generation of discriminating patrons and guests, Jean Contat announced his retirement. That was in May, 1969.

Not surprisingly, the tributes to him were glowing. Peter Ryles, whose twenty-three years' service at the Ritz was spent mostly under Contat, called him a "great hotelkeeper in the true, European tradition — a man who fought every inch of the way for what he believed was right, even if it did at times mean upsetting the staff." Pierre Demers said that his boss had been "feared but very fair." At Contat's farewell gathering, in the Gold and Grey Room, many of the staffers recalled that when he had taken command of the Ritz, they were feeling unsettled, never quite knowing if the hotel had a future or not. They could not forget, they said, how Contat had made the Ritz-Carlton strong again, and that completely on his own initiative he had engineered the staff pension plan which remains a fixture to this day.

"He got me *my* pension," says John Dominique, "and I'll always be grateful for that."

Contat also allowed him his first free weekend in nearly twenty years. Dominique will always remember it: "I went to his office and said, 'Excuse me Mr. Contat, but can I ask you something?' Until then, my only day off each week had been Friday. 'Yes, you can ask me whatever you like,' Mr. Contat said. So then I asked him straight — 'Can I have Saturday and Sunday off? I really need a rest.' And without blinking an eye, he said, 'Of course.' Not long after that, a lot of other guys who'd worked hard at the Ritz got weekends off, too. Mr. Contat saw to that."

Other workers reminded Contat how he had advanced them their wages to help them over financial difficulties. One of them was a man whose wife had given birth to twins. "You're a real man of the staff," he said. It was fitting that as a parting gift Contat's workmates had his four decorations, including France's Légion d'Honneur and a gold medal presented by the King of Yugoslavia, recast into miniatures and mounted on a bar that he could wear when he attended public functions in tails.

Guests were grateful to Contat, too. They wrote in by the hundreds, wishing him well and saying that a long, peaceful retirement would justly reward him for making the Ritz-Carlton a better place. Contat, then sixty-seven years old and beginning to slow down, said simply of his tenure, "I tried." He went home to his farm in Brigham to rear Hereford cattle, ride horses, paint, and maintain memberships in both the Montreal and Lake of Two Mountains hunt clubs. He combined a love for travel with his former profession by serving with the Federal Government's Canadian University Service Overseas plan (CUSO), teaching hotel management in Brazil and Jamaica for three months. Jean Contat died twelve years later from Alzheimer's disease.

"Looking back," says Yvonne Contat, now approaching eighty and still living on the farm, "it was so much fun, and I wouldn't have missed it for the world. The guests loved my husband. They always said that he and I made a tremendous team, and I honestly think we did. But after so many years, we had both had enough. The time had come for us both to live a quieter life."

Contat was succeeded by Fred Laubi, a chemist's son who could never conceive of himself as anything but a hotelier. Born to Swiss parents in Cuise-la-Mott in northern France, Laubi abandoned school when he was seventeen to begin his career by shining shoes and tending gardens in small inns. He eventually became an apprentice chef at the Paris Ritz. When World War II broke out he continued his apprenticeship at the Eden au Lac in Zurich, and then graduated to the city's Grand Hotel Dolder, where he earned his first tip, for peeling a peach. In 1947, he went to work in Florence for a hotel-owning uncle, his best teacher, and ended up managing the Excelsior Hotel there.

After twelve years, Laubi moved to Venice to take charge of the Gritti Palace, which was used as a set for Visconti's film classic, *Death in Venice*. During his tenure, the Gritti was considered the finest small hotel in the world, and the penthouse he and his wife occupied on the Ritz roof in Montreal quickly bore a similar Venetian integrity: Tintoretto hues, Fortuny fabrics and plenty of damask, oil miniatures, and an abundance of rich, warm furnishings.

Fred Laubi's reputation as a hard headed administrator and custodian of the Ritz Idea was well known. He kept a secret file, for his staff's eyes only, in which regular guests were rated VIP, VVIP, or VVVIP. Against each name was written special instructions on how each should be treated; the idiosyncracies and preferences of all important visitors were noted studiously and taken into immediate consideration.

"The most important thing about running a hotel," Laubi often said, "is knowing the craft from top to bottom." Since cooking, like art collecting, was among his first loves, he thought nothing of walking into the kitchen each day to taste the food and tell the chef what spices were needed to improve a sauce. "Canadians are singularly lucky to have Fred Laubi as manager of the Ritz-Carlton," said *Quest*, "for he is one of the world's greatest living hoteliers. Having Laubi at the Ritz would be like having Leonard Bernstein with the Montreal Symphony... In a society where the vulgar and the second-rate proliferate daily, he cares enough to try to do his thing a little better. Fred Laubi believes that a man trying to be sublimely good at anything is a man a little closer to his Maker."

Soon after arriving at the Ritz in January, 1970, Laubi calmly let it be known that he would soon be changing it around — drastically. To those, and there were many of them, who said that the building had been altered and redecorated enough, Dan Doheny countered, "A hotel is like a house. There's always something to be done, and if it isn't done, the place falls apart in no time." By now, both staff and patrons had grown

Fred Laubi, the chemist's son who succeeded Jean Contat as general manager. Laubi abandoned school when he was seventeen to begin his career by shining shoes and tending gardens in small inns. He eventually became an apprentice chef at the Paris Ritz, and went on to manage the Excelsior Hotel in Florence and the Gritti Palace in Venice, making the latter the finest small hotel in the world.

COURTESY OF THE RITZ-CARLTON COLLECTION

so used to seeing the dust and dirt of renovations that they vowed their daily routines would progress unhindered in spite of it. "Life at the Ritz must always go on," shrugs John Dominique, "whoever's in charge. It has to. It stands to reason."

Life did. Dominique and the rest of the staff saw to that. But those human foibles, over which not even the most durable, accomplished Ritz worker had any control at all, continued as well. One October night, shortly after Dominique had been made the Ritz Bar's maître d'hôtel, he was horrified to see a woman bathing nude in the duck pond! A house detective was called. "You can't do that here, Madame," he said. He told the woman to dress, return to her room, and promise never to strip in public again, at least, not at the Ritz-Carlton Hotel. "Actually," says Dominique, "I think she was quite a bit on the nutty side."

Then there was the woman who seated herself in the Ritz Bar just to steal the hotel's ashtrays. It was a good thing for her, Dominique thought, that Judge Collins did not drop in for one his regular return visits. He might have dealt with the incident differently. He didn't tolerate stealing. Nor, it was said, did he have too much patience with women.

Souvenir collectors have always profited handsomely from the Ritz. They have removed almost anything from flatware, plates, and glasses, to paintings, menus, and toilet rolls bearing the Ritz-Carlton crest. At one point, Fred Laubi noticed that soap was missing, too. "We should give people something worthwhile to take home with them," he said, and introduced larger bars and plastic soap cases.

Nonetheless, John Dominique felt it was high time the practice of stealing from the restaurants stopped because it was unfair to other patrons. When he saw the woman slip two ashtrays into her handbag, he made her return them to the tables, and ordered her to stay away from the Ritz.

"You go and buy a couple of ashtrays," he said, "and leave ours alone!"

"You're not going to make a scene over two little things that cost fifteen cents each, are you?" the woman retorted.

"If they cost only fifteen cents, Madam," Dominique replied, "then you can afford to pay for them."

What riled him most was that the woman had not even bought a drink!

Considerably more memorable was the audacious, thoughtless customer who dragged a big black mongrel into the Ritz Bar one lunchtime and seated himself at a corner table, impatiently snapping his fingers for attention. "Tea and toast for me," he told the waiter, "and an open face roast beef sandwich for the dog." He was told, politely of course, that service at the Ritz had never been extended to dogs, and was unlikely to be in the foreseeable future. "We don't have the facilities for any kind of animals, or the staff to clean up the mess they make," a head waiter explained, and the man and his dog departed.

The Ritz's glorious eccentricity is probably captured best, however, by the well known building contractor who, night after night, took his own steaks to the Ritz and insisted on cooking them himself. On one such occasion, while entering the main kitchen, he was accidentally bitten on the arm by the night cook's dog when it leapt into his arms to snatch his parcel of meat. As expected, the management was sympathetic to the patron's injuries, but explained that the cook — an elderly woman — needed to keep her dog at work. It provided both company and protection for her on her long late night walk home.

"That dog's vicious," said the contractor.

"Only with you," a manager said. "Anyway, it's staying where it is because it happens to be the pet of one of our workers. If you don't like it, then you should stay out of the kitchen."

Shortly before noon the following day the customer stalked indignantly back into the Ritz Bar trailing a black and white goat!

"Excuse me, Sir," said the unruffled maître d'hôtel, "but I think it would be better for both of us if you got that thing out of here."

"No," the man retorted with stolid defiance, "it's a customer's pet. And I happen to be that customer!"

He eventually did remove the animal, of course, but not until Fred Laubi had been summoned from his penthouse to mediate.

. Just as customers have remained indelible, so have some of the hotel's directors. In much the same way as Elwood Hosmer found himself something of a celebrity during the 1920s, the 1930s, and the 1940s, so Lord Hardinge made his presence felt at the Ritz throughout the 1950s, 1960s, and well into the 1970s — and with equal conspicuousness. There was one major difference, though. "In the old days when Mr. Hosmer was around," says Denis Laganière, "he couldn't have cared less if the place made money or not. If they only had fifty rooms rented he was actually quite pleased. The Ritz was his private club and that's the way he wanted it. But with Lord Hardinge, things were different. Very different."

Hardinge, the Fourth Viscount, was a huge, overpowering man with a strong aquiline nose, a bristling moustache, and a long, clumsy stride. He fairly charged, not walked, into the hotel and always, to the delight of patrons, with a pink carnation on the lapel of his sports jacket or suit. In the dead of winter he wore heavy topcoats, big fur hats, thick scarves, and gloves like elephant paws; boots, galoshes, or overshoes adorned his large, boat-like feet. Yet, on the coldest day of the year, he was known to be sockless.

"Whether Lord Hardinge had forgotten to put his socks on, or had been too lazy," a former banquet department secretary reflects, "I just don't know. Maybe he simply didn't like socks. What I *do* know for sure is that I found it terribly odd when he showed bare ankles at a publicity meeting soon after I started working there. After a while, of course, we got used to this kind of thing. We had to. That was Lord Hardinge — a real individual, and so beautifully theatrical without having to try to be."

Those who had encountered Hardinge once, however, discerned that the way he spoke sufficed to immortalize him. He had bestowed an aristocratic crispness upon an accent acquired at the Royal Military College in Sandhurst, England, and developed it further while working for a London firm of stockbrokers with the odd sounding name of Kitcat & Aitken. He later perfected his elocution in his job as aide-de-camp to Governor General Lord Willingdon, who brought him to Canada in 1926. There was one part of Hardinge's delivery he could not undo, though: a curious lisp-like impediment that made all his "th"s sound distinctly like "f"s. By this process, "thus" became "fuss" and "three" became "free." In the early 1970s, as the Ritz-Carlton cast studious eyes on its long term finances against a plethora of alterations, this lent itself to some considerable misinterpretation — particularly during the long years that Hardinge was chairman of the board.

To most patrons he was one of them, and unforgettable as the quintessential English Lord at a time when British titles in Canada were viewed with some suspicion. Those who knew him best, however, never questioned his credentials, even when they witnessed some of his unlordly behaviour. Peter Kilburn, who worked with Hardinge at Greenshields, once wrote, "Caryl was noisy, flamboyant, warm-hearted, indulgent, autocratic, rude, and terribly funny," and added, "His abounding energy made it impossible for anyone to forget that he was around."

They couldn't indeed. Hardinge's bluff, idiosyncratic style earned him amused, curious attention well beyond the Ritz-Carlton's public rooms and the Greenshields offices. He was known to the regular guests and staff at the Savoy Hotel in London and, for the Ritz-Carlton, this proved to be more than merely useful. He came to be considered what Dan

Lord Hardinge, known around the Ritz-Carlton as the quintessential English aristocrat. He was said to have been "noisy, flamboyant, warm-hearted, indulgent, autocratic, rude, and terribly funny." His abounding energy made it impossible for anyone to forget that he was around, and he attracted discriminating patrons like himself to the hotel by the score.

COURTESY OF THE RITZ-CARLTON COLLECTION

Doheny once called "a walking advertisement who collected people naturally"; in no time at all he was able to entice them to Montreal. "He was a magnet," Yvonne Contat recalls. "People warmed instantly to Caryl. The next thing you knew was that he had persuaded them to fly all the way to Canada just to sample the Café de Paris — after they had bought him a few drinks in the Maritime Bar, that is!"

That was Hardinge's favourite hangout and he made use of it every day, mooring himself at a corner table to which waiters could deliver the telephone. This in itself could prove to be a nuisance. His Lordship was known to invite friends for lunch, then spend almost the entire meal speaking with business associates in England. Heads at other tables turned not at *what* he said, but at *how* he said it, for Hardinge was rarely discreet, not the least after a big lunch when he was amply buttressed by spirits. "When it came to an argument or a heated discussion," Dan Doheny says, "dear Caryl was not given to the most literary language and, I'm afraid, he used rather a lot of malapropisms."

Nonetheless, whereas Elwood Hosmer turned patrons away, so Lord Hardinge attracted them. Many fitted the Ritz-Carlton mould more than merely adequately and thus became regular customers, and his friends: The Duke of Windsor, for example, whom he had already attracted, and E.P. Taylor, whom he had introduced to Dupré, recognizing that the two men had a common interest — stud farming. From that moment on, and thanks to Caryl Hardinge, Dupré and Taylor cross-bred their horses and became close friends in the process. "I spent more than half my time at the Ritz," Denyse Papineau remembers with a chuckle, "organizing flights and accommodation not for people, but for colts. And Mr. Dupré and Lord Hardinge were behind all this."

By combining his innate talents as a bon vivant with those of a compulsive raconteur, the gregarious Lord Hardinge also ensured that Montreal's most prominent families kept returning to the hotel in abundance, too. One head waiter marvelled that no fewer than five nights a week for more than twenty years, he "could be found in the same chair in the Maritime Bar, drinking well, eating well, or both, with as many as ten people at his table at a time."

No one was more delighted than Fred Laubi. He was about to take the Ritz-Carlton into a new and precarious decade.

CHAPTER ELEVEN

Something Old, Something New

*"The description 'grand hotel'
is only rightfully won after a generation
or more of consummate hospitality."*

THE GLOBE AND MAIL

In October, 1970, ten days after master barman Danny Flynn had marked his twenty-fifth year as a Ritzman by pouring Lord Hardinge a commemorative drink in the Maritime Bar, Fred Laubi launched the restoration program which, he said, would "polish the hotel's prestige image while helping it retain its essentially Continental character." Until then, the hotel had undergone what Laubi considered to be superficial refurbishing. Apart from the transformation of the Grand Ball Room into the Café de Paris and the Ritz Bar, and the lobby being enlarged to incorporate the big foyer, he considered that the changes had been merely "decorative."

Now the Ritz would be completely overhauled, room by room, restaurant by restaurant, salon by salon, bar by bar, for a further $3 million. And with Madame Contat now in retirement, the work had to be designed, and entirely supervised, by a major interior decorator: Henry End of the International Design Centre in Miami, Florida.

Lancashire-born End had consolidated his position as one of North America's most successful and influential hotel and restaurant designers. His work was admired from Kansas City to Los Angeles, and as far afield as Hamilton, Bermuda, and Gafsa, Tunisia, where he had refurbished 175 rooms and public spaces in the Hotel Sidi Ahmed Zarouk. Shortly after settling in Hollywood, California, at the close of World War II, he designed sets for *Joan of Arc* and *Forever Amber*, among other movies; he would lavish his keen sense of drama upon the entire Ritz-Carlton Hotel.

His professional prowess was aptly captured by the magazine, *Canadian Interiors*. The moment it heard that Canada's long surviving privately owned hotel was undergoing such monumental changes, it wrote:

> Henry End is a set designer in the extravagant Oliver Messel and Cecil Beaton tradition. Everything is always a little overpowering but also in faultless taste. His jobs have a sense of occasion — when Aunt Millie can wear her grandmother's hocked tiara, and an International Set party with champagne corks popping, pheasant flown over from the Duke of Buccleuch's moors, and foie gras sent as a gift from the Compte de Paris would seem very much in place there.

Much of the Ritz-Carlton's restoration was overseen by Henry End's chief designer, a lean and loquacious man named George Ray, from from Surrey, England, where he studied both art and architecture.

In the first part of "Operation Facelift," as the management had christened its restoration plan, work was begun on bedrooms and suites on the top three floors. New electrical wiring was installed, with exquisite light fixtures, principally crystal chandeliers. Bedrooms and suites were given extra colour with curtains and upholstery made of bright, European fabrics. About 100 guest rooms, Laubi discovered, had been left without air conditioning when previous managers had surpassed their renovation budgets, and this was immediately remedied. Other rooms still had old black and white TVs, which were exchanged for colour sets. "Who watches black and white television in the 1970s?" Laubi asked. "I don't. So why should the guests?"

Bathrooms were ripped apart and given more up-to-date plumbing and tiling. Many of the hotel's large porcelain bathtubs remained, but those found to be cracked or chipped were replaced "with the biggest we could find," Laubi said. Additional marble shelving and extra lighting were fitted above shining porcelain sinks with gold plated taps. No one, however, dared demolish the high, embossed ceilings or the huge cupboards in the bathrooms and bedrooms. In fact, in some cases, the cupboards were repaired and replaced, and ornamental moulding was actually added to numerous ceilings in suites and public rooms through the entire building.

In November, 1971, a kosher kitchen was installed to cater occasional meals or large banquets. The idea for this, which sprang from a board meeting, was quickly seconded by Lord Hardinge. He had discovered, he said, that a lot of his friends were Jews. Six months later, the attendant-operated elevators were converted to automatic, and work was started on remodelling bedrooms, suites, and salons on the sixth and lower floors.

Shortly afterwards, the lobby was enlarged yet again, according to a design George Ray completed in a single night. He toiled so hard on giving this part of the hotel a new look, in fact, that he forgot to go to bed; office staffers arriving for work at 8.30 a.m. next day were bemused to discover him sound asleep on the board room table in a grey suit and tie, his papers and brushes strewn across the floor.

Under Ray's watchful gaze, workmen soon demolished the glass partition that separated it from the Palm Court. Old moulding and panels were torn away and motifs that harkened back to ancient Greece were fixed in their place. The entire entrance area was eventually given a new personality by George Ray's daring colour scheme: rich black with burnt-amber, burnished gold, and russet. All spilled into the former Palm Court and the elevators, as well as into a large recess housing the cloakroom and washrooms, at the foot of the curving staircase.

The new decor helped accentuate the gleaming brass balustrades, door fixtures, and lamps, and create a feeling of what the hotel called "unpretentious luxury." Whatever it was, it quickly appealed to Hollywood film makers. The newly constructed lobby, and a corner of the Ritz Garden, which Laubi had the good sense to leave intact, were transformed a few years ago to resemble New York City's imposing Russian Tea Room as part of the set for the movie *Dreamworld*.

No sooner was the restoration begun than Laubi, his pursuit of "a better prestige image" firmly in his mind, ordered new staff uniforms. Overnight, dark blue and gold was replaced by neutral browns, dark umber, and taupe, which would make those employees who were visible to the public a part of the decor. Waiters wore suits with vests and a Ritz identification button, the doormen knee length coats with visor caps in summer and double breasted top coats with lambswool hats in winter.

For women, simple A-line, knee length dresses were deemed to be "the most flattering and discreet." Here again, the colours used were various shades of light brown broken by touches of gold. They were compatible with the decor of the silent halls the maids trod numerous times each day. In a concerted effort to remain as old-fashioned as it dared, the Ritz resumed the practice of expecting maids to wear evening uniforms of chocolate brown and white.

As the hotel was being restyled, remodelled, and reorganized, so life inside it ambled on almost unhindered, and Denis Laganière's loyalty to everything the Ritz-Carlton had ever stood for was at last to be rewarded. "We were working like hell," he says, "and the lobby was a mess. Many

A committee of six Montreal rabbis inaugurates the Ritz-Carlton's kosher kitchen, November, 1971, to cater occasional meals or large banquets.

PHOTO BY VARKONS STUDIO
COURTESY OF THE RITZ-CARLTON COLLECTION

times I was sitting in the cloakroom watching the guys rip down walls. 'What am I going to do?' I was thinking. When you're married with kids and you hear a girl is going to take over your job, you start wondering what's eventually going to happen to you."

His apprehension was allayed when, in the fall of 1972 — only weeks before chef Pierre Demers captained the Canadian team which placed fourth in the International Culinary Olympics in Frankfurt, Germany — Fred Laubi sent an assistant manager down to see Laganière.

"From now on," the manager told him, "we want you to be our new concierge."

"Me?" Laganière said. "Me — really?"

"Yes," the manager replied. "You're the best man we've got for the job. Good luck."

For the first time in Ritz-Carlton history, a concierge instead of a head porter would dignify the lobby. Essentially, the two jobs were the same, and always had been, but the title "concierge" would add a definite Continental flavour to the hotel. As he replaced the retiring head porter John Murphy, Laganière, a nimble, puckish man with tousled hair, quick feet, and sharp, darting eyes, would carry this to its fullest. "I was so surprised!" he recalls. "I'd now got the opportunity I'd always wanted, and it brought out a certain strength in me to do something I never thought I could. My life changed. At last I started getting a monthly salary instead of an hourly rate, and not losing pay when I was sick!"

Virtually from one day to the next, Laganière shed the vest he had worn as a cloakroom attendant and began to wear the newly designed concierge's suit. Now, he knew, he could play a larger role in the actual running of the lobby, inflicting upon it his own quality control, which he would monitor studiously. When he arrived at the hotel at 8 a.m. each day, his first jobs were to raise the hotel's flags, update the functions board, and call the first limousines to take departing guests to the airport. Then he was free to consult the black leather log book left by the night porter, for "yesterday's list of overhanging jobs" — chores still to be done.

Typically, the log book told him to make flight arrangements for certain guests, order their theatre tickets, or gather information for them on the next two or three Montreal Canadiens home hockey games. "Anything," says Laganière, "that might save time or provide a little bit of luxury." Numerous times, as César Ritz had stipulated, he chased lost luggage, gave directions, and made restaurant reservations outside the hotel. Most of his day, though, was spent running errands. "My suit will be ready at four," one man said as he left the hotel for a meeting. "Can you pop over to Holt Renfrew and pick it up for me?"

"Certainly, Sir," said Denis Laganière. "It'll be in your room by the time you get back."

When visitors were sick he would call doctors and run to drugstores for prescriptions. He has shopped for and packed, paintings, sculptures, fur coats, bottles of liquor, children's toys, and meat, and all with cheerful dispatch.

Then, he says, there were the people who only checked into the hotel once in a while — "and they'd come back to stay with us after a couple of years and we would still remember who they were. It took years of practice, mind, but it was worth it. We made people feel special and felt good about ourselves doing it."

By now Laganière was taking famous and familiar faces for granted. Many a day the revolving door would spin with the introduction of a visitor who, only a few nights before, the staff had seen on television — Mike Wallace, perhaps, Kathleen Turner, or Christopher Plummer. He or she would now be accompanied by a bellboy, and a porter wheeling a dozen pieces of luggage on an impressive brass trolley.

"Good morning, Mr. Plummer," the Ritz-Carlton's new concierge would say. "It's nice to see you back."

"Good morning, Denis. It's nice to *be* back."

The concierge reflects, "When you've worked here as long as I have, you don't treat famous people like the ordinary public does. You get so used to seeing them and serving them that you treat them like they always wanted to be, as an honoured guest. You don't go asking them for their autograph and things like that. They get that sort of thing from their fans. If they want you to have their autograph, they'll offer it to you."

"No," says John Dominique, a portly, grey, fatherly figure who oversees the Ritz Café devotedly, "but I still get quite excited when I'm reminded where I'm working. Famous people don't fizz on me so much anymore, just the fact that we're working in a place that they love to come. But I'd be very happy to see Tommy Lasorda of the Los Angeles Dodgers walk in. I think I'd be just as pleased to serve him a drink as I would the Queen."

To coincide with Operation Facelift, the Ritz redesigned its graphics, primarily for its letterhead and menus. Ever since Emile Charles Des Baillets' days, its corporate logo had been the "Ritz Lion," whose appearance had never been standardized. On some menus, and in several advertisements the hotel had placed in Canadian newspapers, the animal had appeared fierce and scowling; at various other times it had been benign or smiling. Indeed, over the years since the animal had first been incorporated into the Montreal perception of the Ritz Idea, it had been portrayed in as many as seventeen different ways, and it was high time, Laubi said, for only one.

But which one? "The best," the general manager replied. "The one that will help make people remember us as a class organization."

Artists were assigned to create a new conception of how the Ritz Lion should look in the 1970s, and the version finally chosen resembles one that is quickly associated with medieval heraldry. It shows the lion rearing up determinedly, and somewhat ferociously, in a posture that has come to symbolize the Ritz-Carlton's unyielding determination never to live through impoverished years again, and to fight off those intrusions that threaten to detract from all it stands for.

Unquestionably, the major of these was the modern vice of informality, against which the Ritz had begun to struggle valiantly. It was becoming increasingly difficult as time moved on. Other hotels had either never adopted formality, or had long since abandoned it, succumbing to waves of public taste and opinion. At the Ritz-Carlton, however, every effort was being made to retain formality as an integral, lingering component of the original Ritz formula.

While the formal-wear-for-dinner rule had long since been relaxed, the hotel still expected men to wear jackets and ties in its public rooms. Rather than turn bare-necked offenders away, head waiters could offer them one of a several ties the hotel had bought for this very purpose; but the Ritz firmly refused to invest in a stock of jackets, as Contat had once suggested it should. That, the directors felt, was going too far. "If our male patrons are insensitive enough to arrive for drinks or a meal in, say, shirtsleeves or a sweater — well it's impossible," Fred Laubi shrugged. "They must leave. You see, our regular visitors have always known the rules here, and have welcomed them. They *expect* to see other patrons nicely dressed in our public rooms."

It was against this backcloth and amid this continuing philosophy of keeping the Ritz quaintly old-fashioned and conservative that, in July, 1972, John Dominique was horrified to notice a British rock group, the Rolling Stones, trying to enter the Café de Paris in bomber jackets and jeans. The group had checked into a sixth-floor suite and, to maintain its privacy, rented the entire floor. The management, meanwhile, expected the worst. "Quite frankly," says Peter Ryles, "we were afraid that these guys might attract hords of fans who wouldn't appreciate the hotel and end up wrecking it."

Once, the Rolling Stones decided to risk being hounded by fans, to eat in the Café de Paris. As soon as they were hungry, they barrelled through the lobby, now rubble-free at last and sparkling with what *Canadian Interiors* called "a sense of drama and surprise," and approached the restaurant, where they had reserved two corner tables.

They never reached them. They had been perfectly welcome to register in the hotel under the names of "P. Ginger" and "Biggles" to help hide their identity. The management had agreed to that. But to be seen jacketless by other patrons in its main dining room? This, was another matter; it could not be tolerated at the Ritz — even for the Rolling Stones. "Excuse me, Gentlemen," said Dominique crisply, "but would you all be so kind as to return to your rooms for whatever jackets and ties you may have brought with you? I think our regular dining room guests would prefer that."

Taken by such diplomacy, it should be recorded, the group obliged. At the Ritz-Carlton Hotel they were no trouble at all, and Peter Ryles would be the first to admit it. "They were decent guys," he says. "They really were. And when they left their suite it was just as clean and tidy as it was when they first moved into it."

Israeli foreign minister Abba Eban was among the next group of celebrities to choose to stay at the Ritz, as he had on several previous occasions. He arrived in May, 1973, while restoration work continued on some of the lower floors, to stay in the Royal Suite. He was suitably attired for it in a blue pinstriped suit, and was just as friendly as ever, even though he was tired.

It was around 1.30 a.m. when Peter Ryles took Eban and his wife to their suite. They, and several advisors, secretaries, and bodyguards, had checked into the hotel two-and-a-half hours late because of a flight delay. Peter Ryles knew that only too well. He had waited behind especially to greet them.

In those days, the Ritz-Carlton's night chef worked only until midnight, but Abba Eban and his entourage was not only tired, but hungry. "Can you get us all something to eat?" he asked.

"I didn't want to let the Ritz down," Ryles says, "so I decided to do the best I could and produce a meal there and then."

He got the key to the main kitchen from the night manager and, reliving his days as a floor waiter, instantly set about preparing a hearty breakfast of eggs, potatoes, and toast for twelve people. Because all the hotel's food is freshly prepared each day, he saw nothing he could serve for dessert until he came upon a bowl of fruit salad, which he ladled into cut glass dishes. With tea and coffee, it was an acceptable meal indeed.

"That was very good," Eban said. "By the way, when does this hotel serve breakfast?"

"Breakfast, Sir?" Ryles said. "But haven't you just had it — early?"

"I'm always hungry," Abba Eban said. "Always."

Notables continued to flood into the Ritz-Carlton Hotel for their dinners and private meetings even though some of the mezzanine public rooms were still being redesigned. Almost without exception, they were unperturbed by the mess. Governor General Jules Léger, Yehudi Menuhin, Prime Minister Giullio Andriotti of Italy, the premier of Venezuela, and film actress Gina Lollobrigida all savoured the kind of hospitality that was still a growing legend. Then, on Sunday, July 18, 1976, after a day at the Olympic Games, Queen Elizabeth and Prince Philip stopped by on only two hours notice.

Concerned for her safety following scattered but angry demonstration against the Royal visit by members of Quebec's separatist movement, the Queen's security staff advised her not to return to the Royal Yacht to rest before her state banquet that night, but to check into the Ritz, where the function was to take place. Each member of the hotel's staff likely to work near her on such short notice, underwent a hasty official security check. The management, principally Fred Laubi and Daniel Doheny, met the Royal couple in the lobby and accompanied them to a third-floor suite where they could bathe, relax, and dress before attending the banquet in the Oval Room at eleven o'clock that night.

One of the Queen's first considerations, though, was to entertain her security men and women at a small reception, which was held in the freshly decorated Blue Room. "I was really in a terrible mess this time," Peter Ryles remembers, shaking his head. "I didn't have the heart to serve the Queen's people drinks in the glasses we used for other guests."

He called Fred Laubi, who had gone upstairs to his penthouse. "Can't we serve the Queen and her people drinks in *crystal* glasses?" Ryles asked. "I mean, we've got to do something a bit different and special for her."

Laubi agreed. "Of course," he said. "If it's glasses you want, come up right away and I'll lend you whatever you need."

Back in the Blue Room, where Daniel Doheny was talking to the Royal staff, Ryles set out Fred Laubi's Italian crystal glasses (almost identical with those he had ordered for the Gritt Palace), on a crisp white tablecloth and asked, "May I get you all a drink?"

"No, thank you so much," said Prince Philip, "we've brought our own."

Most of the liquor required for the reception had already been delivered. In one sweeping movement, however, the Prince drew a bottle of Beefeater gin from a briefcase like a cavalier drawing a sword, and plunked it onto the table.

Ryles suspected that his offer to pour drinks from the Ritz bar had been refused for security reasons, and understood perfectly. By the time members of the Royal family check into a hotel, their menus — like the one already drawn up for that night's state dinner — have been arranged well in advance. On their arrival, their food and drinks are prepared under strict supervision so as to lessen the chances of sabotage. In fact, as Ryles watched the Queen's butler serve her a gin and tonic, RCMP officers and city detectives were sampling the banquet food in the kitchen — and enjoying every mouthful. "Just a formality," oine policemen explained. "We all know that the Queen can trust the Ritz."

"Well, is there *anything* I can do for you, Your Majesty?" Ryles persisted in the Blue Room.

"No thank you," said Prince Philip brightly, as the Royal butler handed him a dry martini, "everything is just fine."

It wasn't with Ryles, the room service manager, though.

Returning to the Blue Room after the reception to escort the Queen and Prince Philip backto suite 310, he was pained by the notion that they may not have been properly received. "Why on earth," he was thinking, "haven't they been given the Royal Suite? They should have the Royal Suite!" On checking that day's lists of reservations and registrations, he discovered that because the hotel had not been advised in sufficient time that the Queen and Prince Philip were arriving, the Royal Suite had been given instead to Liberace, who was playing at Place des Arts.

"Just imagine," mumbled a manager. "We've got the Queen in 310 and Liberace's doubtless relaxing in bubbles in one of the Royal bathrooms!"

Laubi said, "Had we known in good enough time that Her Majesty was coming, of course we would have reserved the Royal Suite for her. That goes without saying."

There was nothing unusual at all about entertainers staying in the Royal Suite. Like superstars of sport, an increasing number of them discovered that they could actually afford it. Maestros Franz-Paul Decker and Zubin Mehta, and singer Harry Belafonte were among those who rented it often. Usually, the suite was reserved weeks and sometimes months ahead of time, for politicians, important industrialists, and heads of state. Every provincial premier slept in its big four poster bed during the 1970s, as did Louis Rasminsky, governor of the Bank of Canada, Governor General Roland Michener, and the presidents of Mexico and Argentina.

More often than not, though, celebrities were quite happy to indulge themselves in an ordinary Ritz suite, and the British actor Oliver Reed was no exception. He arrived at the hotel with a flourish in October, 1977, and was more than happy with rooms 601 and 602. Peter Ryles says he will never forget him.

"Are you in charge of room service?" Reed asked him.

"Yes," said Ryles. "I have been for some time."

"Good," said Reed.

At that, he took a $100 bill from his pocket, tore it into two pieces, and pressed one of them into Ryles' hand. "That bit's for you," Reed said. Then, tucking the other part of the bill into his pocket, he added, "You will get this only if I get my dinner — in half an hour."

Ryles couldn't get down to the kitchen fast enough. "Stop everything!" he roared, as he swept through the big swing doors.

He gave the chef $20, placed Reed's order, and told the story of the actor's arrival. The kitchen staff agreed unanimously that $100 was far too good to miss and the meal, a plate of smoked salmon with steamed vegetables, was instantly prepared. Ryles looked on with one eye on his watch and the other on the sous-chef who was laying out asparagus, carrots, and little pieces of sweet potato as if he were crazy-paving a driveway.

His shoulders square with pride, and with six minutes to spare, Ryles placed the meal on a trolley. He wheeled it into the service elevator and then along the hallway to the actor's room. Oliver Reed, freshly showered and perfumed, opened the door in a Japanese bathrobe and declared in a voice that was almost certainly heard by all the guests on that floor, and possibly the one above, "You're under arrest!"

Ryles looked bemused. He had produced the meal on time. What more did his guest expect from him? He was relieved to see Reed's malleable face quickly crinkle into a smile. Well satisfied with room service, he gave Peter Ryles a friendly pat on the back, and the other portion of the $100 bill.

Such was thirty minutes in the working life of one of the Ritz-Carlton's venerable department managers, and no one ever dared tell him that his assignments were boring or uneventful. If Peter Ryles had not seen or heard it all, Fred Laubi certainly had.

All the same, in the fall of 1977, when restoration was all but

Fernand Roberge, the Ritz-Carlton's ebullient chief administrator.
Champagne corks popped at an Oval Room party on the night of November 15,
1977, when 600 guests bade farewell to Fred Laubi, and welcomed his
successor. At the age of only thirty-six, Roberge became the Ritz-Carlton's first
French Canadian general manager, and its youngest ever.
He is now executive vice-president and a director.

PHOTO COURTESY OF THE RITZ-CARLTON COLLECTION

complete, he told his staff he would be departing to manage L'Hôtel de Paris in Monte Carlo. His plans for the Ritz, he felt, had been achieved, and it was time to move on. "Before Fred Laubi came along to breathe fresh winds into the sometimes arid conservatism of the Ritz," said *Maclean's*, "the hotel had taken on a legend of stuffy eccentricity. Now all that was changed."

A hasty search for a successor began, and one day shortly after announcing his resignation Laubi met Fernand Roberge, the exuberant young general manager of Montreal's Hotel Bonaventure, and told him of his impending departure.

"Who's taking over from you?" Roberge asked casually.

"They haven't found anybody yet," Laubi replied. "Are you interested in the job?"

"Maybe," said Roberge. "Maybe."

The Bonaventure, then part of the Westin chain, had considered sending Roberge to San Francisco to manage its recently-built St. Francis Hotel, but he had other ideas. He wanted to remain in Montreal and was more than merely encouraged when, a few days after meeting Laubi, he received a telephone call from Dan Doheny, who invited him to meet one of the Ritz-Carlton directors. "He and I would be very interested in talking with you," Doheny said.

In only days, Fernand Roberge was ushered into a reliquary office at Greenshields, where none other than Lord Hardinge, his pink carnation precisely in place, had seated himself stiffly behind a large desk.

"So you think you can run the Ritz," he glowered.

"You're damn right I think I can," Roberge replied impulsively. "Damn right!"

"Good," said Hardinge, taken aback with the young man's intrepidity. "That's very good."

The outcome was that on the bitterly cold night of November 15, 1977, champagne corks popped at an Oval Room party at which 600 guests bade farewell to Fred Laubi, and welcomed his successor. At the age of only thirty-six, Fernand Roberge was hired as the Ritz-Carlton's first French Canadian general manager, and its youngest ever. He burst upon Canada's oldest privately-owned hotel with panache, zeal, and purpose, and a fund of ideas for administering it in modern times.

Like virtually all his predecessors, Roberge came with experience drawn from hoteliery's most arduous ranks. He was from tiny Laurierville, Quebec, about twenty-five miles from Thetford-Mines, the son of the general merchant who supplied the neighbourhood with everything from

René Gounel, who joined the Ritz as its manager two months after Roberge arrived, settling in as the perfect compliment to him. "I make quick, gut-feeling decisions," Roberge says, "and René follows behind me with an incredible eye for detail." Gounel is now general manager.

PHOTO COURTESY OF THE RITZ-CARLTON COLLECTION

meat, vegetables, and bicycles, to shoes, hardware, and plants. His grandfather, Eusèbe Roberge, the riding's member of Parliament, owned the large house opposite the village church, and after his death the family ran it as a guest house.

This gave young Fernand the taste for hotels as a career and, at fourteen, when his family moved to Quebec City, he spent his weekends and summer holidays at Motel de Laurentide, working alternately as a busboy, bellboy, waiter, or bartender. At the age of twenty, he attended L'Ecole Hôtelière de Lausanne for three years, worked for a year as assistant manager at the Queen Elizabeth Hotel, Montreal, and then became an assistant manager at Miami's Biltmore Hotel. Just when it was built, he joined the Hotel Bonaventure as rooms division manager. He was twenty-six. Four years later, he occupied the general manager's office.

Fernand Roberge arrived at the Ritz as it was beginning to lose money again, largely because competition was stiffer than it had ever been. A glut of hotels, including the Bonaventure, had been built for Expo '67; by the mid-1970s, many more had sprung up to accommodate visitors to the Olympic Games. Now that both Expo and the Olympics were over, the fifty percent increase in the number of rooms these hotels provided far exceeded the demand.

According to the Hotel Association of Greater Montreal, a hotel needs a sixty-five percent occupancy rate to break even. Yet, in December 1977, the association's membership, which includes all major city establishments, reported an average rate of only thirty-eight percent. The problem was compounded by the election of a Parti Québécois government, which severely crippled tourism and sent thousands of English Montrealers — many of them longstanding Ritz patrons — out of the province for good.

Despite its trademarks of elegance and quality, and after having invested considerably in renovation, decoration, and restoration, the Ritz-Carlton had only a thirty-four percent occupancy rate for January, 1978, and Roberge began a struggle to turn business around. To help him, he called upon a former Bonaventure colleague named René Gounel, whom he had first met in Calgary in 1966 and hired in 1967 as the Bonaventure's assistant front office manager.

Gounel joined the Ritz as its manager two months after Roberge, and settled in quickly as the perfect assistant for him. A lot has evolved since then, though. Roberge is now the hotel's executive vice-president and a director, and Gounel has been promoted to general manager. They work as a duo in harmonious cordiality.

"I make quick, gut-feeling decisions," Roberge admits, "and René follows behind me with an incredible eye for detail. He's the guy who says, 'Hold on a minute! We'd be better do it this way.' And he's usually right."

Gounel throws open his hands in semi-apology. "Maybe it's my nature," he says, and it doubtless is. He is worldly, seemingly imperturbable, and decidedly European, with one foot rooted firmly in the old school tradition of hoteliery, and the other in Montreal in the 1980s. "In Europe," he adds, "we tend to be a little more cautious and try to analyze all the implications. We don't jump into things." But, he concedes, "I make a lot of fast decisions, too, which are always based on my experience."

That experience stretches back to Nice, where René Gounel grew up. He learned his business by attending a hotel school for three years and by working in the evenings and during holidays. The next two years were spent as a waiter at the Bermudiana Hotel in Hamilton, Bermuda, where he learned impeccable English. He later spent a year at Quebec City's Manoir St. Castin, first as a dining room captain and then as a desk clerk, and another few months as a room clerk at the Calgary Inn, where Roberge had gone to interview him.

Now together at the Ritz, Roberge and Gounel assessed its financial dilemma as gravely as Frederick Collins had reviewed the accountant's books back in 1939. Although business at the hotel had gradually improved — by 1978, the average yearly occupancy rate was fifty-six percent and, by 1980, nearly seventy percent — the hotel had lost more than $1 million of $8 million-worth of anticipated revenues. The debt was spiralling, and business was declining; the exuberant Roberge was challenged to halt the slide and recover what was lost, and more.

It was a challenge, indeed. In retrospect, the Ritz was suffering through Montreal's worst-ever hotel slump, in which the so-called "luxury establishments" were the first and most acutely affected. The dilemma was certainly not aided by the world wide recession which followed. Roberge and Gounel vowed to meet this obligation head on.

Shrewdly, they realized that the Ritz-Carlton Hotel had moved into a new age in which competition was fierce and was likely to remain so for many years to come. Their hotel was still the best in Montreal, they felt, but certain aspects of it needed drastic improvement. As Gounel says, "The product was not as good as it could have been, not by our standards, anyway." Systematically, he and Roberge made a list of both the hotel's strengths and weaknesses. They realized that it still had a superb reputation, and worked from that point on. Instead of cutting expenses and trimming back service, as other managers had so reluctantly been forced to do, they took a different approach. Even though Fred Laubi had invested heavily in new staff, increased services, and carried out physical improvements to the building, Roberge and Gounel realized that they would have to augment his efforts, whatever the cost, thereby making the hotel more competitive while upholding its standards.

One of their first projects was to commission a Montreal marketing firm to conduct a survey which asked 100 upscale French Canadians, and as many upper income English Canadians, which hotel would be their first choice when making reservations for their clients. The survey also asked participants which hotels they would choose for themselves as the site of an important private dinner or a wedding reception, and where they immediately thought of going for fine dining. Their responses provided a variety of insightful answers and spurred Roberge and Gounel to devise numerous "vitalizing plans," most of which were launched simultaneously and immediately. All were designed to make the Ritz-Carlton's services far better known and more accessible.

First, the two men recognized from the survey that although their hotel had a fine reputation and was well known, it needed to be streamlined. This meant that the Ritz had to be led into the computer age, which Roberge and Gounel considered an investment that would pay for itself many times over. "If we were to hold our own in an increasingly busy marketplace," Roberge reflects, "there could be no half measures."

Computers were installed to record inventory and stock, and to pay wages and bills; for the first time ever, front desk clerks tapped out registrations on an electronic keyboard, and, as guests checked out, pressed two or three keys to print out their bills.

The most crucial element of this, however, was that guests' needs, which previous managers has diligently recorded in notebooks, were also now available at the touch of a few buttons, in computer files that could be accessed only by senior management. Computers, then, began to keep up-to-date data on the history of all clients — solely for their comfort — from the frequency of their visits and the rooms or suites they preferred to sleep in, to what they expected from room service and what meals they enjoyed most in which restaurants, and how they usually asked for their food to be prepared. "We wanted the hotel to remain exquisitely traditional," Gounel explains, "while modernizing the back of the house to refine and broaden service."

He and Roberge then concluded that they needed aggressive marketing

The Royal Suite bedroom. It has panels of white silk on its walls,
a white corniced ceiling, and a marble floor that sprawls beneath a sunburst
of gathered, off white silk. The bedspread and bedskirt are of a co-ordinated
fabric, and the furniture, made in France, is a mixture of the Louis XV and
Louis XVI styles.

PHOTO COURTESY OF THE RITZ-CARLTON COLLECTION

techniques to ensure that the hotel was constantly being mentioned in the media. So they increased their marketing staff from two people to ten, and opened a sales office in Toronto. Their efforts were aimed at reaching out for a broader clientele. Indeed, throughout its entire history, the survey showed, too, the Ritz had been perceived as a hotel run by Europeans for Europeans, but with a local patronage that was exclusively English Canadian. The French Canadians had been left out.

"Absolutely!" says Montreal writer François Smet. "We always stood in awe of the Ritz as a place where we couldn't afford to go, and a place that was frequented by so-called foreigners with whom we had nothing in common. This had to change."

True, Montreal businessman Paul Desmarais was often to be seen in the Café de Paris with clients or political leaders, and Maurice Duplessis had made the Palm Court his second home. But Smet, author of a television drama about Duplessis' life, says, "Desmarais hails from Sudbury, Ontario, and, rightly or wrongly, was never perceived as a true French Canadian, which he really is. And Duplessis? He hung out at the Ritz because he didn't want French Canadians, the people who entrusted him with power, to see him at his antics — drinking extravagantly and having the province's richest Anglophones among his closest friends. He knew the staff there would keep quiet about that. Besides, before the liquor laws were changed, the Ritz was the only place in town that would discreetly serve him a drink without a meal on a Sunday."

Roberge and Gounel wanted the Ritz to be more readily accepted by the French Canadian population at large, and they embarked on a plan to make it so. Roberge led this drive, he says, by first seeking to attract the French-Canadian "elite" he had known back at the Bonaventure — young Québécois professionals whom he felt were "rising stars about to become the big guns." As soon as they could appreciate the Ritz's history and ambience, and afford its prices, he hoped, they would become fixtures in its public rooms alongside the English.

To attract new and younger patrons in the bloom of their careers, the Ritz had to introduce extra amenities. Or, as Roberge says, "We had to fix the place up." He and Gounel ardently began to modernize the hotel further while preserving not only its turn-of-the-century Continental character now, but also the fine remodelling that had already been done. To anyone who argued that the Ritz-Carlton had been refurbished, decorated, and restored enough and had always been attractive, Roberge had a quick response: "Yes, I know. But where are all the new people going to go?" He remembers, "The Ritz Café didn't appeal to them, the

The Royal study walls are padded and covered with bottle green moiré, the same material from which the curtains are made. The beige ceiling is decorated with a green-gold and bronze trim, and the furniture, upholstered in green, gold, and bronze tufted leather, was imported from England. Note the fine Louis XV desk.

PHOTO COURTESY OF THE RITZ-CARLTON COLLECTION

Maritime Bar was too small, and the hotel had no night life. René and I had to do something about his, and fast."

By late 1978, they were already addressing these needs. They enlarged the Maritime Bar by forty percent, and, in that part of the basement that had once housed the Ritz Café at Night and the kitchen where the Air France meals had been prepared, they introduced the moderately priced Intercontinental Restaurant and a brand new piano bar called the Grand Prix. All this added a further $2 million to the $3 million already spent by Fred Laubi.

Only time would tell if the investment was worth it. Nonetheless, when the new public rooms emerged, it was just cause for celebration. On February 8, 1979, the management threw a huge cocktail party that stretched well into the following day and brought Lord Hardinge back from a vacation in the Bahamas — just to satisfy himself that decorators had not displaced his "private" table in the Maritime Bar. They hadn't, of course. They wouldn't have dared to. "Viscount Hardinge's table, which he has occupied for many years," the *Gazette* reported solemnly, "remains in its appointed place."

With the Ritz marketing staff hard at work and business generally showing signs of booming again, Roberge and his fellow directors decided to enlarge and redecorate the Royal Suite. That was in the spring of 1985. The suite now has four bedrooms, two complete kitchens, a master dining room, a study, a grand salon, a reception room, a dining room, and seven marble bathrooms. The job of creating the decorations and supervising them fell yet again to George Ray, whose frequent visits to the hotel had since made him a regular patron in the Ritz Bar. He did an impeccable job indeed, choosing furniture and accessories to honour the Ritz heritage, while conveying the warmth, comfort, and individuality of a luxuriously appointed home.

The Royal bedroom is predominantly white, with panels of white silk on its walls, a white corniced ceiling, and floors made of a classic French pattern of Italian carrara marble inlaid with marble from Belgium. The focal point is the bed itself. It sprawls beneath a sunburst of gathered, off white silk and is surrounded by silk hangings — salmon on the outside and silver-grey on the inside — suspended from a ceiling cornice. The bedspread and bedskirt are of a coordinating fabric. The furniture, made in France, is a mixture of the Louis XV and Louis XVI styles.

In the adjacent Vice-Royal bedroom, the walls are covered with a light aubergine Italian wallpaper. The curtains and bedspread, imported from France, are of aubergine cotton prints. The canopied bed is dressed with

In the Royal dining room, an eighteenth-century crystal chandelier from Ireland is suspended over a Louis XVI table that seats eight people. The ceiling and walls are both of sepia canvas. Montreal artist George Di Carlo, whose talent is also displayed in the Maritime Bar, has decorated the room with a scene of a horse in the Amazon.

PHOTO COURTESY OF THE RITZ-CARLTON COLLECTION

matching drapes, and a small sitting area is decorated with sage green sofas.

The walls in the third bedroom are adorned with pale pink silk; the paint work is in a light, matching lavender, and the bedspread and drapes, which complement the walls, have a decidedly Japanese influence in their design. The furniture is mainly in the style of Louis XVI, finished in off white lacquer.

The Royal guest room is equipped with a king size bed covered with a cotton print bedspread in shades of beige, red, grey, and blue. The furniture comprises mainly French and English "period" pieces upholstered in grey-blue velvet.

The main Royal bathroom, with its pinkish-grey porcelain fixtures which are gold plated and imported from Germany, has a European bidet, a direct-dial telephone, and a whirlpool bathtub. In a second Royal bathroom, where the gold plated fixtures are set in silver-grey porcelain, there is a cedar sauna.

Except for its pink marble floor — Rosa Aurora, imported from Italy — the bathroom in the Vice-Royal suite is similar to the Royal bathroom. A second one there is lined with light travertine marble and has an oak ceiling and rosewood cabinets; all the remaining bathrooms are in Rosa Aurora marble.

The Royal study walls are padded and covered with bottle green moiré, the same material from which the curtains are made. The beige ceiling has been decorated with a green-gold and bronze trim, and the furniture, upholstered in green, gold, and bronze tufted leather, imported from England. The room is given a "classical" atmosphere by a Louis XV desk, two Louis XVI étagères, and an eighteenth-century English coffee table.

Here, though, the focal point is a sound system complete with a tapedeck and two colour television sets hooked to a VCR. Encased in a wooden cabinet, the system pipes music to all Royal Suite rooms, each of which has its own separate set of controls.

The velvet-walled grand salon in the Royal Suite is predominantly grey with a marble fireplace, and a blend of furnishings in the Renaissance, Louis XV, Louis XVI, Japanese, and Chinese styles. The dining room walls and ceiling are both of sepia canvas on which Montreal artist George Di Carlo, whose talent can also be seen on the ceiling of the Maritime Bar, has painted a scene of a horse in the Amazon. An eighteenth-century Irish cut lead crystal chandelier is suspended over a Louis XVI dining table that seats eight people. The chairs are in the Regency style, and the decor is completed by a baroque sideboard and a set of bitter-green velvet chairs.

Silk — light green this time — has been used yet again in the reception room. The furnishings here consist mainly of a marquetry table that can accommodate eight diners, too, with what decorators call "Chinese Chippendale" chairs. A sitting area has several Louis XV *bergères*, a steel, glass topped table, and a comfortable sofa covered with rich grey-blue jacquard.

Among the first to sleep in the new Royal Suite were Governor General Jeanne Sauvé, Juan Antonio Samaranch, president of the International Olympic Committee, Brian Mulroney, actress Eva Gabor, Italy's Prime Minister Bettino Craxi, and former United States President Gerald Ford.

Enlarging the suite certainly enhanced the Ritz-Carlton Hotel, but meant the immediate loss of seven guest rooms, reducing the number from 247 to 240. True to form, though, Fernand Roberge, who has cultivated a distinct taste for luxury himself since leaving tiny Laurierville to take on the hotel world, is unruffled. "The rewards far outweigh the disadvantages," he says. "We can now pamper *ourselves* a little by boasting the most luxurious, prestigious accommodation for royalty in the country."

CHAPTER TWELVE

Modern Times —
the Best of Times

"Above all, that's what has made this familiar
Montreal landmark what it is today —
a symbol in an age when such symbols are in short
supply, of refinement and gracious living."

CANADIAN HERITAGE

The extra money and thought that Roberge and Gounel devoted
to Operation Facelift was eminently well invested, as was the annual
sales and marketing budget of $1 million that both men felt was necessary
in 1985 to achieve their ends. That January, the monthly business
magazine *Revue Commerce* selected Roberge as its Man of the Month for
"saving the Ritz," and many people firmly believed he did just that.

True to his plan, new patrons had soon poured into the hotel by the
hundreds — big-spending executives like Roger Landry, publisher of *La
Presse*, Ronald Corey, president of the Montreal Canadiens, the
developer Maurice Pinsonneault, Marc Bourgie, who owns a chain of
funeral homes, and Laurent Beaudoin, president of Bombardier Inc.,
who became a director. Each was credited with drawing other French
Canadians into Ritz public rooms, as well as many English clients and
friends.

The effects of Roberge's solicitations, and the massive publicity
campaign, were enormous. Business tripled. In 1977 an average room
cost $45.55 a night and the hotel's occupancy rate was a mere forty-five
percent. By 1986, however, it was a healthy seventy-seven percent and,
on average, a room cost $128. Like François Dupré, the audacious son
of Laurierville had given the Ritz-Carlton a new life.

A lot of the success can be attributed almost directly to the hotel's
rejuvenated public rooms which, like all the Ritz-Carlton's restaurants

and bars, have established themselves among the most distinguished and popular in all of Montreal: the new Intercontinental Restaurant, which today serves casual dinners in three charming European settings — a Normandy auberge, an English pub, and an Italian trattoria — and the Grand Prix bar, a trendy, elegant, nightspot which offers generous drinks and fine piano music from late afternoon until the early hours of the morning. As befits the Ritz, one of the Grand Prix's two pianists is Count Robert de Sibaud de St. Médard, who performs under the professional name of Robert Marsan, to honour his native Mont-de-Marsan, a charming town nestled in the hill country of Southern France, about fifty-five miles from the Bay of Biscay.

Fifty-two percent of the Ritz-Carlton's revenues come from the sale of food and beverages, and its kosher kitchen, supervised by the Jewish Community Council of Montreal, offers sophisticated cuisine under the laws of Kashruth. It is so busy as to account for sixty-five percent of the combined kosher kitchen business in all Montreal hotels. In retrospect, Lord Hardinge was right to have seconded and promoted it among his friends.

So was Jean Contat when he began to enlarge the hotel's wine cellar from 3,000 to 5,000 bottles. Today, the cellar is bigger still. It contains $500,000-worth of stock that includes 16,500 bottles of wine and an assortment of other spirits and liqueurs — sixteen different apéritifs, for instance, eight sherries, nine types of port wine, twenty various brands of Scotch whisky, twelve makes of gins, twenty-four brandies and cognacs, and more than 200 miscellaneous liqueurs — and is universally acclaimed as one of the finest cellars in the land.

But as good as it is, the wine cellar is by no means everything to the Ritz-Carlton. To remain viable and competitive, the hotel needs to continue to average 175 guest room rentals a day, well exceeding the fifty-odd with which Emile Charles Des Baillets had to content himself in an age that saw many permanent residents move out, and hardly anyone take their place. In this respect, Fernand Roberge and René Gounel agree with Frederick Collins' astute assertion made back in the 1940s — that a hotel's strength depends not on who drops in for a meal or a drink only to go home and never to return, but on who actually stays there. Nonetheless, Roberge and Gounel believe that to enjoy long-standing success over the next seventy-five years, it is imperative for the Ritz to continue to attract Montrealers as well as visitors from afar.

"The local environment is integral to *any* city hotel," Gounel says. "If you don't do well there, you are facing a very major weakness."

"Quite right," says Roberge. "The locals are the locomotives. They are the people who come into the Ritz Bar and the Grand Prix every day, bringing other customers with them, and telling the rest of the world how good you are, how much you care, and what fine meals and drinks you serve. 'I'll meet you at the Ritz,' they say, and business snowballs."

The Ritz-Carlton Hotel has proved this. Its in-house studies have consistently shown that most of its room business is generated by patrons who lunch or dine in the Maritime Bar, the Café de Paris, or the Intercontinental Restaurant, sip drinks in the Ritz Bar or the Grand Prix, organize private dinners and their children's wedding receptions in one of the hotel's twelve banquet rooms — then recommend the hotel to others.

Besides telling out-of-town friends and clients what makes the Ritz-Carlton special, patrons are quick to extol its other virtues, such as its proximity to the centre of the city. Visitors find the hotel within easy walking distance of Montreal's most fashionable and original boutiques, as well as its fine museums and art galleries. In fact, clients of the stature of Harry Minden and his wife Beryl book rooms at the Ritz expressly to shop for art or to attend exhibitions at the Montreal Museum of Fine Arts.

But there is much more to staying at the hotel than conveniences such as these, and Roberge and Gounel have never doubted exactly what it is. Numerous people who frequent the Ritz still attach special value to being "seen" there and, accordingly, they vie for what they consider to be the public rooms' most strategic positions.

One of these, in the quiet Ritz Bar (which offers one of the best lunchtime salad bars in the city), is a spot near the entrance. A seat there ensures that patrons can be easily recognized from the foyer by others as they enter the hotel from Sherbrooke Street. It is also said to be socially advantageous to enter the bar simply to sip afternoon tea, or to occupy any one of the fifty or so plush red chairs when waiters serve early evening drinks against a background of soft piano music.

Here, not long ago, one of Montreal's best known millionaires was "seen" so drunk that a waiter, Turkish-born Mike Ucok, boldly demanded his car keys, then checked him into a room. "You are not driving your car tonight, Sir," Ucok told him.

"Well, how do I get home?" the man asked.

"You're not going home," the waiter replied. "You're staying right here."

The following day the millionaire handed Ucok a cheque for $500,

The lobby as guests see it today, its brass gleaming, its marble floors shining more than ever. The entire entrance area has been given a new personality by George Ray's daring colour scheme: rich black with burnt-umber, burnished gold, and russet. The decor is warm and friendly and helps accentuate the brass balustrades, door fixtures, and lamps.

PHOTO BY ARNOTT ROGERS

and told him, "You saved my life." The money was refused, of course. "I was doing my job, that's all," the waiter said. "I was doing what I would expect other people to do for me if I'd had too much to drink."

In summer, many of Montreal's old moneyed families consider a table in the Duck Garden ideal for public view. But not just any table. It should be as near as possible to the French windows that open from the Café de Paris, where socialites linger over lunch or indulge themselves in an early supper.

Besides being a rendez-vous for cocktails, the basement Maritime Bar is a superb spot for seafood as well. Patrons who go there, either for a hearty business lunch or an intimate dinner, are almost certain to be noticed by Montreal's stockbroking and legal establishments. For businessmen, the Café de Paris provides a significant venue for a so-called "power" breakfast. This, says the *Financial Post*, "is the first meal of the day taken in public, generally in an upscale restaurant or hotel dining room. Some people meet solely to transact business; for others, being seen in a classy restaurant is the objective."

Guests who sleep at the Ritz, however, do so not because its rooms are among the best in the city, or to be "seen" there. Nothing, they confess, surpasses being remembered, recognized, and acknowledged by the staff — an integral part of the simple art of pampering, coddling, and making people feel important, that was advocated and exploited by César Ritz the former shepherd all those years ago. It is as applicable at the Ritz-Carlton today as ever it was.

"There's no point in denying it," says Roberge. "Our clients enjoy the ambience we provide and the tremendous status that goes with it. So we are still selling a total environment, of the kind Monsieur Ritz espoused." Most other hotels, particularly those that belong to chains, so obviously lack this atmosphere, he is brisk to point out, because they cannot lay legitimate claim to a long, colourful tradition. "Some of them are starting to develop it, though," Gounel adds. "But for the moment, they are still too young."

Generally speaking, these hotels have yet to acquire what Roberge calls "staying power, the ability to create an environment into which people constantly yearn to return," consequently, they cater mostly to "one night stands." At the Ritz-Carlton, however, clients are still apt to book rooms for several days — even weeks — at a time, just as they have since doormen began doffing their hats to the very first visitors on that cold morning of January 1, 1913.

More than anything, Ritz-Carlton visitors and patrons alike continue

The Palm Court, where moulding and panels were torn away and replaced by motifs that harken back to ancient Greece, creates a feeling of what the Ritz calls "unpretentious luxury." Not long ago, Hollywood filmmakers transformed the lobby and the Palm Court to resemble New York City's imposing Russian Tea Room—part of the set for the movie *Dreamworld*.

PHOTO BY ARNOTT ROGERS

to savour what distinguishes the hotel and makes it unique — that which has remained essentially unaltered and kept the hotel afloat through those long, difficult times. "The key to running a good hotel," says Fernand Roberge, "can be found in three things — service, service, and service. And it must never cease to be exquisite."

The perfection of this is uppermost in his mind as he administers a staff of 500 people who, he says, keep the Ritz what it is, and what it always was. It includes forty-two chambermaids, thirteen housemen, eleven night cleaners, a valet, five laundry workers, ten barmen, forty-seven waiters, thirty-three busboys, thirty-five stewards, thirty-five *commis* and *chefs de partie*, and a dozen chefs and pastry cooks who are part of a seventy-person kitchen team. At two Ritzers to one room, it provides the highest staff-guest ratio in Montreal, and one of the most impressive in North America. "At the Ritz-Carlton, where the elite seem to meet," wrote a *Miami Herald* reporter, "we lunched in sumptuous style with as many waiters at our table as there were customers."

The managers protect this statistic like the crown jewels as they seek to preserve and enhance the hotel's reputation as being essentially small and European. So do the directors, who have always reflected the absolute class of the Ritz, its affluence, tone, and direction. When Charles Hosmer and his associates first formed their company back in 1909, building the hotel two years later with $2 million, it had four directors who came and went as their other business pressures subsided or increased, and two more who were recruited later. Ritz-Carlton Inc., the owners, however, have eighteen, each of them a modern-day counterpart of the original founders, and equally as driven by a dream. Theirs is an array of affluence and good fortune indeed, and until he became Opposition Leader on June 11, 1983, Prime Minister Brian Mulroney was part of this.

The president of Ritz-Carlton Inc., and a shareholder, was Philippe Cambessédès, a dapper Parisian financier with sharp flashing eyes and a shy smile, in whom the Dupré legacy lived on, uncompromisingly. He was appointed to the board in 1968 by Anci Dupré (to whom he had been a financial advisor), to represent her interests in the Ritz following the death of her husband. Until then, few of the Canadian directors of Ritz-Carlton Inc. knew who Philippe Cambessédès was. His presence and popularity, however, were soon very well established.

Then there was George Marin, also of Paris, who, although in retirement, was widely recognized as the world's finest hotelier. He was the general manager of London's Dorchester Hotel, and later both the manager and a director of Dupré's Hôtel Georges V and his Plaza Athénée. That was soon after he had suffered through arduous war years in Nazi captivity — like Cambessédès, who fought with La Résistance.

An officer in the French army, George Marin was interred in the Colditz prison camp; Philippe Cambessédès was among only 1,100 men who survived Dora, a satellite of the feared concentration camp at Buchenwald. During his two years there, from June, 1943, to May, 1945, he was forced to work on a production line that manufactured V1 and V2 rockets used by the Germans to bombard London. It was an assignment he tried unsuccessfully to sabotage by inserting the wrong parts into the wrong places, or by not installing any parts at all.

"Both these men," reflects Daniel Doheny, who himself had been a prisoner of war, in Eichstätt, Germany, "brought to our meetings world class expertise, a congenial spirit, and an open heart always so understanding of the human predicament."

Other members of the Ritz-Carlton board, besides Beaudoin, Kilburn, Doheny, and Roberge, included Frederik Eaton, president, chairman, and chief executive officer of the T. Eaton Company Limited; lawyers E. Jacques Courtois, Georges Perreard, Jean-Pierre Imhoos, Neil F. Phillips, and Wilbrod Bherer, a former president of Canadian Vickers; Allan A. Hodgson, chief financial officer of Alcan Aluminium Limited; investor broker Thornley W. Hart; Jeremy H. Reitman, president of Reitmans (Canada) Limited; the retired Geneva banker Pierre de Boccard; Charles Baker, chairman of the Ontario Jockey Club; and the amiable Prince Constantin von und zu Liechtenstein who, among his colleagues, had by far the smallest investment in the Ritz-Carlton Hotel — one solitary share.

The prince carried enormous influence, though. Back in the 1930s, while a member of the Cambridge University ski team, he began to befriend the "cream" of European society; it is said that he has since come to know nearly every European monarch, as well as innumerable aristocrats like himself, whom he never failed to encourage to stay at the hotel during their North American travels.

Early in the winter of 1988, the corporate make-up of the Ritz-Carlton changed. The hotel was bought by a consortium headed by Daniel Fournier, coincidentally another of the up-and-coming French Canadian businessmen Fernand Roberge had once attracted to the hotel. Now, Roberge attracted Fournier not so much to dine in the Café de Paris and enjoy a quiet drink in the Maritime Bar, but to wander through the hotel's quiet corridors and reliquary public rooms — as one of its five new owners.

It is a story of quiet success. Six years before he put together a package that would enable him to become a Ritz partner with some of Canada's most influential men, Fournier had no capital whatsoever. In fact, when he gathered a group of friends in his living room and brought them into his fledgling Equidev Inc., he told them, "We don't have any money to pay you, but if we all work hard, one day, maybe, we will have." But by the time he was able to make a bid for the hotel, Fournier headed a team of aggressive, ambitious co-workers and advisors each of whom was just like himself — under thirty-five, a bachelor, and an upstart Québecois investor well on his way to becoming a multi-millionaire. Fournier himself had risen to become the chairman and a major shareholder of a real estate empire worth some $150 million.

Slowly but surely, he and his men had also begun to change the face of downtown Montreal for the good, delighting in every moment of it. "These friends," said a CTV current affairs documentary on Fournier that was aired shortly after the Ritz-Carlton take-over bid was announced in March, 1988, "are a close-knit group, well educated, bilingual, and brimming with imagination. They are driven by the idea that if it isn't fun, it isn't worth doing."

For Daniel Fournier, the fun part came when he commanded attention as a dynamic young Francophone realtor who was actually daring to buy up those institutions that were once the exclusive domain of the English — the ailing, 110-year-old Windsor Hotel, for example, which he transformed into spectacular office space. To a large extent, it was what Fournier calls "ironic attention," for he never purposely set out to acquire only those institutions that were perceived as being inherently Anglo. It just happened that way. Nonetheless, until then, he had remained virtually unknown outside Quebec, and was completely unperturbed by it. He had thrived, after all, solely on the affluent, free-wheeling business climate in the city he dearly loved.

"There's no place I'd rather be than in Montreal," Fournier says. "The doors are always open here and I don't feel cliques. I sense an exciting, aggressive feeling of, 'Let's move. Let's progress.' That's what we are going to do."

The Windsor Hotel project, which cost $40 million, was quickly acclaimed across the world for the way it installed new life and new character into an old, seemingly unwanted building. It thrust Fournier among the country's most celebrated developers and had Montrealers asking who he was.

He was born on Ile Bizard, just west of Montreal in 1954, but when his parents divorced, he moved to neighbouring Pierrefonds with his mother and sister. At sixteen, he won a scholarship to take his last two high school grades in Exeter, New Hampshire. Later, and again on a scholarship, he entered Princeton University, where he majored in history. While there, he won a Rhodes Scholarship and went off to Oxford University to study law. In 1977, between his first and second years at Oxford, he returned to Canada to satisfy his love for athletics, and played thirteen games as a tight-end for the Ottawa Rough Riders.

Former teammate Tony Gabriel says that as a player, Fournier, who had been a first-round choice in the Canadian Football League draft, showed "great potential." But the big, shy realtor-investor remembers, "I stopped playing before I knew whether I could make football my career or not. Maybe, if I'd hung around the Rough Riders for another couple of seasons, I would have found out. But that was out of the question. My law professor was telling me that it made more sense for me to profit from my experience at Oxford, and live up to what I promised when I accepted my scholarship. He was right, of course."

So Fournier earned his degree and returned to Canada, not to practice law — he never did — but to work as an assistant to Montreal financier Lorne Webster at his Prenor Group. Then, "to purposely avoid any kind of job that was salary-oriented," he joined a firm of realtors owned by Jonathan Wener and, while there, shared in both the risks and the fortunes. One day shortly afterwards, while admiring a collection of Auguste Rodin sculptures in Paris, the idea came to him to reach out on his own by forming Equidev, and he has never looked back. "The scope and size of real estate and investment projects may change," Fournier says, "but the principle of them remains. By taking properly calculated risks, I was engaging in what I felt was absolutely right for me — a truly entrepreneurial experience."

He was, indeed. The same week that he sold his interests in the Windsor Hotel, he acquired Ogilvy's, Montreal's oldest department store, renovating it at a cost of $7 million. Now the likeable entrepreneur, who stands a robust six feet two inches tall and weighs 230 pounds, only seven pounds heavier than he was as a Rough Rider, could add the Ritz-Carlton Hotel to his growing list of acquisitions. And, just as he maintained tradition at Ogilvy's by ensuring that the corridors were trodden several times each day by a bagpiper, as they had been for more than sixty years, so he vowed to keep the Ritz as a first class hotel, even to the extent of planning some additions to it, south on Drummond Street to de Maisonneuve Boulevard.

"My word is my bond," says Fournier, confessing to instantly shying away from any deal that smacks even remotely of being shady. "I would never take the profits from anything unless it was straight. You have to look at yourself in the mirror every morning."

Fernand Roberge felt that Daniel Fournier was the right kind of man to be a Ritz owner, and approached him to become so. It was no secret that the hotel had been up for sale for two years, and Roberge took it upon himself to find a buyer, locally. "Dan has high standards," he says, "and knew the right kind of people who would help shoulder the risk." From then on, Fournier began forming his team of purchasers, separate from those in Equidev — men who shared his business philosophy, men who revered the old place as a fine Canadian institution. Then came the laborious, intricate work of actually "closing the deal." It involved eight months of intense negotiation with the Ritz-Carlton's owners who, mysteriously, had always remained obscure.

Few people ever knew that when Anci Dupré died in 1976, she left nearly all of the hotel's shares in a Liechtenstein-based foundation which, among the many other charities it sought to help, rehabilitated ex-convicts the moment they left prison. This foundation had seven holding companies, all registered in Panama, and Fournier and his partners had to negotiate with each separately. The deal was further complicated because, while the holding companies owned 61.9 per cent of the shares, three Canadians together held a crucial 17.4 per cent. They wanted all the other shares to be acquired by the new investors first so that they would be assured of getting a top price for their own later. The balance of the shares in Ritz Carlton Inc. was obtained from other shareholders holding smaller numbers.

Negotiations for the Ritz-Carlton owners were handled in Geneva by Prince Constantin von und zu Liechtenstein, Pierre de Boccard, and attorneys Imhoos and Perreard; in Montreal, they fell to lawyer Jean Pierre Ouellet. He acted for Placements Sherbrooke-de-la-Montagne which, having outlived its usefulness as the consortium's holding company, was dissolved just weeks before the old directors of Ritz-Carlton Inc. said goodbye to the hotel at a dinner party in the Carlton Room on January 19, 1989, and welcomed their five successors.

Apart from Daniel Fournier, the directors now include Fernand Roberge and Derek A. Price, the trustee of what is well known in Montreal as "the McConnell family fortune." At the time of the sale, Price, a member of the Quebec City pulp and paper company family, was chairman of Starlaw Holdings Ltd., the McConnell's investment company, which once held twenty-five per cent of the shares in FP Publications. Until it was wound up in the late 1970s, FP publications owned, among several other enterprises, such newspapers as the *Globe and Mail* and the *Montreal Star*.

As a young boy, when his family travelled to Montreal, Derek Price stayed at the Ritz-Carlton, bounding recklessly through its corridors as though it were his second home. But as he grew older, he came to respect the old place as a heritage building, and a reminder of "what Sherbrooke Street could and should have become." In his decision to invest in the Ritz then, he says unabashedly, "there is a feeling, a spirit, of being able to contribute something to the well-being of a pristine place."

Other Ritz owner-directors are Pierre Shooner, president of Le Groupe Cooperants, owners of Guardian Trust, the depositary for the offer, and Galand Willard Gordon Weston, one of Canada's richest men. "It's very important for us, and Montreal, to keep this hotel going," says Shooner, who teamed up with Fournier to transform Ogilvy's. "It's one of those places that has to be protected."

Galand Weston agrees, and Fournier says of him, "We are very lucky to have garnered his support, his influence, and his power." In 1987 alone, Weston's holdings — they include Weston Bakeries, the Loblaws chain of grocery stores, E.B. Eddy Paper, (the manufacturers of White Swan products), the chocolate company William Neilson, BC Packers, and Holt Renfrew — recorded North American sales worth more than $11 billion. Work, however, is only a part of Weston's life. He plays hard, too — polo with Prince Charles — and, like all his friends at the Ritz, has a deep-felt respect for historic sites. He owns a one-room log cabin near Collingwood, Ontario, a castle near Dublin, and Fort Belvedere, an English country estate where, in 1937, Edward VIII abdicated.

With the encouragement of men like these, Fournier was eventually able to buy out all the Ritz-Carlton's shareholders, virtually in the same way as François Dupré had started to take control almost to the very day forty-nine years before. It was a deal worth some $39.5 million, and it promised to maintain the Ritz not only as a European-styled hotel, but as a timepiece. So, fittingly, in its seventy-fifth year, the hotel had come full circle. Leaking into newspapers in October, 1988, to be officially announced two months later, the sale ensured that the Grande Dame of Sherbrooke Street was finally being returned to where she had started out. She was being entrusted to owners of absolute integrity who were not only Canadians, but, with the exception of Galand Weston, who hails from the salubrious Toronto district of Forest Hill, lived and worked in Montreal.

From the outside looking in — beyond the fluttering flags and the fortress-like limestone and granite walls, and those twinkling lobby lights — nothing appears to have changed at the Ritz-Carlton Hotel. ("Life," John Dominique reiterates, "will always go on, remember, whoever's in charge.") Every morning at seven o'clock, Fernand Roberge, a picture of chunky but sartorial elegance, usually in a dark, flannel suit, but sometimes in a sports jacket and a Ritz tie, walks briskly through the lobby and into the Café de Paris for breakfast before attending the first of several meetings convened throughout the day. René Gounel is invariably with him to help him plan his schedule. Their first job is to review the previous day's reports which show how many people checked into the Ritz, who among them will be staying, and for how long. They study, too, each department's revenues and what the security officer had to deal with the night before, mostly who lost what and where, and who complained that a waiter had dropped food on his or her clothing.

"We try not to spill too much sauce on people's suits or dresses," says Gounel, "but if we do, we clean it up."

Clients' comments, made on cards left in rooms, are carefully answered, analyzed, then filed. "From these," Gounel says, "we can discover all those things we are doing right and, much more important, those we may be doing wrong."

After a long evening in one of the hotel's bars, a client reported, he awoke the following day with the mint chocolate a maid had left on his fluffed-up pillow the night before covering the entire side of his face. "In future," he suggested, "chocolates should be left on the night table!"

The management sympathized with the man's dilemma and promptly instructed its maids to ensure that whenever he was in the hotel, his "Goodnight Candy" was placed "where he would immediately see it, but not sleep on it."

Every Wednesday morning in the board room, which was used as an office by Philippe Cambessédès when he visited Montreal four times a year, the hotel's seven division heads meet to review the week, exchange ideas, and brace themselves for what is to come. These divisions are Rooms (front office, bellboys, garage, beauty salon, and housekeeping); Food and Beverage, by far the largest section, which incorporates all restaurants and bars, the kitchens and dishwashing facilities, and the

Executive chef Christian Lévêque in a busy corner of the white main kitchen.
One of his biggest assignments was in January, 1988, when the Oval Room
and the Café de Paris were closed to the public so that nearly 600 staffers and
their spouses could sit down to dinner—to celebrate the Ritz-Carlton's
seventy-fifth anniversary.

PHOTO COURTESY OF THE RITZ-CARLTON COLLECTION

banquet department; Marketing (public relations, advertising, and sales); Finance (accounting, payroll, and pensions); and Personnel (staff selection and training.)

As a follow up, the thirty heads and assistants of every restaurant, bar, or department meet in whichever small banquet room is available on Thursday afternoons to discuss their own specific areas: what they may need to meet the growing demand for their services, and how they can make these better. It is a goal that must never slip from reach. The Ritz-Carlton's bars and restaurants, after all, are known and revered throughout Montreal, and they must continue to be so.

"Next to service," says Roberge, "comes the quality of our food."

Many critics believe that Ritz cuisine is unparalleled in Canada. The Café de Paris serves lunch and dinner in the elegant Ritz way, thanks to fine cooking and a corps of graceful waiters, and must retain its place in the hierarchy of Canadian restaurants; during the summer months, the Ritz Garden strives to provide a pastoral setting for breakfast, lunch, "le five o'clock tea," and dinner al fresco.

Ducklings, bought for $2 each from the same Eastern Townships farm, still enliven the garden's flower-fringed pond between mid-May and mid-September, depending on the weather, and are exchanged for a younger batch every three weeks. "They're cute when they're young," says Roberge, "but if they get too big, well, they aren't so exciting for the guests." As they fatten, and fatten they do because guest persist in feeding them, the hotel gives them away to patrons with ponds.

Resident ducks are rounded up at night by a busboy who paddles into the pond wearing Wellington boots to shepherd them into a heated shed against the garden's southern wall. It is a Ritz spectacle, indeed — an agreeable side show. At the height of summer, the job is often done when the garden is still thronging with customers sipping their last drinks, and they cheer as the birds elude their captor. They cheer even louder when he tumbles flat on his face in the water, sending the ducklings scurrying in several directions in a flurry of fluffy white feathers.

When the weather turns cool, the birds' nightcap is cognac-laced milk. Either that, or fine Napoleon brandy — neat! And in the morning, they are fed from the previous night's table scraps, which always include the best croissants, muffins, sweet rolls, Danish pastries, and vegetables doused in champagne sauce, before being returned to their freshly cleaned pond.

Just as coveted as the hotel's restaurants, are its facilities for business meetings and banquets. The Ritz-Carlton has twelve meeting rooms

The Oval Room is set for a banquet. It can seat about 500 people, and often
has to. The hotel caters for fifteen functions and 400 guests on one busy day;
during one good year, it will cater 5,500 functions and prepare 170,000 meals.
The Oval Room is popular for large weddings and famous for state banquets.

PHOTO COURTESY OF THE RITZ-CARLTON COLLECTION

which range from the Canadian Suite, which has seating for eighteen, to the Oval Room and the Palm Court, which can jointly hold 550 people. On a busy day, the hotel caters for fifteen functions and 400 guests; during a good year, it will cater 5,500 functions and prepare 170,000 meals.

Staff pride in particular tasks is unswerving. The chef who replaced Pierre Demers had spent an entire decade at the Ritz making nothing but sauces. Another kitchen worker was promoted to waiter after having specialized, for eighteen years, in washing only the hotel's glasses. Every afternoon the steward's staff hand polishes more than 300 pieces of silverware, including a huge, egg-shaped roast beef trolley, a replica of one used in all Ritz hotels as and when they were opened around the turn of the century.

The hotel's furniture, much of it antique and chosen to convey the warmth and individuality of a well-appointed home, has never for a moment been profaned by varnish, and never will be. It is French-polished in the hotel's workshop, which remains on the tenth floor. "Our clients enjoy our old furniture," says Roberge, "but they also like to sleep well — not on the beds of yesterday, but in those of today. And they'd better be king size!"

Part of Roberge's modernization was to introduce for guests small but vital comforts — terrycloth bathrobes, French toiletries, and bathroom scales; large umbrellas in case of rain, are always placed in rooms. A newsstand and gift shop, and secretarial and translation services are available in the hotel, too, with hair-styling, pedicures, and massages in the Ritz-owned beauty salon which has processed the likes of Marlene Dietrich, Maria Callas, the Baronesses Rothschild, Zsa Zsa Gabor, Governor General Jeanne Sauvé, Flora Macdonald, and Lady Hardinge, who is a regular customer. Similarly, same-day laundering has always been part of the Ritz Idea, as has a complimentary shoeshine, a job which falls to a former valet with Claridge's, London. He is comfortably resigned to having to hand-clean an average of fifteen pairs of shoes daily, as he has for nearly forty years at the Ritz, leaving the remainder for the night bellman to do.

Since Roberge has taken charge of the hotel, guests also recognize the presence of technology: remote-control colour TV sets, radio alarm clocks, electric hairdryers, magnifying make-up mirrors, and complimentary video movies. They find, too, a mini-bar and an individual Norwegian-made electronic room safe that accommodates a briefcase. A microprocessor, powered by the hotel's electricity supply but protected by a back-up battery, allows each guest to program his or her own six-digit locking combination and alter it at will.

By handing out courtesy copies of the *Gazette*, *Le Devoir*, *La Presse*, and the *Globe and Mail* each day, the Ritz-Carlton began to add more "little touches of luxury" to make itself worthy of hoteliery's highest recognition — five stars. But then, it has never forgotten its place or abandoned its mandate to be first class and luxurious by adding what Roberge calls "the simple little things that a lot of other hotels forget."

Whatever the changes he and Gounel made to the Ritz were administered in style. The two men have always been determined to keep their hotel "classical," with its turn-of-the-century Continental character firmly intact. In other words, they have been intent on seeing that the Grande Dame of Sherbrooke Street harkens back to a more gracious age, and that contemporary patrons will love her for it.

"In the final analysis," says Roberge, "it all adds up to a feeling you give to a customer, an ambience, an Old World charm with fine service that can't be found elsewhere. So you must keep as much of the old as possible and mix it with the new with utmost care and precision, and you must always see that morale is high because the attitude of the staff makes all the difference in the world. It is something, a special feeling they acquire which is passed on to customers. It is instantly passed down to the customers before anything else, and it makes them comfortable, at ease."

Employees can be prouder than ever to work in the hotel. "To be a Ritzman," says Denis Laganière, "means you have to anticipate and be prepared to do a little, sometimes a lot, more than other places will do. If it only takes a couple of hours of our lives to make someone happy, why not?"

Just as César Ritz would have wanted, he books theatre tickets, calls in baby sitters, arranges car rentals, updates the functions board, and tends to visitors' other needs as and when they arise. A few years ago, a departing businessman inadvertently picked up the wrong briefcase and headed home. On his own initiative, Laganière immediately called a taxi and ordered the driver to give chase. He finally exchanged the briefcases on a busy highway just a couple of miles from Montreal International Airport where, in only minutes, the man was due to board a flight to Los Angeles.

Not long afterwards, Laganière saw Prince Karim Aga Khan IV sitting in the lobby and, completely unprompted, handed him a glass of water. "I just saw the poor Prince sitting there in a sweat," he says, "and to me, he looked so thirsty."

When Laganière is absent, he has two assistants: Italian-born Tommy Ciriello, a Ritzman with twenty years service, and Marianne Moore, one of the growing number of Canadian concierges who are women. They follow in distinguished footsteps. Through good times and lean, their predecessors — the hotel's head porters — recall having walked dogs, called cabs for celebrities like Lee Majors, David Niven, Yehudi Menuhin, Moshe Dayan, and Igor Stravinsky, and ordered tickets to the National Ballet of Canada for Pierre Cardin.

Such actions have not gone unrecognized. "César Ritz would be proud of his namesake," said the *Denver Post* — and promptly proclaimed the Ritz-Carlton North America's best hotel. "This conservative, small hotel on Montreal's Sherbrooke Street is as Ritzy as its surroundings...and its concierge department is one of the best and most efficient in all the world."

Denis Laganière shrugs off the compliment. When he first became a Ritzman more than forty years ago, a severe man with a monocle told him gruffly, "Never say no to a customer. Always say you'll try your best." Laganière has never forgotten it.

Sophia Moscoutis, for nearly fifteen years the housekeeper, would be the first to agree with the man's advice. Like Marcelle Gohier three decades before her, she always insisted that her staff, installed on each of the hotel's ten floors, should address guests by name and never consider their requests peculiar, even when they were. To this day maids continue to tidy rooms twice, sometimes three times, daily. Bedclothes are folded back neatly at night and the "Goodnight Candy" is positioned with care on a fluffed-up pillow. A running list is still reverently maintained of those guests who need allergy-proof pillows, special mattress wedges, or anything else that might remind them of home.

Nor is the maids' work always confined to guest rooms. They have frequently hand-washed shirts and ironed them, and, like the concierge department, undertaken the odd shopping spree with "the compliments of the hotel." Sophia Moscoutis always said fervently, "If we can't find a little moment to do something special for someone else, after all, our life will never be worth living." And she remained true to her word.

Not long before she retired in 1987, her phone rang. It was actress Sophia Loren, who was staying in the hotel's Royal Suite with her husband Carlo Ponti and their teenage son between long stints on the Montreal set for the movie *Angela*. "Would it be possible," the actress asked, "for me to have some cooking utensils so we can cook our own pasta?"

"Of course you can," said the housekeeper. "No problem at all."

That morning she sent out a colleague to buy a complete set of pots and pans so it could be delivered to the Royal Suite that afternoon. Loren was delighted. "Believe me," she told the floor waiter, "this is no ordinary hotel. It really isn't!"

It was never intended to be. What was originally launched by those Golden Square Mile tycoons who had a propensity for all things good, has mushroomed beyond our wildest dreams. The hotel is constantly receiving requests from film companies wanting to use it as a setting, particularly its lobby and garden. But to Fernand Roberge and René Gounel guests, not movies, will always come first, no matter how fussy or demanding they may be, and they have proved it time and time again.

On Sunday, January 10, 1988, the staff was rewarded for its efforts. The Ritz-Carlton closed the Oval Room and the Café de Paris to the public so that nearly 600 workers and their spouses could sit down to a gourmet dinner with champagne to celebrate the hotel's seventy-fifth anniversary. The meal was served by those staffers who volunteered to work for their colleagues — they were given gift vouchers that entitled them to a dinner for two in the Café de Paris later — but the only work Ritzmen like John Dominique and Denis Laganière did that night was to fetch their wives a drink.

As the Ritz-Carlton prepared for other seventy-fifth anniversary celebrations, it was told, by New York publicists, that British actor Richard Harris wanted to stay there for a few weeks while he performed in the Lerner and Loewe musical *Camelot* at Place des Arts. Harris, said the publicists, insisted on having a suite with a bar-sized refrigerator, and a king size bed placed so that it had direct ventilation. The bedroom windows had to have blackout curtains to prevent daylight from waking the actor should he decide to sleep in. His bedsheets had to be thoroughly rinsed — "in clear water and with at least one full washing machine cycle" — and were not to be changed during his stay, unless he wanted otherwise.

On his arrival, Harris expected to find one non-fat yogurt (preferably Weight Watcher's or Dannon's), three quart-sized containers of non-fat milk, a "hand-sized" banana, and one box of Bigelow's Sweet Dreams herbal teas. For breakfast, he preferred John McCann's porridge, for dinner small servings of chicken or turkey breast, fish (salmon, cod, or sea bass) served with brown or wild rice, or a combination of all three. These meals were to be accompanied by brewed decaffeinated coffee or breakfast tea, and Evian spring water.

"Experience has shown," said the publicists, "that if there are going to be any problems, they generally are a result of the person who is handling the telephone for room service, or the staff in the restaurants not being informed that special foods are available."

Problems? At the venerable old Ritz-Carlton? Food has always been such a priority there that in whichever of its restaurants guests or patrons choose to eat, they can be sure that the string beans, turbot, or caviar they order have all been‹d‹imported from Paris that week, and that the wild rice, an option with many Ritz dishes, is Prairie-grown and has been flown in from Winnipeg.

Understandably, then, Richard Harris got everything he requested. But what was unusual in that? Such indefatigable care and conscientious attention to detail that has appealed uncompromisingly to those statesmen, aristocrats, opera singers, entertainers, and prize fighters, and anyone else who could afford to stay there. "I greatly enjoyed my recent stay at the Ritz-Carlton," former British prime minister Edward Heath said in a letter to René Gounel. "I am most grateful to you and your staff for all you did to ensure the comfort of my stay. Your kind welcome and excellent service were greatly appreciated. It was good to be back again."

A few days later, a letter arrived on his desk from Senator Royce Frith, who had arrived at the hotel from his home in Ottawa, tired and without his baggage, which had been misplaced by an airline. Night concierge Marianne Moore traced the luggage and had it delivered to the hotel. She also made arrangements for the senator to depart Montreal early the following day, by train. The senator said:

> Thank you for the extraordinary hospitality you provided on the evening of October 5 when I unexpectedly had to stay over in Montreal. Miss Moore, your concierge, and other members of your staff, effectively solved all my problems on the spot and the beautiful suite you offered was a most appreciated bonus.
>
> The Ritz has been my first choice in Montreal all my life beginning decades ago when my daughter went to Trafalgar School for Girls. I have not been in Montreal as frequently during the last few years, but when I am, I always like to think of the Ritz as a home.

Many do and many will, for Sophia Loren was right. The Ritz-Carlton is *not* an ordinary hotel, and those far sighted investors from the Golden Square Mile who envisioned a world class establishment modeled after the very best anywhere, would be eminently proud of how it has evolved.

The Queen Mother arrives at the Ritz for a 1988 state banquet. She is being greeted by Fernand Roberge. Royalty has frequented the hotel since Edward Prince of Wales began staying in the Vice-Regal Suite in 1919.

PHOTO COURTESY OF BUCKINGHAM PALACE

Still independent and privately owned, the inimitable old Ritz been a member of The Leading Hotels of the World since the late 1940s, and has garnered numerous honours: the American Automobile Association's coveted Five Diamond Award, for example, and *Mobil Travel Guide's* Four Stars for "distinguished achievement in service, cordiality and overall quality." The citation said: "Outstanding — worth a special visit."

A journalist once asked Fernand Roberge what he would say if he met César Ritz? "After all," she said, "Monsieur Ritz showed us all what service and luxury could really be, and how it could be applied to hostelry. He gave you and other Ritz administrators before you something to strive for."

Roberge paused and searched for words. "I would probably be in awe of César Ritz," he replied finally, "because of what he has done. He was a pioneer of fine, luxurious hotels with standards of quality. He was to me someone who had so much foresight into what luxury really was. 'You did a super job, Monsieur Ritz, in your era,' I'd tell him, 'but now I must adjust your creation to mine.'"

That, Roberge contends, is how it will go on. "Fifty years from today," he adds, "people will be taking what I and all those other managers before me have done, and making it more applicable to the times in which *they* live. Things are always going to be a little different at the Ritz."

Indeed, time must never stand still at the Ritz-Carlton. Nor must the ardour that has made it what it is. Over those long, lean years, the hotel has survived as an inseparable part of Montreal life and a haven of European hospitality virtually untarnished by generations. Dignity and good taste must never cease to prevail, which the owners know only too well. Hence, also like Sir Charles Gordon, Charles Hosmer, Sir Montagu Allan, and Sir Herbert Holt, they have unanimously agreed to plough all profits back into the hotel, not so much as to keep it going now, but to improve it as a bastion of refinement and elegance.

The original founders had no choice, of course, because they presided over a hotel that was famous but poor. Today's directors, however, are intent on preserving an image and backing it with quality amenities that are unsurpassed. "We must continue to refine the product and make it as competitive as possible," says René Gounel, "and this cannot be achieved without the new owners' commitment." Today, this philosophy has made the Ritz-Carlton famous, successful, and assured of another, less turbulent seventy-five years.

"Truly," says Prime Minister Mulroney, "there is a certain magic that greets all who pass through the Ritz-Carlton's door. More than a famous hotel, it has welcomed numerous personalities who have shaped history, bringing to mind images of the golden years of Montreal." Dancer Gene Kelly called the Ritz "genteel and stunning." Film actor Trevor Howard found it "decent, civilized, and warm," and a fellow performer, Robert Mitchum, agreed with a visiting writer named Barbara Moon who summed-up the hotel neatly when she wrote, "At the Ritz, service is a leisurely, loving, handcrafted thing, extravagant of steps and time."

The most fitting tribute of all, however, and one which the staff has striven hard to live up to, has come from *Canadian Interiors* which, in recent times has watched the bastion grow, forever changing its interior, and forever refining its amenities. "The Ritz-Carlton," the magazine has reported unabashedly, "is the Grande Dame of Montreal hotels — and the standard by which other Canadian hotels are measured."

AWARDS AND HONOURS

Over the years, the Ritz-Carlton Hotel,
and members of its staff, have garnered
innumerable awards and honours for everything
from cuisine and service to hospitality and decor.
Here are some of the more recent ones:

- Despite the continuance of considerable restoration work in 1972, the Quebec Government's Department of Tourism rated the Ritz-Carlton "Five Star Plus."

- In October, 1972, Chef Pierre Demers captained the Canadian team which placed fourth in the International Culinary Olympics in Frankfurt, Germany.

- In 1972, Chef Pierre Demers was chosen Canada's Chef of the Year by chefs from across the country.

- In 1974, in Banff, Alberta, Chef Pierre Demers, a past president of the Sociètè des chefs de cuisine du Quèbec, was among the invited delegates who attended a convention organized by the World Association of Cooks' Societies.

- In 1976, the Ritz-Carlton received one of the most distinguished ratings a hotel can be given — the American Automobile Association's Five Diamond Award. It has received this every year since.

- In 1981, the *Mobil Travel Guide* assigned the hotel four stars for "distinguished achievement in service, cordiality and overall quality." The citation concluded, "Outstanding — worth a special trip."

- In December 1983, following a poll by more than 100 prominent bankers, the Ritz-Carlton was ranked by the firm Institutional Investors as one of the best hotels in the world.

- In December 1983, the Ritz Garden menu was rated the best hotel menu by l'Association des restaurateurs du Québec.

- In December 1983, the Ritz-Carlton maître d'hôtel John Dominique, and concierge Denis Laganière, both won the American Express Hospitality-Hospitalité award for achieving "the highest level within the Canadian Hospitality Industry," and for "dedication to service." Other winners, in 1984, 1985, 1986, and 1987 were Nick Karras and Alice Manso; Bruno Persechino and Tommy Ciriello; Antonio Punilhas and Diane McLellan; Vidal Hernani-Gomes and Christine Boulanger.

- In January, 1985, the magazine *Revue Commerce* selected Fernand Roberge as "Man of the Month" for "saving the Ritz."

- In both 1986 and 1987, the Ritz-Carlton's L'Intercontinental Restaurant was awarded a bronze medal by the Ministère de L'Agriculture des Pêcheries et de l'Alimentation du Québec, in the "Cuisine de type familial" category.

- On May 24, 1987, in San Antonio, Texas, the Ritz-Carlton Hotel received The American Gold Star for Tourism, an award given by Business Annotative Directions.

- On November 18, 1987, the Quebec Government's Ministry of Tourism designated the Ritz-Carlton Hotel as Quatre Fourchettes for culinary excellence.

INDEX